# The Scenic Art

Also by Hugh Hood

Novels:

*White Figure, White Ground* 1964
*The Camera Always Lies* 1967
*A Game of Touch* 1970
*You Cant Get There From Here* 1972
The New Age/Le nouveau siècle
I: *The Swing in the Garden* 1975
II: *A New Athens* 1977
III: *Reservoir Ravine* 1979
IV: *Black and White Keys* 1982

Stories:

*Flying a Red Kite* 1962
*Around the Mountain: Scenes from Montréal Life* 1967
*The Fruit Man, the Meat Man and the Manager* 1971
*Dark Glasses* 1976
*Selected Stories* 1978
*None Genuine Without This Signature* 1980

Non-Fiction

*Strength Down Centre: the Jean Béliveau Story* 1970
*The Governor's Bridge is Closed* 1973
*Scoring: Seymour Segal's Art of Hockey* 1979
*Trusting the Tale* 1983

# HUGH HOOD

## The Scenic Art

Stoddart

Copyright © 1984 Hugh Hood
All rights reserved

No part of this book may be reproduced or transmitted in any form or by any means, electronic or mechanical, including photography, recording, or any information storage or retrieval system, without permission in writing from the publisher.

The author gratefully acknowledges the invaluable assistance of the Canada Council and the Ontario Arts Council in the completion of this work.

First published in 1984 by
Stoddart Publishing
A Division of General Publishing Co. Limited
30 Lesmill Road
Toronto, Ontario

CANADIAN CATALOGUING IN PUBLICATION DATA

Hood, Hugh, 1928-
   The scenic art

(The New age = Le nouveau siècle ; pt. 5)
ISBN 0-7737-2023-5

I. Title.   II. Series: The New age ; pt. 5.
PS8515.049S28 1984      C813'.54      C84-098887-7
PR9199.3.H66S28 1984

Manufactured in Canada by Webcom Limited

*For the Dean of Women and the
Academic Principal
of Redneck University
Barbara and Don Mulroney
From the Head of the Creative Writing
Department
With Love*

# 1

In the first season at Stratford that tent sang all the time, like Don Giovanni, in a sustained *legato* baritone pitched somewhere around the B an octave and a semi-tone below middle C. When he came to describe theatrical life under canvas, a year or two later, Tyrone Guthrie considered the music of the temporary structure Wagnerian, the fabric sail-like, marine, the whole enterprise tabernacular, reminiscent of both Arks:

> In a high wind the gallant Tabernacle rocks and creaks like a windjammer at sea. Rain drumming on the canvas roof makes a most glorious Wagnerian effect but it completely, if temporarily, obliterates the puny competition afforded by the actors. A more solid structure is clearly indicated.

Whether reviewed under the figure of the Ark of the Covenant, a Holy of Holies, or that of Noah's saving vesselful of animal pairs, the primitive tent of the Stratford, Ontario, Shakesperian Festival, sacred and saving as it might have been, only enjoyed the canonical life of three years, being supplanted in 1956 by the solid handsome permanent edifice for which the founders of the Festival had long prayed.

In the beginning though, canvas, masts, guy-wires, rigging, made their weird music day and night in the summer weather, never more sonorously than in the weeks before the opening, when daily experiments were being made by the rigger and his crew to ascertain the correct tensity for every rope in every atmosphere. As Guthrie later suggested, management of the fabric was precisely like rigging and sailing a ship, and no frolicsome sloop or cutter, or somewhat larger rig like brig, barque, brigantine or barquentine, but the whole wide-spreading suit of sails for a full-rigged three-masted ship. Sailors speak almost involuntarily of singing in the shrouds: we associate ships with musicality and with the tabernacle, naturally and innocently. The tent at Stratford was certainly a Holy of Holies for some of us: for others it seemed exactly a ship on a doubtful voyage. It had a master, Skip Manley, whose name rang with nautical and even naval associations. Brought in from the United States early in the spring of 1953 by the governors of the Festival with a great, in fact an unrivalled reputation in his field, Skip Manley was precisely what his nickname said he was, skipper, captain, director of the whole vessel. Nothing could be done without him or before him. He was a kind of precursor or John the Baptist to the events in the tabernacle. It would not have been possible at any time to say of whom he might be the forerunner.

Guthrie thought the music of the tent Wagnerian, which reveals much about his conceptions of the histrionic and theatrical. To many of us who were observers of the scene, Mozartian associations seemed immensely more appropriate, the voice of the tent more assimilated to *dramma giocoso* and the atmosphere of Salzburg and Vienna than to the more heroic—and at the same time heavier and less gymnastic—operatic conceptions of Bayreuth. What went on there during the first year might have had heroic elements and grave shadows, but the substance of the action was unquestionably jocose.

The conductor, the leader of the band, the skipper, was a man who had learned his craft in an astonishing variety of public entertainments. I'm not talking about Guthrie but about Manley, the man upon whom Guthrie and Guinness and Irene Worth and Tanya Moiseiwitsch and Cecil Clarke and Jacqueline Cundall depended for life. Without Skip there would have been no Festival and he knew it and rejoiced in it. He was a lean man, a wiry man who wore at all seasons an ancient faded fedora-shaped straw Panama, its pale yellow hue suggestive of long ages passed under hot sun. Skip was then in his early forties and had spent most of his life working on tent shows, a circumstance at once obvious to anybody who watched him in action. The governors of the Festival had

# The Scenic Art

found his name exactly where you'd have expected them to see it, in the pages of *The Billboard*. They were fascinated by the notion of giving the first few seasons' entertainments under canvas; it seemed a romantic and un-Canadian thing to do, having a circussy and even revivalist air about it. When they thought the matter over, they realised that an extraordinary variety of performances, as well as exhibitions of more serious intention, could be delivered in tents.

Chautauquas! Literary, musical, poetic, deeply moral and uplifting undertakings, justifiable from their gravity and their origins in upstate New York, not very far from Stratford, Ontario! Designed to bring illustrations of high thought and noble feeling to a provincial populace, the Chautauquas, founded in 1874, flourished under canvas for nearly a century, and served as an example to the Festival governors, and as one of Skip Manley's training grounds. A tent is always in some sort a tabernacle, "a wooden framework covered with curtains" as the dictionary tells us, transportable, suitable for warm climates, evocative of nomadic desert existence: rugs, dates, syrupy coffee, dancing girls, miracles, heavy fate.

Circusses under the big top.

Medicine shows.

Political rallies complete with circus clowns and the embrocations of the itinerant herbalist, and approximately the same audience.

Sporting events. Boxing matches, the occasional cockfight.

Above all revivalism, the evangelists, the miracle cures, the outcries, bruised hopeful souls, confessions.

Why, thought the Festival men, tents are positively Shakesperian! And they were dead right. You could give any kind of show, as Shakespeare does, in a tent, as long as summertime conditions were in play. Tent shows will not do in Canada after Labour Day, nor much before Victoria Day, which is why the first season was so compressed, so much a triple-distillate of raw happenstance, two-hundred proof experience. But in such a time what dreams might come! Skip Manley was himself a Shakesperian figure and might have figured largely in one of the late romances, perhaps that fantasy of old Britain, *Cymbeline*. He had raised tents for religion, politics, sport, for aerialists, hootchy-kootchy girls, horses: all good friends of Shakespeare. In June of 1953 he bestrode the narrow cockpit of western Ontario like a colossus, and Tyrone Guthrie, not normally a docile man, waited upon Skip and did what he told him to do.

You don't simply pour a foundation and put in your seats and hoist your tent. You have to make friends with your winds, know where they come from and at what time of day. You have to know your mean temperatures at all hours, your rainfall. Your kinds of crowds, whether dignified or excessively happy or rowdy or turbulent: religious, circussy, sporting, political. For your political crowd, sirs, is not your religious crowd, nor yet your connoisseurs of pugilism nor your shrill children. Who will be in the tent and when and how many, in fine weather or in tempest, in heat, in hail, rain, sleet, God save us, in snow?

Skip Manley had to know all about these matters, intimately, as they affected his rigging, just as the skipper of a white-winged vessel must know his crew, his passengers, his cargo, tides, winds, seas, all these variables in a systematic relationship whose lines of control shift with the air. I can see him now, standing on the already yellowing grass, waving his arms and calling out to his under-riggers as this portion of canvas or that was hauled part way into the air, then allowed to droop and flatten on the ground, when another section of the fabric would be lifted and aired. This wasn't some pup-tent from Canadian Tire, but almost a square mile of heavy, terra-cotta-coloured, aromatic, stiff, thickly-sized web, tough enough and thick enough that you couldn't bunch it in your fingers, it took two powerful hands to crush the canvas into folds, and those hands would come away smelling richly of the sizing and waterproofing, coloured too by the excess of dye. The big top had to protect more than fifteen hundred people from the weather—the number in attendance at a sold-out performance; that first season was almost a hundred-percent sellout. And though about sixteen-hundred and fifty souls could crowd around the elegant three-sided thrust stage, no single member of the audience was seated more than sixteen rows of seats from the playing area.

# The Scenic Art

The stage, the auditorium and the tent—and the excellent choice of plays—conspired to make the opening season a special, almost unique time in Canadian life, overpoweringly exciting, symphonic. Perhaps more than anyone, Skip Manley threw this image of the Toscanini-like over those weeks in June and early July, as he stood on a wooden crate, a kind of outdoors podium, and waved his arms in a set of signals apparently traditional in the profession. He used his feet as well as his arms, curious kicking motions of either leg seeming to suggest release of these guy-lines, tightening of those.

On Anne Street, not more than three hundred yards from the site of the tent, I could look down from the front bedroom window during the first weekend of our honeymoon and watch Skip and his crew as they carried out the last manoeuvres prior to hoisting the canvas definitively into place. This was only a few weeks before the first performance of *Richard III* was to be given, with Alec Guinness personating the celebrated monarch whom small-part actors hired for the season delighted in calling "Crookback Dick." Opening night was to be Monday, July thirteenth, not very long after Midsummer's Night, perhaps one of the two or three most momentous dates in contemporary Canadian culture-history, and it was rushing towards us at a dizzying rate. All the stakes were on the table; the actors had been hired and the production crew engaged, the seating and other structures of the auditorium planned and constructed with ghastly speed, immoderate haste as some felt. There had been second thoughts, but second thoughts entertained after the *fait accompli*, a singularly un-Canadian form of behaviour. Most great decisions are taken in Canada some time after the bankers have been over the estimates and the lawyers have vetted the legality of the proposal and the intentions of the proposers and the wording of the prospectus. These petty precautions had been elided; now the poured concrete of the seats and the tent underpinnings was in place; contracts had been signed covering the actors' engagements; costumes and props were being constructed in an old mop-and-floor-polisher factory and warehouse several miles across town, always called The Workroom, the capital letters audible in the speaker's voice.

In this place there laboured a young Englishwoman named Jacqueline Cundall under the title of Assistant Production Designer. She was the strawboss of the The Workroom, chief co-ordinator of props and costumes; her young women painted kirtles and surcoats and shields in a variety of heraldic patterns somewhat modernised in a line reminiscent of the work of John Piper. Fleurs-de-lys, English roses, thistles, and more recherché devices, spiders, unicorns, crocodiles. The crocodiles were uncalled-for in the designs, but Islay Strathdrummond (gamesome lass) painted them all over the shield carried in one scene by Adam Sinclair in *Richard III* and they passed muster as legendary mediaeval beasts among critics of the production, Herbert Whittaker, Nathan Cohen, even the astute and picky Walter Kerr. They may have identified them at a distance under fluctuating lighting as lizards or armadillos or some other creatures from romance, if indeed they noticed the crocodiles at all. I seem to recall that Adam had a line of dialogue in the production, but not a line that might cause any critic to focus his attention on its speaker, however briefly. Something along the lines of, "Help, ho!" or maybe "To horse!"

Myriads of such artifacts, orbs of unwonted size made of gilded toilet-tank floats, sceptres sparkling with all the rubies of Malabar and Moon, had to be prepared under conditions of drastic inefficiency and inadequate cost-control, by people who quickly acquired a specific and expert understanding of narrowly limited tasks. Letty Millen, for example, a woman of nearly thirty, highly competent and experienced as a teacher of interior design at Central Tech in Toronto, a graduate of the Ontario College of Art of a decade's standing, passed ten days from early morning to dusk in cutting out hundreds of tiny rosettes from bolts of cheap felt, painting them, then passing them to a woman at an adjoining bench who pasted them on other lengths of cloth, sometimes felt, sometimes muslin. Letty considered herself lucky to have this job, luxuriated in it, the proximity or at least the putative proximity of the famous stars and leading actors of the company, the genuine proximity of the small-part actors and the extra ladies and gentlemen, the circumstance of being in on the whole intoxicating undertaking from the start. Maybe the intoxicants were inappropriate for Letty. She fell at once and lastingly in love with Roly Ducane who was at least four or five years her junior and himself uncertain about his amative propensities, as he used to call his sexual inclinations.

Roly had had a juvenile lead at some primeval period in an eighteenth-century comedy, some curtain-raiser like *Miss In Her Teens*, in which the words "amative propensities" had been used to describe his character's pursuit of the ingénue described in the play's title. The words had stuck in his head and he often used them to indicate the problematic nature of his oscillations between poor Letty and Adam Sinclair, with whom he shared quarters, restricted as to size and pressingly inconvenient as to bathroom, on the top floor back of the same house on Anne Street as ours. Me and my Three Graces.

For it must be admitted that my lodgement in Stratford was of an equivocal kind, at least in the terms of the epoch. Married on the morning of the day I came to Stratford, Thursday, June fourth, 1953, and fatigued, even exhausted, as one is on his wedding-day, by a long automobile ride from Stoverville to Toronto, the subsequent train ride from Toronto to Stratford, and the taxi ride from the station to the house on Anne Street in Dave Williams' cab, I found myself on that first night projected into the middle of a strange *ménage à six*, the like of which Stratford had not seen until that time. There were my Three Graces—as they hated to be called— Islay Strathdrummond, Letty Millen, and my darling Edie, late a Codrington, "of that ilk" as Islay would have said, now a Goderich, who shared the most commodious of the quasi-apartments on the upper floors of the Anne Street house. And there were Roly Ducane, Adam Sinclair and I. Six was plenty!

Take Islay Strathdrummond for one! Edie had mentioned this young person in a series of letters written to me from Stratford in the weeks immediately preceding our wedding, and I had assumed that her unusual Christian name was pronounced to rhyme with "mislay" or "this way," with the stress on the first syllable, but this wasn't so. She called herself something that rhymed with "Twyla" or "while a" and often received letters addressed to Miss Aila Strathdrummond. As this pronunciation of her name was so regular and common, and the misspelling so wholly accepted, even by her old schoolfellows of Miss Edgar's and Miss Cramp's, I think that the simplest way out of the confusion is to give her name as "Aila" since that is the sound I imagine when I think of her.

When I found that this musical Christian name was actually spelled "Islay," which wasn't until I had known this lady for quite a long time, I realised that the mere look of the name, the quaint, unpredictable spelling and the sounds it suggested, put me in mind of all those charming British film comedies about the Outer Isles, written by people like Eric Linklater and Compton Mackenzie and directed and produced by Alexander McKendrick "of that ilk," and of the large Hebridean island of that name. Gentle satire of some of the congenital Scotticism found in parts of Ontario and very strongly around English-speaking Montréal, suggested itself insistently as one thought over the difference between Aila and Islay. Movies like *I Know Where I'm Going*, which were deservedly popular for decades in Ontario, were invariably invoked by the lady's incarnation in print, not so much by her person. One thought of Rum, Muck and Eigg, of Skye, of the Kyle of Lochalsh, of the isle of Islay itself, and all the rest of those romantic Hebridean places and scenes, when one thought of Aila (Islay) Strathdrummond, picturing her as some isolate laird's daughter smelling of tweed and peat smoke and baptised in the unblended malt. Her actual physical appearance was radically unlike the associations linked to her exotic name. She was simply a rich Montréal girl, a Westmount child, innocent of the contamination of higher education. She had been "finished" by Miss Edgar and Miss Cramp, had thereupon spent a season or two in the French cantons of Switzerland and afterwards returned home to pursue polite classes in drawing and painting under the aegis of the Montréal Museum of Fine Art, classes by no means destitute of guidance by justly famous directors, but not so concentrated or demanding as to excite high ambitions and the inclination towards excellence of execution in the breasts of the students, invariably women, who attended them. You could draw from the life at the MMFA, or learn the rudiments and even some of the subtleties of colour relationships, while making those first hesitant strokes in oil. Few students of talent remained long in the MMFA classes, for one reason or another, though several talented women passed through them.

I don't think that Aila Strathdrummond took her two years at the MMFA classes very seriously; she seems to have been waiting for some son of a whisky baron or millionaire tobacconist or newspaper publisher to seek her hand. She would accept him, whoever he turned out to be, and they would live somewhere near Summit Avenue, occasionally visiting her parents, who lived in the Château—or was it the Trafalgar? I never can remember. She could not, at that time, have been a more characteristic product of her background, and I fear that the first summer in Stratford did much to suspend or obliterate entirely those wholesome early influences. Aila seemed an exceedingly comely little Highlander or Hebridean, not so little neither. She had attracted attention from the interviewing committee which had visited Montréal in the winter of 1952–1953, seeking representative young persons to fill the junior production appointments at the Festival. It was thought necessary to have a few Montréal people on staff—the whole enterprise had an engaging air of improvisation as of a church entertainment—because Montréal finance, the Montréal rich, to put it crudely, would certainly be called upon at some time in the near future to lend a hand in support of the infant undertaking, if any kind of permanent establishment were to be mooted. Aila heard from friends at the MMFA that the interviewers from Stratford would be at the Windsor Hotel on certain dates in February. She went to the specified room number during the appointed hours, gave her name and address, either the Château or the Trafalgar. The address, her appearance, her Museum connections, her excellent French which came into play once or twice in the course of conversation, impressed the committee very favourably, and three weeks later she received a letter offering her an engagement on the design staff for the first season, which she promptly accepted. When she arrived in Stratford in mid-May she went at once to a billeting office that the Festival management had established in aid of its young people. There she was directed to the home of a Mrs. Roop on Anne Street where she might find colleagues with whom she could share accommodation. It was tacitly assumed by all parties that the salary paid by the Festival was more an *honorarium* than a *merces*; nobody could be expected to live on it without sharing an apartment, flat, or bed-sitting room with one or two other parties.

At Mrs. Roop's house, just up the slope from where the tent was about to be installed, Aila met Letty Millen and Edie Codrington who were already acquaintances, though not by any means close friends. They had had the same instructor in the Interior Design courses at OCA, though a decade apart. In Mrs. Roop's shadowy spacious downstairs hall the three women decided to share living quarters for the summer, if the second-floor flatlet described to them by the householder should prove all that she claimed. Upon inspection it proved to be slightly less than that. The water ran rusty into the bathtub for some seconds after being turned on; this phenomenon continued the whole summer. And the bathroom had to be shared with two other girls who had the smaller flat across the hall, which meant that five people, and after I moved in six, had to share a single bathroom. It was fortunate that the toilet was housed in a separate adjoining cubicle; otherwise congestion in the bathroom might have been seriously inconvenient. As things were, this minor logistical difficulty caused some surprising shifts and circumventions of ordinary propriety. It was not long before the two girls across the hall were suspected of bathing, or at least showering, together.

This always seemed like perfectly good sense to me, and even rather fun, but it gave great offence to Letty Millen. She was also much put out by Aila's declaration that she no longer minded not being able to run water into the basin while she was peeing.

"I didn't use to want to be heard. Now I don't care," said Aila. She considered this a step towards personal liberation, according to Edie who told me the story later on. It wasn't that Letty minded people hearing other people pee. What she minded was discussion of the subject. There were other confusions and, to adopt appropriately Shakesperian idiom, other alarums and excursions in connection with constricted lavatory accommodation which finally attained the status first of high comedy, then of comic cliché. Then we all grew tired of jokes about the bathroom and let the matter drop, except when the squeals of unconcealed rapture from the girls across the hall, once they had managed to scramble into the shower, grew too intensely expressive to be ignored.

"Those two aren't Lesbians," Letty Millen would assert, her lips firmly compressed between each irritated speech. "They're just playacting." She seemed to consider Lesbianism a hard-won honorific status, though in no degree herself inclined that way. "It's an unearned dignity," she would declare.

It didn't materially help matters that one of the girls across the hall, actresses they were, was called Lizzie Holcombe. Her roommate, still at that epoch Brenda Schatzenberg of Toronto, was in process of trying to decide which of several alternatives should become her stage name. She was hovering between Fitzalan and Conquest in those first days. Letty used to lie awake nights listening to her murmuring the two names in the front bedroom across the hall. "Brenda Conquest ... Brenda Fitzalan. Brenda Fitzalan ... Brenda Conquest." A choice had to be made before the printing of the first Festival programs. Not very long after Mrs. Roop got those five young women crowded together in the two cramped flatlets on her second floor, around the last day of May, 1953, poor Brenda finally achieved a command decision. She scrapped both her names for histrionic purposes, chose her second given name, Sadie, and an entirely new, wholly fictitious, family name, emerging from her chrysalid state as *Sadie MacNamara.*

It is as Sadie MacNamara, of course, that she has become famous. At the end of May in that first season she was just an extra lady, making brief appearances in both *Richard III* and *All's Well.* I can't remember for sure whether Lizzie Holcombe had a line in either play. I rather think not. But she did appear onstage in the crowds, and at one point in rehearsal was given a long cross and a curtsey before the king in *All's Well* as part of the complex blocking of a crowded court scene. Neither of these girls was as well known then as afterwards, but they qualified quite distinctly as actresses within the meaning of the act, as it were. They had the characteristic professional disdain for mere members of the production staff.

"Oh you're on props," said Brenda Schatzenberg to Edie Codrington, the first time they met, thereby making, if not an enemy at least an adversary for life. Even her transformation into Sadie MacNamara and epiphany in the Festival cast-lists under that name, at about the same time that Edie was metamorphosed into a Goderich, even her chastened realisation that Edie was now very proximately related by marriage to Canada's Nobel Peace Prize winner, the celebrated MP for East Gwillimbury, wasn't a sufficient alteration in the two girls' relationship for Sadie and Edie to become true friends. The rhyming echo of their names didn't help matters either. There they were, stuck across the hall from each other on the least satisfactory of terms, in very constricted space.

Mrs. Roop, in common with most of the other homeowners of Stratford whose premises allowed of rental subdivision, had decided to get in on the business of housing Festival staff for as long as the going was good. She emptied the top two floors of her three-storey home of all traces of Roops. Then the second floor was divided with lightning speed and liberal use of beaverboard into two flats sharing a common bathroom and toilet. The larger of the two, not really a very large unit in itself, was made up of two big rooms, plus a sunny kitchenette, some big closets, and a pretty screened balcony on the north side of the house, with a wooden staircase leading down from the balcony to the side drive. Garbage cans could conveniently be carried down this staircase, and apparently it met local fire regulations about emergency exits, though made of old dry wood and presumably highly inflammable. This was the accommodation shared at first by Letty, Aila and Edie, afterwards by all four of us in decidedly inconvenient circumstances. Edie and I fastened upon the large front bedroom

# The Scenic Art

which luckily had a door opening onto the centre hall. Letty and Aila were stuck with the middle room and a pair of perfectly comfortable but somewhat obtrusive daybeds. These daybeds were a bone of contention all summer. Every time Letty and Aila complained and urged that we switch rooms, Edie and I would exchange sighs and moon over each other and our friends would be obliged to concede that they hadn't the heart to shift from their nuptial chamber a married couple who might just as well be honeymooners. The place was too small for the four of us, though I found the experience of living on terms of the closest intimacy with three women stimulating in the highest degree. It was with relief and intense anticipation, however, that Edie and I moved back to Toronto and our place on Yonge Street in the fall.

The other second-floor flat consisted of two smallish rooms without any kitchenette space or balcony, rather commodious lodgings for Lizzie and Sadie when they were left alone, but impossible to cope with when they were forced to extend overnight hospitality to visitors, which is what happened when Edie and I arrived from Stoverville on the night of the fourth of June, ecstatically happy and resolved to oust Letty and Aila from the apartment for the first weekend of our life together. Heavens, but their noses were out of joint, but there was nothing else they could do. They had to agree to doss down with the actresses across the hall, at a time when the distinction between cast and crew was starting to irritate everybody in the house, including Roops.

The element, I am almost impelled to write, of class distinction which was in play between cast and crew was exacerbated by the discovery early made by Lizzie and Sadie that the new husband of one of those props people across the hall, that snotty Codrington bitch, or Goderich, or whatever she called herself now, was a man who knew the actors on the third floor very well, seemed indeed to be the intimate long-term friend and counsellor of one of them, the promising Adam Sinclair, already much discussed in the town as one of the new young Canadians who would go far in the profession. His reading of "Help, ho!" or possibly "To horse!" had distinguished him in the eyes of his young associates. There was talk that he might be given another line or two in the usual shuffle of bits of dialogue during the cutting of a Shakesperian chronicle play in rehearsal. One bright morning later in June, Tyrone Guthrie took Adam by the shoulder and told him to move over here, just here, and shout repeatedly "They come, my liege," though the line will not be found in the text. A bit of audible gag meant to give shape to the rumble of crowd noise. This action by the director gave Adam a sharp increase of renown among his peers; he was now seen to be a rising young actor. Lizzie and Sadie were not best pleased to find that the stuck-up little Mrs. Goderich was married to somebody who, in addition to being the son of a great man, was intimate with Adam.

There were two bed-sitting rooms up on the top floor, and a bathroom, and Mrs. Roop turned these to good account. She had four young actors packed in up there, Adam and Roly Ducane in one bed-sitter and two more young men in the other. The second pair were talentless blokes whose names appeared in the cast-lists of the first season in the smallest lettering at the very bottom, often thereafter in CBC-TV Drama credits. Neither managed to project much sense of himself in 1953, but both were always available to swell a scene or two, and were in constant attendance at the sempiternal party which was in progress on the Thursday night when Edie and I installed ourselves in the second floor apartment and commanded Letty and Aila to bunk in with the ladies across the hall.

"Pair of sluts," said Edie of the two budding actresses, through tightly clenched teeth, "serve 'em right." I have to laugh as I think over the situation. Sadie in particular, as events of the later summer abundantly demonstrated, very much wished to display herself as a worldly-wise, richly experienced woman of the theatre. She would like to have been able to prove and sustain a Lesbian relationship with her apartment-mate for professional reasons, and in the early days of their joint tenancy the thing was attempted, but despite the pinchings and squealings in shower or tub, neither Lizzie nor Sadie seemed able to manage more than qualified enthusiasm for a permanent sexual relation with a person of

# The Scenic Art

the same sex. Both of them remained extremely interested in the behaviour and emotional orientation of men, particularly the four men lodged on the top floor at Mrs. Roop's. They might even have been described, in the prejudicial language of the day, as boy-crazy. No amount of flopping around in the bathtub succeeded in expunging this inclination. After all, they were very young women.

All these complexities were winding themselves into little snarls while Edie and I were getting ready for our wedding. I knew nothing about them. I had barely heard the names of Edie's roommates, in fact had only begun to realize that Edie had mentioned the name of Letty Millen to me during flying visits to Toronto or Stoverville. I thought that she might have spoken what I recalled as the name of a girl who lived down our street when I was a child of six, the first girl I'd ever been able to focus on as a person in herself, separate from the covering cloak of background and circumstance in which a young child drapes everything but his immediate family. Could Edie's new roommate be the same Letty Millen whom I had adored from afar when I was hardly more than a baby? Time would tell. Who were all those other mysterious figures swimming around in the treacherous waters of Stratford like highly-coloured exotic tropical fish? I realised all at once, as we were being driven from the railway station to Mrs. Roop's house in Dave Williams' De Soto (*Dave Williams De Soto Taxi Service, Stratford, Saint Mary's, Tavistock: Speedy Efficient Transportation*) that I was about to be dropped with a great splash, as from a considerable height like a circus performer, into this tank of green illuminated fluid in which gold and scarlet and silver creatures of unimaginable shapes and habits swam round and round agitating slender fins, looking at me out of the sides of their heads with curiously impassive eyes: the denizens of the theatre.

It was now well past ten o'clock. I remember giving Dave Williams two dollars and refusing the change for a thirty-five cent ride, thus making a friend, as it turned out, for life, or for life up to now. Always wise to insert that qualification. I thought of Dave in those days as somebody much older than I, but he was actually no more than four or five years my senior; he'd inherited the taxi business, three cabs, five drivers, from his dad, only a few months before the Festival opened. I saw a lot of him that first summer. I used to sit with him in the dispatcher's office while Edie was working, chatting about Stratford life and the landslide business the cab company was doing.

I don't know why I gave Dave a dollar sixty-five tip for a thirty-five cent ride. I know that I was so tired that I was hysterical. Edie and I were laughing helplessly and falling all over ourselves; we'd had a long long day. I kept rolling up like a cigarette paper on my forefinger, then unrolling, the slip of paper which Mr. Codrington had passed to me hours before, as we took our departure from the wedding party. "You always need a bit extra," he had murmured in an aside clearly intended for my ears alone. The piece of paper was a certified cheque for a thousand dollars, and Earl Codrington was perfectly right. We did need a little extra. You can take it as a general maxim or guide to life that no matter where you go and how long you stay, outgo will at least marginally exceed available resources.

Dave Williams drove off wearing a pleased smile, leaving us standing on Anne Street in front of Mrs. Roop's place. At our backs some two hundred yards down a gentle slope lay the huge tent, now draped over the cement underpinnings to which it would be guyed when fully erect. We stared at it for some moments hand in hand in the fresh spring night, wondering what the future held for us. All at once several bright lights came on at the Festival site and a series of shouted commands and replies floated to our ears, mingled with rich oaths and other expostulations. Like a woolly mammoth or outsized elephant, a whole section of the tent rose miraculously from the ground, a huge blister swelling strangely from a freshly dressed surface. Then there was motion under the canvas; workmen seemed to be adjusting the length and angle of an interior mast. You could hear a distinct musical note, not the baritone sonority of later summer but a kind of flutelike whistling, altering in pitch as the height and shape of the elevated section shifted. It was at this point that I made the observation so often quoted back to

# The Scenic Art

me by Edie in later years, finally put into wide currency by the great Kenneth Williams (no relation to Dave) in *Carry On Camping*.

"It isn't getting it up," I muttered as though to myself, "it's keeping it up that counts." Edie squeezed my hand and giggled. She now began to reveal a distinct taste for humour tinged with eroticism, nothing too blue.

"How sweet the moonlight sleeps upon this bank. See how the floor of heav'n is thick inlaid with patines of bright gold," I said, remembering the line from time spent studying *Merchant* with Bea Skaithe when we were in Grade Eleven together, the year the war ended.

"Shut up, Matt," said Edie, "there isn't any moonlight." It was true; the light was coming from the floodlights on the Festival site. A further round of shouted exhortations drifted to our ears and the bulge of the tent collapsed. A tractor came into view, hauling a line like an umbilical cord leading to the tent's insides. All at once the floodlights were switched off and darkness descended. The music of the breeze under canvas was silenced. Other voices succeeded it.

"Edie, Edie, you got here, you old married lady, let's see you."

This was Aila Strathdrummond, bouncing down the outside staircase with a brown-paper sack of garbage in her hand. She deposited this handful beside a row of garbage cans in the driveway and rushed forward. Above us, lights came on in the second floor windows; another young woman peered down from the front bedroom.

"That's Letty," said Aila breathlessly, "straightening out your room, the honeymoon suite, goodness." She stopped and looked at me as if she'd said something embarrassing, which she had.

"Come on upstairs and let us see you," said Aila, leading us along the row of garbage cans, all crammed full, empty whisky and beer bottles the most prominent feature of the collected refuse. A definite odour of hops hung over them.

Aila forced a lid onto one of the cans.

"God, what a party," she said brashly. She led the way up the stairs and into the flat by the kitchen door. I got no very definite impression of the kitchen as she led us through it and into the sizeable middle room which had several shabby easy chairs distributed around it, as well as the two daybeds on which Aila and Letty proposed to sleep that night. We proceeded into the front bedroom, which was to be our dwelling for the rest of the summer. I liked it. There was a good big double bed. All I wanted to do at that moment was to visit a toilet, then fling myself into that bed and sleep for about a month. Only the first of these goals proved feasible for some hours. There was a long conversation, several cups of surprisingly excellent coffee, and settlement of the question of how the flat was to be shared, to be gotten through before we retired to rest.

"Let me take those coats and bags," said Aila helpfully. Letty advanced into the bedroom and stood by the doorframe. "More light?" she asked, pushing a switch. The room went all bright pink and white; the walls were papered in a floral motif reminiscent of birthday cake, scrolls, rosettes, the lot. Letty advanced into the room and I took a good look at her; it was the same person without a doubt as the brisk fair-haired eleven-year-old Canadian girl who had so beguiled me on Summerhill Avenue beside the bus-stop in 1936, the object of Mr. Busdriver Smith's covert affections, therefore related in a peculiar way to Mildred and Marigold Smith, my high-school near sweethearts. I had one of those sudden intimations of the immense complexity of even the most provincial, parochial society as I gazed at her. The crisscross of relations amongst Letty, Mildred and Marigold, and therefore Bea Skaithe, Edie and me, involved many more people than just the six of us. Aila was on her way to joining us, I saw, and so were the girls as yet unknown across the hall, whose aid now had to be invoked. I felt the cruel toils of modern life winding themselves ever more tightly around me as Aila and Edie passed out through the door of our bedroom into the hall. I heard them tapping on the door across the hall. It was opened, and they went inside. Feminine voices were now raised in declaration and protest. I stood motionless, looking Letty over. It was plain that she didn't recognise me, though she was scrutinising me narrowly.

"You're the Goderich boy, aren't you," she said doubtfully. "Which one are you? I believe I know your sister."

"Amanda?"

"Yes, Amanda Louise. Such a sweet name, I always thought."

"I'm the middle child," I said. "I've got a brother Tony, a couple of years younger than me. I don't think you'd have known him."

This remark seemed to displease her slightly.

"I was twenty-eight my last birthday," she said quickly. "I'm not much older than you are."

"Going on six years," I said. I was much too tired to make polite conversation.

She eyed me more closely. "Didn't you used to hang around the bus-stop and try to sell my mother magazines?"

I laughed weakly.

"You must be 'dirty-face'," she said accusingly.

"What?"

"That's what I used to call you. You used to ask Mr. Smith for bus transfers, didn't you? And you were always sort of sticky?"

"OK," I said. "We needn't go into all that right now."

"You were terribly cute," she said. "I used to want to take you and wash your little face. I used to want to mother you."

I found this an unsatisfactory attitude, on my wedding night, from an older woman now virtually a stranger. On the simple dogmatic grounds of the modern mind, its Freudian baggage included as wanted on the voyage, I realised that this particular night should admit of no mothering, either from my own mother or from anybody else. I was all through with this goddam mothering, I figured. I was now a married man, not some woman's little boy.

The voices on the other side of the hall mounted in volume; some sort of debate seemed to be in active progress. It was midnight. I longed for sleep. "So I was cute and you wanted to mother me, great, terrific," I said, rather abruptly. "If you want to mother me tonight would you do me a favour and leave the bedroom to Edie and me?" There was an evilly contorted parody of Freudian orthodoxy in this outright appeal which pleased me even in my nearly drunken state. Psychoanalytic method derives its categories from theatricality: the slow revelation of the guilty secret, the stripping away of costume, rôle, concealment. "Aren't you and Aila going to let us have the apartment for our honeymoon?" I asked.

"How long do you want it for?"

"Give us till Monday morning. Four nights alone together."

"And then we can move back in?"

"Certainly," I said, with great suavity.

Letty turned on her heel and went out into the adjoining room, where she seized two pairs of pyjamas and an outsized teddy bear. Then she marched back through our bedroom and into the hall. "The bear belongs to Aila," she said as she exited. "She won't get to sleep without it." I watched her disappear into the flat across the way. The squeaks and squawks of five females rose to an ingeniously orchestrated pitch. Edie's level menacing tone dominated the arrangement, but I could also make out a clarinet-like legato of appeal from Letty. In moments all was still, and Edie came back. The door of Lizzie and Sadie's place closed behind her and calm returned to the second floor. The four-man drinking session on the top floor apparently continued, for I heard occasional raucous shouts and bits of repeated dialogue. Somebody hollered something about glorious summer and this sun of York. Edie fell into my arms, kicking the hall door shut as she executed the action. We moved towards the bed.

It turns out that over-excited exhaustion is no bar to sexual love. Neither of us got to sleep that night until about four-thirty. It was beginning to get very light on Friday morning when troubled slumber descended. I kept dreaming of the big tent, imagining that I heard the cries of the rigging crew. Imagining gradually gave way to reality, somewhere about noon. I came awake with a jump to find myself stark naked, running with sweat, the day immensely sultry and the chorus of voices from across Anne Street growing louder, if anything, than the cries of the five outraged women across the hall on the previous night. I wondered confusedly if life at the Festival was going to include an unending sequence of outcry, view hallo, haro, havoc. Should this prove to be the case, one's nerves seemed destined to remain at taut pitch.

Edie was sitting on the window seat, eating a peach and rubbing juice from her chin. She had no clothes on. I went over and seized her and made her put the peach down. We went back to bed. I don't think I ate anything that day. Letty and Aila kept knocking on the doors to the apartment; we wouldn't let them in. They attempted a diversionary raid up the outside stairs, which was fiercely repulsed by Edie. I heard Aila bellowing, "I only want a clean pair of panties." On Friday and Saturday night we were treated to a brilliant display of heat-lightning. As we lay in each other's arms, we saw the walls of our room brighten up silently, eerily, again and again, with light from the west. It looked as if we might be treated to one of the June thunderstorms characteristic of the region. But Sunday morning came and passed, and Sunday afternoon, and the only thunderclaps we were forced to acknowledge were the truly thunderous blows upon the door to our apartment made by some emissary from The Workroom who insisted that Edie must must MUST come over that evening to make another orb for King Richard. Edie giggled and perpetrated a coarse jest about Richard III's balls which made us both hysterical. I was holding her down across my knee, kissing the small of her back and her bottom, when she said that about Richard's balls. The association of balls and buttocks was fixed for me from that instant. I rubbed my cheek ardently across her bum. The person outside insisted. Edie rolled away from me onto the carpet, stood up, and conversed briefly with our caller. Then she came over to me and put her hands on my cheeks. She wound her arms around my neck, placing my face between her breasts. We embraced closely. I felt my knees buckle.

She whispered, "I've got to go."

"But this is our last night alone together."

She struggled into her painting clothes, a neckcloth, plaid shirt, paint-stiffened jeans. I don't think she was wearing a bra. She caught my eyes on her breasts and grinned. "All girls over there," she said. "Not to worry."

"I'm not so sure."

"There's none of that in The Workroom. Mostly hard-bitten old married ladies. I'll be back in a couple of hours."

"What do you have to do?"

"I've got to gild another toilet-tank float."

"What?" I could feel myself drowsing off.

"I'll explain later. You have a nice nap, like a good little boy." She vanished from my sight. I tottered to the bed and fell on it, not bothering to put on my pyjamas; the room was muggy and ill-ventilated, one window shut, the other half open. I was too tired to go and fling them apart. I slept.

I woke again momentarily sometime around eight-thirty or a quarter to nine. It wasn't quite dark yet. At that time of year it doesn't get completely dark in Stratford till after nine-thirty. But it was by now twilight. The flickering heat-lightning was coming more frequently and making a fantastic moving picture in the shadowy bedroom. I dozed, imagining Edie, her legs and arms and breasts and bum. What a girl! My cock was engorged and hot and felt . . . well, I hate to say this, but 'thrilling' is the right word. I had never felt so male.

All the funny humane language of sex ran through my head. My wife is a good lay, I thought, and I thought all the other things too. I'm no prude. Holding my wife in my arms was completely different from talking about girls out behind the barn . . . not that I've ever been out behind any barns with anybody. When you've got the actual woman naked and panting in your arms and you're kissing each other and she's playing with your cock and you're squeezing her ass and kissing her nipples and the real love is there, that's the best of sex. I never much went for one-night stands. As I was lying there thinking of all these matters I felt myself becoming stiffly erect and excessively stimulated. I thought of the gorgeous round peachy smoothness of Edie's bottom. I wanted to kiss it and kiss her stomach around the navel. I ejaculated suddenly and copiously. My body moved rhythmically up and down; the climax lasted some time. When I fell asleep the second time it was a deep sleep and I didn't wake again for a couple of hours, when a loud clap of thunder sounded overhead. It blended with my dreams.

Lightning flashed on the walls, not heat-lightning but the reflection of great flashes of chain lightning. There was a new presence in the atmosphere, a new sound which I couldn't at first identify, the long deep sonorous bass-baritone singing of the tent. Skip must have got it up at last, I thought. I chuckled silently, feeling the sticky wetness between my legs. More lightning. I got more awake and suddenly realised that I was no longer alone on the rumpled bed. Except for the flashes of lightning there was no illumination in the room, and the sound of the approaching storm, the repeated cannonade like celestial bowling-balls, orchestrated in harmony with the pedal point supplied by the theatrical erection — I mean the tent, no joke intended — confused me so that at first I didn't hear the sighing and whining coming from my bedmate. Edie's back already, I decided, lifting myself on a shaking elbow. Somebody was caressing my damp thighs and — horrors — my rear end, as though I were a girl. There was a momentary interruption of the rolling thunder and I identified the sighs and murmurs of my companion as those of a male. I sat up instantaneously, and it wasn't easy on the soft mattress, and glared into the shadowed hollows of the rumpled sheets and the big pillows. Whoever this person was, he was the wrong way around: his head was down around my knees, and I suspected that I was looking straight at his sexual members. This was totally disaccommodating. Cries began to clarify themselves.

"Oh Matt, I've always loved you, don't send me away. Oh Matt, you're so beautiful."

Nobody in my life had ever told me I was beautiful; it's a groundless assertion. Actually I'm a funny-looking man.

"Matt, I've waited so long for you to come. Why did you take so long, oh so long?"

I was having a hard time finding the light switch. There was a lamp on a bedside table but I had got my feet caught in the tangled bedding and I couldn't quite stretch far enough to reach it. I certainly didn't want to have to cope with the harsh overhead lighting, which was like the illumination in an interrogation room, where the good and bad cops take turns questioning you. Afterwards they beat you with rubber hoses.

"Who is this?" I whispered. I wasn't sure that Aila and Letty were still across the hall; they might have found entry and even now be tossing on narrow daybeds in the next room, restless themselves and slightly feverish because of the tempo of life in this turbulent environment. The person beside me gave my buttocks a painful squeeze.

I said, "Now cut that out," and it made me think foolishly of Jack Benny. I almost found myself saying, "Rochester, oh Rochester!"

My companion pinched me painfully. I suppose this was meant as an endearment, but it stirred no affectionate response in me. I'd have bright pink marks on my bottom, I figured, hard to explain to Edie. What might she conclude from such evidence?

"All right, who are you, what's the trouble?" I said. I knew who it was, all right. I managed to sit up on the billowing mattress, and the other party sat up eagerly from the opposite direction, facing me.

"Oh darling Matt," said Adam Sinclair, and he took me in his arms and kissed me full on the lips. He smelled overpoweringly of a mixture of many drinks, among which rye whisky appeared to predominate. There was a tang of vomit as well, and of something else, perhaps a cosmetic of some sort. His mouth and breath were far from sweet. He lurched suddenly to one side, inadequately positioned on the soft bed. I had to grab him or he'd have fallen right over on his head. I found myself, to my horror and amazement, with my arms around him, a posture which I was reluctant to preserve. Should I slap his face? The gesture seemed too much like that of a terrified woman. I would speak daggers to him, but use none.

"All right, Adam, come off of it, eh? Just stop the nonsense and wake up. What the hell do you think you're up to anyway?" Overhead a rush of raindrops sounded distantly, like brushing on the heads of the snaredrums as the parade moves off; the tent continued to sound its deep B.

He clutched me, hung on tight. I couldn't make out his face but now that I was awake I thought that I recognized the

# The Scenic Art

outline of his form. The voice was certainly his. "Oh Matt," he gurgled, "the sight of honeymoons is so upsetting."

Well, I mean to say!

"Oh God, Matt, when I saw you come in the other night with that big blonde. . ."

"Caramel. Her hair is too dark to be called blonde."

He said brokenly, "I saw her under the street lights. She's a blonde, Matt. Take it from me. Maybe strawberry-blonde, but you can do anything with a good rinse. She might even be a brownette. They're so mendacious."

"What?" I said, falling sidewise on the sweaty messy bed. I'd have given anything to go back to sleep, but the second I lay down he started fumbling at me from behind. I could feel him pressing himself against me and I was almost frightened. I don't think Adam could ever really frighten me. He got his arms around me from behind and his hands were slipping around on my wet chest. A ring he was wearing caught in my chest hair and yanked some out. It hurt like hell.

"Why can't you be nice to me like you were when we were small? You used to stop them from pulling my pants down. You used to help me get dressed afterwards. It was as bad as a gang rape."

He was quiet briefly, and I began to hope that he would go to sleep. If the smell of liquor was anything to go by, he must have been soaking up the stuff since the middle of last week; there had certainly been a party in progress on the night we'd arrived. Thursday, Friday, Saturday. This was Sunday night. He'd been into the sauce for at least four nights and maybe a whole lot longer. I didn't see how he could attempt anything more tonight except a few fervent clutches and the occasional passionate declaration. Passionate declarations won't kill you. I could feel his body relaxing, sinking into the mattress behind me. He began to breathe deeply; was this some clever ruse or was he really dropping off? How as I going to get him back upstairs?

The more he relaxed, the more he pressed against me. I could feel his knees pressing in against the backs of my knees, making them flex. His stomach and his pelvis kept snuggling in against the small of my back — to put the matter as delicately as possible. I'd been the object of several heavy passes before this from persons of all sexes, as it were, every imaginable stripe of sexual persuasion, but nothing quite so explicit. He was cuddling me and I think he was starting to be erect.

"Lemme go, Adam!" I said, horrified, but he was either genuinely asleep, in a somnambulistic state, which I doubted very much, or he was faking slumber to beguile me into acquiescence. Another sheet of rain washed across the remote roof; it would have sounded very romantic in slightly different circumstances, say with a girl. Not to panic!

You have to remember that there was a lot of thunder banging and booming around while all this was going on, sometimes quite close and sometimes further away, approximately over the quarry near Saint Mary's. People on the Festival staff used to drive to the quarry after the performances to swim under starshine or moonlight, often in the nude, sometimes right through a June thunderstorm. There were probably some of them there at this moment, slipping and sliding around in the lightning flashes, on and off the rock ledges, spray phosphorescent in the irregular light, a very cinematic conception. I wished that I was someplace like that instead of held down in this grubby bed with a deeply frustrated small-part actor clinging to me.

"You were much nicer to me when we were in *Othello*," crooned this Shakesperian voice behind me, and I had to giggle. Of course he was awake; he knew perfectly well what was going through my mind. Adam might be a homosexual or he might not. I suspected that his homosexuality was largely assumed as a rôle, a kind of protective colouration he considered essential professional equipment, as Edna Millay held that all one's nice friends were homosexual. Party clothes, like the skin-deep Lesbianism of Lizzie and Sadie across the hall. You never can tell. His mention of the Hart House production of *Othello* suddenly jolted me sharply awake, because I remembered it very well: the lousiness of my own performance in a small but crucial part, the engaging good looks that Adam had somehow miraculously conjured up for his rôle. He played Cassio, a bigger and more important part than mine but not the sort of part in which an actor normally shines, especially when you consider the nature of the rôles assigned to the other male principals. Cassio is really a feed for Iago and Othello. You might call him a Don Ottavio character; it's basically a light tenor part. But Adam had managed to make himself seem an exciting model of male beauty and soldierly bearing. That was the first time that I ever realised that he might have great talent — so rare in Canadian life — because he had never shown any kind of ability to conceal or modify his rather peculiar appearance when we were kids together, living on Summerhill Avenue. Everybody in our family used to call him, "yon wee Scotch farrrttt" or "Putty-face."

When my brother Tony invented the nickname "Puttyface" to characterise the child Adam Sinclair, he showed astonishing artistic prescience. He had only been describing, as he thought, the peculiar shape and texture of the flesh on the little neighbourhood boy's cheeks, something like a dried apple, something like a hazel-nut. There were already at six or seven years of age deep laugh lines around the corners of his mouth and below the round cheeks, and around the eyes. It was an old face for a child and an exceedingly mobile and expressive one, though I didn't realise this at the time. Tony knew, though. At three or four years, he could judge the plastic changeable potential of such a face. It wasn't that Adam's cheeks were rubbery and a bit grey, though they were, it was more that they supplied a blank surface on which any number of subsequent personations might be inscribed. I have known one or two other cases of extraordinary transformation of one's personal appearance. I remember little Angie Robinson, Esther Robinson's baby sister, Angela Mary, to give her the formal baptismal names, who at the age of five or six was one of the ten princesses on the last run of the SWLS from Westport to Stoverville. Many years after that first magical appearance in my own annals, Angela Robinson moved to Montréal where she apparently effected an almost total change in her looks, habits, character, which she was able to sustain for some years, though not permanently. When she was living in Montréal, according to my informant, Maura Boston, Angela had changed herself so completely that quite close friends from childhood days in Stoverville found her impossible to recognise during chance encounters in the province of Québec. She had altered her name, her dress, her profession, her language, opinions, sexual comportment — she lived a pretty free and easy life there for a while — in such a way as to approach the state of multiple, or as we say, "split" personality. This wore off after a time, and Angela married quite conventionally, returning to Ontario in a later phase, apparently in much chastened state.

I think that the metamorphoses of Angie approached, though they did not quite equal, the extraordinary change I encountered in Adam Sinclair, when I finally got into the University of Toronto in the autumn of 1948. My own circumstances had been in a highly fluid state ever since the end of the war. All the way through my first three years of high-school I had fondly imagined that I would eventually don the uniform of one of Canada's fighting services. I had longed for the day to come. I saw myself transformed into an adult of infinitely more impressive appearance and capabilities than anything adolescence had proffered. I greatly wished to change my life, my circumstances, though never my true parentage.

Freudian family romance requires that children, especially boys, regard their parents of record as unspeakably unworthy of them: the actual parents are drab, quotidian, engaged in plebian work. Their kids long to have the grandeur of their fantasies justified by the discovery that their true parents are not the bland couple who live in the same little house as they do. The true parents must be kings or queens or movie stars, or God Himself. No great hero ever admits that the people who raised him can be anything but foster-parents; when this denial forces its necessity upon him, the hero wanders off about his imagined father's business: Oedipus, Gatsby, Moses, all in their different ways the children of God.

But suppose the child has a king or queen, a great athlete, a very rich and handsome young man or woman — or both — as parent of record? What do you do for family romance if you find the old couple who live in your house to be more glamorous, more charming, more interesting than you? Or can children ever make this terrible discovery? Yes they can. I did. I never believed that there were "real" parents somewhere in the world or in the heavens more valuable, interesting, charming, glamorous, than mine, though there were lots richer. When I found myself, in the fall of 1950, the son of the first Canadian winner of the Nobel Peace Prize, I felt justified in this judgment. I knew that I was privileged to be the child of Andrew and Ishy. I'll give a late example of their magnanimity: they didn't take me to Stockholm. I couldn't have sustained the trip. Amanda Louise went along, and apparently had the hell of a time. She still raves about a particular little meatball on a toothpick that some Swedish prince or other, Carl Gustav or Bernd, offered her at one of the receptions.

It isn't for their meatballs that one admires the Swedes, but for their generous commitment to international movements towards peace and human rights which compel the consciences of us all. I'm not a great fan of Swedish culture. Their painting cuts no ice with me. It is cold, cold. But they are a humanitarian people, generous where humanitarian concerns are in play. The actual prize money which accompanies the Peace Prize is a pretty large amount. I never knew for certain exactly how much it was in 1950, but in later years newspapers quoted sums in six figures. Of course my father gave the prize money away. It may have been around a hundred thousand. Gave it to the Secretary-General of the UN to help finance UNRRA programs in resettlement. How can you entertain the classical family romance narrative about a parent who gets to do that sort of thing?

And she was just the same. "Now that your father has a steady job, the first he's had in ages..." she'd grin at us, saying these things. Such a sense of happiness, such a belief in beatification, at having Andrew Goderich back from wanderings in foreign parts, that her kids felt the warmth reflected on our faces, almost to the point of discomfort. That particular line of dialogue surfaced when I was first beginning to pay court to Edie in the autumn of 1952 when my father had just been elected to Parliament in a by-election. Should I explain the joke? My father didn't get back to Canada after the war until the middle of 1948, just at the time that I was struggling to get enough money together to register at university. I had finished high-school in the spring of 1947, lacking a passing grade in one subject for university entrance, which I obtained a little later on. While preparing for the necessary supplemental examination, I decided to work for a year to raise some money while I tried to keep track of my father, wondering all the while when he would finally be free to come home.

In May, 1948, Paul-Edouard Martin, the first general secretary of UNRRA, died suddenly of a heart attack, and his post was offered to my father, who declined it. He returned to Canada immediately after the death of M. Martin, just about the time that I managed to squeeze into university. I think he felt that he'd interrupted my growing-up by causing me to spend most of 1947/48 working in a series of dead-end jobs. I've never thought that. I liked those jobs.

"Tell me again what you were doing while I was at the UN."

"I spent the summer of '47 working on a farm near Collingwood. After that I worked for a fur-blender and dyer for a few months, till my nose gave out."

"That would be smell of the dye?"

"Right! Golly, how it stank!"

"What else?"

"I was an office boy for the Treasury Department, working in an Unemployment Insurance Commission office."

"Very useful experience, that. Anything more?"

"I quit the U.I.C. when we heard you were coming home, and I just bummed around on the Island for a summer."

He said, "I feel as though I'd disinherited you."

"No, no."

"Tony hasn't gone to university."

"It wouldn't suit Tony."

"I guess not."

"Was it such a great amount of money after all?"

"What, the prize?"

"Yes."

"I don't know the exact amount. I asked them to send it directly to Mr. Lie. I couldn't have taken it, you know."

"Yes, I do see that."

"You aren't going to lose by it, Matthew. All the same, I do now and then feel as though I'd done you out of something. You were only a child when I left and now you're a man. I missed your teens."

"Well sir," I said, "an awful lot of fathers missed their kids' teens in the nineteen-forties."

"I stayed away far too long."

"But you're back for good now, aren't you." We had this chat the day after he was elected to Parliament.

"I could lose in the general election, I suppose, but it isn't likely."

"Are you thinking about a place in the CCF leadership? Foreign affairs critic, something like that?"

"I'll tell you what I'm doing," he said with a guilty grin. "I'm learning Chinese. Don't tell your mother."

"Oh God!"

"Did you like farming?"

"What?" I said. I'd lost the thread. "Oh farming, you mean when I was in Collingwood? Yes, I liked it. I loved it. But I wouldn't be able to spend my whole life doing it. I probably wouldn't have enjoyed it so much if I'd known I was going to spend the rest of my life on the same farm."

He said, "You're better off as you are." I could see that his mind had gone on to something else.

"Are you thinking about another book?" I said accusingly. He gave a start.

"Don't you think three is a nice round number?" he said.

"Depends. The last one would be a tough act to follow. I often see copies of it in bookstores."

"I still get royalties from it. I didn't give them away. I've made money out of *Sin Quantified*. It seems odd."

"And now you've got a steady job."

"That's your mother's joke."

By the time we had this conversation I'd graduated from the university and begun my MA courses, including the course that took me to the country around Stoverville where I met Edie, Valerie Sherbourne, little Angela Robinson, Mrs. Codrington, and the rest of the cast of characters in that strange pastoral that re-directed the course of my life. I never had any idea in 1948, when I began university, that my father had any qualms about having left his children fatherless for most of the forties. In May and June, that year, when we were anxiously awaiting his homecoming, we were simply consumed with curiosity about what he would look like. None of us had seen him for seven years — which makes this narration sound like a fairytale. He went to England late in 1941, and even after the war was over we had no direct contact with him until mid-1948. There were frequent letters after he got back to Switzerland from the near East. We kept seeing news photos and an occasional picture in *Time* or *Life*, but he stayed on in Europe until Paul-Edouard Martin died and then returned to North America, where he was famous as the author of *Sin Quantified* which had appeared in late 1947.

The book appeared simultaneously in three languages, in Zurich, Geneva, Paris, London and New York in September 1947. The New York publishers sent my mother several copies just before publication. I remember reading the book during my lunch hours while I was working for the fur blenders and dyers on King Street West. I took one of the advance copies to work with me one day, and sat down in the workers' lunchroom at noon to take a look at it. Most of the people in the fur business in Toronto at that period were Jewish. Mere courtesy prompted me to cover the boards of the book with a brown-paper wrapper. I prised the fresh crackling unbroken spine open and read the first lines:

> The crime of murder has always been disallowed by the weightiest of human prohibitions. It is the one action everywhere taken to be taboo. The special kinds of murder and their names, parricide, matricide, the name of self-murder and that of the innocent infant, suicide, infanticide, have been the subjects of our greatest works of literature. No action is worse, we think, than murder, because the freely willed extinguishing of a human life destroys a witness to history, a window on the universe. But now we see that there is a kind of action that is worse than murder, deserving another

name, a crime for which perhaps reparation cannot be made. It is a crime which excises a history from history; it cuts the conscience and the testimony of a holy people — as every people is holy like this particular people — out of the book of life. It crushes and proposes to obliterate millions of witnesses. It wounds the centre of the body of humanity. It is today called genocide, race murder. What is to be said of it?

That was the first day I ever understood anything about race murder. I tore my eyes from the page with a struggle and looked out onto quiet King Street. A streetcar went rocking past. The vile stink of the dyers' vats in the workroom next door made me feel sick. I took another bite of my peanut-butter sandwich as the foreman sat down beside me.

"What are you reading, kid, another murder mystery?"

"Yeah," I said, not looking at him, "more or less."

There was an unfamiliar accent to the text, much of it embodied in a series of reconsiderations of *Beyond the Pleasure Principle* and the thought of some of Georg Mandel's associates and pupils who had survived him. The war-crimes trials—those of the chief Nazi leaders—had ended less than a year before. Many of the lesser leaders were still being tried; in some cases indictments were in course of preparation. The term DP was current in Canada, often opprobriously as in the expression, "fucking DP." Movies like *The Search* and, a little later, *The Third Man*, and political action like the founding of NATO, give the tone of the period. *Sin Quantified* has for a reader of today something of the air of a period piece. I don't say that to trivialise the book. There can't be any such thing as holocaust-chic.

But *Sin Quantified* had an undeniable vogue and made a lot of money. In fact the royalties were pretty much what we lived on for the next several years, all the time, in fact, that I was following the Honours Course in Art and Archaeology from the fall of 1948 until I graduated in 1952.

Almost the first person I saw, without even suspecting who he was, when I arrived at the university, was Adam Sinclair. He had ensconced himself so firmly in a chair at one of the front-window tables at Murray's in the Park Plaza, among his little coterie, that the waitresses had given up trying to make that particular space available to other diners from eleven in the morning until about three in the afternoon. It seemed as though this very special young man was always sited firmly in the window, observing the passersby acutely, now and then giving a teeny wiggle of the fingertips at some strolling acquaintance. I acquired the habit of the mid-morning Murray's coffee-break just as soon as other Vic freshmen and freshwomen, and I wondered for quite a time who this uniquely privileged undergraduate might be. I knew he must be an undergraduate because he was about my age, and I'd seen him at a distance advancing slowly up Avenue Road towards Bloor Street in the very first mornings of the term. He seemed to have gathered around him at his table in the window a little group or band of about six regular companions; faces came and went but the total number of *le petit cénacle* probably didn't exceed ten, most of whom came to Murray's several times weekly. They had some indefinable quality in common, and this one chestnut-haired young gentleman was certainly in some sort their leader. It must be stressed that the little band was in no sense simply a crowd of homosexuals, with the roguish humour and the self-conscious posturings of many such gatherings. Adam himself at no time in his life displayed obviously effeminate mannerisms. His appearance at that time was perfectly unexceptionable in all respects. He did not, however, preserve any resemblance to his childhood avatar. Gone was the persecuted, tearful look, gone the easily removed short pants and, presumably, the tattered underpants upon which so many indignities had been visited.

He was in short unrecognisable. His hair, from being a mousy blonde, had unaccountably darkened to a rich near-auburn, I suppose really a chestnut colour, and was certainly brushed and coiffed with great care each morning. It had a natural wave and lay thickly, low on his forehead. His complexion bore no hint of adolescent blemish. As a child, I hadn't realised that he had the smooth clear skin that resists unsightly acne scarring. He had somewhere learned to carry himself so that his clothes, not expensive or outré in style, sat well on him. He might have been one of those fortunate people whose body is close to a standard size, who can therefore buy clothes off the rack which seem tailored to measure. On those first days in our contemporaneous university careers, Adam might wear one of his several tweed jackets or blazers, and flannel trousers of a distinctly darker hue than was usual at the time, not what was later called charcoal grey, but a medium-to-dark grey which suggested English tailoring; these pants were Daks. The position and shape of his hands, relaxed and folded with composure on his morning coffee table, suggested the ministrations of the manicurist, as his neat head suggested careful barbering. He was taking care of his appearance, that was all, something that no other person of my age group had quite learned to do. I believe that he had attended some sort of radio college or professional childrens' school, while at the same time attaining the necessary educational standard for university entrance, a minimal standard, as he later communicated to me.

"I promise you, Matthew, I could scarcely spell 'cat.'"

He and his friends would chat endlessly over their coffee about some matter that plainly provided them with a totally absorbing interest. Nobody outside the little band had any idea for the longest time who these people—all young men—were, until the first Hart House Theatre production of that season, when it developed that they were "the theatre crowd." Always known by that phrase, words spoken not at all in mockery by my callow acquaintances, but with envy and something like awe. This was a perfectly reasonable tone for the excluded to adopt, because several members of the theatre crowd were persons of real, provable, talent. It was some time before they were able to recruit any young women to their circle, for reasons which had nothing to do with sexual discrimination. Opportunities for young women to acquire an absolute minimum of professional training in the theatre arts were if anything fewer than those available to young men in the Toronto of 1948. There were occasional dance classes here and there, and one or two teachers of elocution, but no theatre school that anybody remembers. Some primitive education in dramatic speech might be acquired in acting for the radio—if you could find engagements in radio-drama productions. That was where Adam got his start. He began his professional career as soon as his voice broke, as a teen-aged announcer on radio shows produced by the Harry "Red" Foster advertising agency for department-store mechandising accounts. He picked up a good deal of vocal technique by listening to the great radio announcers of the day: Don Wilson, Harry von Zell, Ken Carpenter, Bill Goodwin, Truman Bradley, and the single Canadian whose voice had made an impact on a whole generation of budding actors, Lorne Greene. Adam went through his Lorne Greene phase about the time of our first months in college. When you came into Murray's you might hear his voice, pitched down around his shoetops, booming "good-morning" in a throbbing bass-baritone. Later on some of the waitresses at Murray's confided to me that it was Adam's voice that got him his front-window table and the almost undivided attention of the restaurant hostess, her attendant ladies, and a whole horde of women who used to come in for coffee around ten-thirty to listen to Adam talking to the rest of the theatre crowd.

"I had to work for years to get rid of those radio tricks," he said later. "I sounded like Chaliapin hollering down a rain barrel."

Adam had plenty of that quirky, self-mocking, miniaturising, playful humour that English theatre people affect. "His tiny mind." "A chorus of naked ladies." "Not to worry." "Bob's your uncle!" "Why, whatever for?" "Oh don't touch that girl, you don't know where she's been." It makes me chortle to recall how sharply Edie and Letty Millen deplored and rejected this comic tone, which was apparently the only mode of colloquial expression available to the English production people who got the Stratford undertaking off the ground.

"If Jacqueline Cundall says, 'Cor chase me Aunt Fanny up a gum tree,' to me one more time, I shall strike her," said Letty to me one night just before the Festival opened. And it was always like that. The English theatre possessed so many peculiar folkways and traditions of speech, physical comportment, artistic judgment, that only Canadians with an immensely strong sense of personal worth survived their influence at Stratford. By his late teens Adam had understood

# The Scenic Art

the quality of self-protective irony characteristic of the English theatrical profession, mastered it, and begun to think of discarding it. He had a prior task however; he had first to disembarrass himself of the accents of Lorne Greene and learn a form of speech appropriate to the classical theatre—in the event tinged with much fake Shakesperianism—finally arriving many years afterwards at a way of talking, on stage or off, which was simply his own, sounding neither Ontarian, Shakesperian, Yankee or what you will. He has a great voice, and a very flexible voice; he can sound like anybody. But it isn't a voice that you'd pick out in a crowd as a Canadian voice.

In 1948 he sounded like a younger Lorne Greene, and he had friends who sounded like young John Drainies, like young Laurence Oliviers. There was even one poor child who had trained himself—much like a parrot—to sound like a young Donald Wolfit. A mistake. He never got anywhere in the nascent semi-professional theatre which was beginning to put out tiny shoots around the University of Toronto, in its component colleges and more importantly at Hart House Theatre, which is where I had my first professional contact with Adam Sinclair and "the theatre crowd."

Like most people of my generation I thought vaguely from time to time that it would be fun to be an actor in the movies or on the stage, and I had had the casual brushes with theatricality one encountered in high-school, singing in the chorus of a Gilbert and Sullivan production, prancing about in skits for a Christmas entertainment. I had failed as a band singer and was sure that solo performance was not my cup of tea. I might however have the pleasure of being in a show without being noticed and therefore without feeling the pressure of nervous tension which was the product of fitful, low-intensity, adolescent egotism. In my first university term I tried out for a part in a one-act play which was being produced at Victoria as part of a two-night Drama Weekend to be mounted in Hart House Theatre on otherwise open dates. The usual one-acters were produced: *Pullman Car Hiawatha* and *The Happy Journey From Camden to Trenton* by Thornton Wilder (later a frequent observer of Stratford goings-on), *Fumed Oak* from Coward's group of short plays *Tonight at 8.30*, *The Valiant*, *Waiting for Lefty*, *Aria da Capo*, and a lesser-known work called *Lucifer at Large* which was the entry from Vic. There was a sizeable part in this piece for an allegorical figure who personates Time. You can see what kind of play it is. Time sits at the side of the stage and offers a number of philosophical comments on what is passing before him. The play derives in method and argument from the magnificent short plays of Yeats, but it is a poor and distant version of its exquisite models.

I got myself cast in the part of Time. I didn't have to move around onstage, a requirement which would have betrayed my shrinking and egotistical embarrassment and my total lack of any thespian talent. I just had to sit at a small table well downstage-left, and read from time to time the philosophical observations allotted to this allegorical figure. I have a clear voice and excellent diction and I was not too bad at all in the part, the only sort of part I could have attempted with the smallest hope of success. I was even noticed by some of the "theatre crowd" who attended this drama weekend as informal talent spotters, and ticketed by them as a possible recruit. These one-act productions had been put on by the second echelon of theatrical folk at the university, those whose limited talents and/or modest ambitions confined their activities to their local college scene. The really talented undergraduate actors and actresses gravitated immediately to the major university theatre, Hart House Theatre, then and for many years afterwards under the direction of the exceedingly able Robert Gill.

The college theatre functioned as a bush league or training ground for freshmen and sophomores who, if they exhibited any gift for the stage, might later read for a part at one of Mr. Gill's casting calls. The system was exceedingly democratic. Robert Gill would announce his selection of four plays for the forthcoming season in the spring of the previous season, and would hold auditions for them at the end of the academic year. When I was at the university, the announcement of the choice of plays for the coming year was a major event on campus, and would be written up in *The Varsity* in close and accurate detail. Actors and aspiring neophytes all over the immense campus would examine the range of parts and possible castings with strained and concentrated attention. There was invariably a relatively new play from the American theatre, a translation of a European classic, Ibsen or Chekov perhaps, often a Shaw play or something by one of his contemporaries—but not Wilde—and a play by William Shakespeare to finish the season. The Shakespeare play was always produced in early April, just before the end of the academic year, and was the high point of the theatrical season in Toronto for a large number of people. The only professional productions available in the city at that time were touring shows, travelling companies from the U.S., with stars like Tallulah Bankhead or Madeleine Carroll, which played at the Royal Alexandra.

It's hard to remember how wholly denuded of dramatic production was the Toronto of the late forties and early fifties. Robert Gill's productions at Hart House, Ibsen, Chekov, Shaw, Shakespeare, routine fare as they might seem now, were like a gift from God to a large number of the citizenry, and they received a correspondingly large amount of attention from the Toronto press. The city was fortunate in its possession of two really excellent drama critics, Nathan Cohen, and Herbert Whittaker who came to Toronto from Montréal in the spring of 1949. Most North American cities of middle size without any local professional theatre, a Cleveland or Minneapolis, would have been lucky to possess a single writer on the theatre of any gifts. Toronto had two. Whittaker and Cohen had serious presentable qualifications as drama critics; their work in the pages of the *Globe and Mail*, the *Star*, sometimes on the radio and later on television, contributed an enormous amount to the growth of the Canadian professional theatre.

The mere presence too of the physical building at Hart House, the cosy underground theatre buried beneath the enormous student union, simple possession of a working theatre which seated about four hundred and fifty people when sold out, with more or less adequate dressing rooms and the beginnings of a lighting system, with wing space, some sort of budget, and a shrewd management team, helped as much as the presence in the city of Cohen and Whittaker to breed the group of actors and actresses who finally created the professional theatre in English-speaking central Canada.

Once or twice in the winter of 1948/49 I was addressed by some person unknown to me, in the JCR at UC or in Murray's or in the Vic coffee shop, as a potential brother-in-arms.

"You're Matthew Goderich, aren't you?"

This was at least a year before my father won that damn' prize.

"That's me."

"I saw you in *Lucifer at Large,*" they would say, "and you were good."

That was a bit of an overlay. I hadn't been good, but I had managed to sit still and read my lines clearly and audibly. Good is something else.

These folks, always at least a couple of years older than I, some of them much older than that, seemed to be following a script. For the next thing they always said was, "Are you going to read for Gill?"

And I always said, "That's not till next spring, is it?"

Then one day one of these people, a girl of about twenty-one, which seemed enormously adult to my youngish eighteen, said to me, "There's a small part open in Gill's *Othello,* which you'd be just right for."

This was already January. Rehearsals for *Othello* would begin quite soon. One wonderful aspect of the Gill productions was the way in which they were always meticulously rehearsed. Robert Gill paid special attention to the management of crowd scenes and the encouragement of players who took small roles; there was always plenty to do for anybody in a Gill Shakesperian production. I was in four of them at different times, *Othello, Romeo and Juliet, Julius Caesar* and *Henry IV-i,* and in three of those plays I had small speaking parts. There was enough happening at all times to keep me and the

# The Scenic Art

other small-part actors, walk-ons and crowd, abudantly busy. After this women mentioned the opening spot in the forthcoming Shakespeare piece to me, I thought I might do worse than read for it. Why not? Couldn't do any harm.

So the next afternoon about two o'clock I walked down the stone steps to the stage entrance of the theatre and pulled open the heavy oak door. The interior was deeply shadowed, cavernous. I found myself facing a blank wall with a sloping and gentle descent at my left hand. I heard distant voices. In a moment I came to the management offices where Mr. Gill and the business manager, Jimmy Hozack, had their quarters. There was a reception booth next to the doorway, in which a striking blonde lady was seated behind a glass partition. She asked me very politely, in fact indulgently, and with that come-hither quality which so many people connected with the theatre seem to possess from birth, whom I wished to see. I told her that I had an appointment with Mr. Gill at two-fifteen.

"I don't see how that could be," she said, looking puzzled. "He's supposed to be working with the stage carpenters all afternoon." She came out from behind the glass and went into a further office. I heard her say, "Did Bob say anything about Mr. Goderich, Marian?" They were so overwhelmingly polite and helpful that I was fatally won over. A stout man with a beaming face and a slender woman with a dark face came out of a recess with the original blonde. They stood looking at me speculatively, and with great friendliness.

"Bob said to be here at two-fifteen?" asked the stout man. I nodded.

"See if there's a note on his desk, Marian," commanded the stout man. He came forward and took me by the elbow. "Come into Bob's office."

I felt embarrassed.

"Bring him in, Jimmy," called the dark woman. "There's a reminder on the memo pad."

We entered a room that I already felt to be holy. Afterwards I spent many happy hours there, though I never had the least claim upon Robert Gill as a protégé of talent, or as a writer on theatrical subjects. A moment or so after I entered his office, the director himself came into the room, smiling apologetically.

"I'm sorry to be late, Mr. Goderich. I've been in a wrangle with Jack and Terry all the forenoon and I haven't had a moment. Would you mind terribly if I were to eat a biscuit and drink a cup of tea while we chat? Perhaps you'll join me?"

I never drink tea, but at that moment I'd have died for him; he was incredibly approachable and decent. "I'd like some tea," I said, half choking as I spoke. The little office was a gallery of theatrical delights, the customary signed photographs with the characteristic emphatic lighting and the compliments annexed to the signature. I recognised several celebrated faces: Cornell, Alfred Lunt, Maurice Evans, Donald Cook, Ina Claire. Robert Gill wasn't an Englishman but a Pennsylvanian who had attended the theatre school at Carnegie Tech, then performed in summer and regional theatres and in a few small parts on Broadway, before finally inclining towards direction, in university theatre.

Of the hundreds of people I've known at one time or another who were connected with the theatre, Robert Gill was beyond any doubt the man most perfectly suited for the position he had made for himself. He was the most patient man of the theatre imaginable. He allowed himself, in the course of any production, one major loss of temper, and the company always knew just when it would come—during the last rehearsal before the technical rehearsal. He never lost his poise at a juncture when serious consequences might have ensued, never during the arduous and seemingly endless technical rehearsals, never during one of the two full dress rehearsals he allowed during a production. So the last run-through in rehearsal clothes was always the moment when he permitted himself the luxury of a teeny tantrum. I can hear him so vividly in my mind's ears, if there are such things. I see again the smooth, carefully waved light brown hair, and the very faint resemblance to the Frog Footman in the line of profile and chin. God, but he was an attractive person, the politeness, the careful attention to what you said, the roomful

# The Scenic Art

of memorabilia, the programs, posters, maquettes, the ends of makeup with which one shelf was strewn, all the apparatus of the theatre, and that fatal, persuasive courtesy—you couldn't forget any of it. He might have been the most sheerly winning man I ever knew.

He eyed me over the teacups with the composure of a mandarin. I gulped down mouthfuls of the hot unsweetened tea from a big cheap restaurant cup, one of those pale thick cups with the broad and narrow green rings around the rim. He handed me a biscuit and put one in his mouth whole. "I was in need of refreshment," he said in a joky affected ladylike voice. "I believe it is customary to take some light refreshment at this time of day."

"Cucumber sandwiches," I said smiling.

"Ah," he said. "Would you mind standing up and walking across the room and back? How tall are you?"

"I'm not certain." I mentioned some inaccurate statistics.

"Do you know anything about stage makeup?"

"Not a thing," I said cheerfully.

"You'll need a bit of facial hair in the part," he said, and I began to feel very excited. "Now the great thing to remember about false hair is to comb it out carefully and use much less than you think you're going to require. If you don't comb it out, it'll go all kinky, from having been sold in those little tight bunches." He told a brief anecdote about a friend's mishap when playing Lear. Inadequately combed out, the monarch's false beard had curled back into itself in the first scene in such a way as to shoot out at a ninety-degree angle from the chin and lips, in an unintentionally comic effect which destroyed the balance of the production.

"You'd be wise not to come on like that."

"I understand."

"Plenty of people in the cast to give you advice, that is, if you don't mind asking. I check makeups in the first dress anyway."

He was thinking of giving me the rôle.

"The man who was to play Lodovico, Roly Ducane, a very promising young man, broke his leg during the Christmas holidays," said Mr. Gill.

"No he didn't, Bob," called a voice from the next office. "He sprained an ankle."

"Oh, was that it? Thank you, Marian. In any case, he can't do the part. Lodovico is an upright man in the prime of life, somewhat younger than Othello, at least as I see him. He must seem energetic, decisive . . . do you know the play?"

"I'm afraid not." We'd never been assigned *Othello* in highschool and I was not a constant reader of Shakespeare.

"It's a small part in the context of the play, but a major part from Act Four, Scene One, down to the curtain. He's a kinsman of Desdemona's who comes in at the beginning of Act Four with letters, and new orders for Othello. While Othello is reading his letters, Lodovico, who has to be an upright, active, vital man, walks with Desdemona, and Othello is immediately suspicious of him. It's a strong scene."

"I can see how it would be."

"He has a lot of short speeches in the scene. Are you a quick study?"

"A what?"

"Do you learn lines easily?"

I said, "I'm told I've got a pretty good memory."

"Excellent. Well then, Lodovico comes in again briefly in Act Four, Scene Three, and his big scene is in Act Five, Scene Two right at the climax. He has several big speeches and the very last lines, the curtain lines. I want you to read the longer speeches now."

"What, right here and now?"

"If you don't mind." He handed me a blue-backed, student's edition of the play, open at the last scene, and took up another copy, much marked in green ink. "I'll read the other parts," he said. "Take it from, 'O Desdemona! Desdemona! Dead!'"

He read this exclamation with a sudden power and emphasis that startled me. "Where is this rash and most unfortunate man?" I cried angrily.

We continued with the reading, right to the end of the play, then he said, "You've got an excellent voice, very promising for the stage, and you would probably be an excellent radio actor. Can you project?"

# The Scenic Art

I looked at him blankly and a quiver crossed his face. "You haven't had much experience, have you?"

"None to speak of."

"To project is to produce and deliver your voice so that you seem to be speaking in a normal tone, but the voice carries to the back of the theatre. It's a technical trick; most beginners learn it easily, you'll see."

In this he was wrong. I never learned to speak from the diaphragm and ventriloquise so that my slightest intention could be heard in the third balcony. Adam, on the other hand, mastered this aspect of the stage actor's craft at once, quite effortlessly.

"How old are you?" said Mr. Gill.

"I'll be nineteen in April."

"Lodovico might be thirty-five or forty. He has to have presence. Are you certain you can give me presence? You seem a rather unassuming person—not a bad thing in its way, but unhelpful for most actors, onstage or off, unless they're persons of genius. Just read through the last lines again."

I went through them with all the feeling and expression I could muster, ending with a kind of cadence or dying fall on the line, "This heavy act with heavy heart relate."

"We've got to work on that," he said. "I know it's a couplet, and it's obvious and embarrassing. We don't want the audience to think we've lapsed frivolously into rhyme. I think the line has to be taken slowly ... slowly ... but extremely clearly. We can't cut it either. It's rather a famous line. One shouldn't cut the closing speech. I'm giving you the part, you know. It's probably the fourth most important part, after Othello, Iago and Cassio. Three scenes, maybe thirty speeches. A few of them might be cut in the performance text, but don't worry about that. Everybody loses some lines in a modern Shakesperian production. Somebody might say that Roderigo had a better part, but I don't think so; he's a weakling, easily fooled, not very masculine, a juvenile's part. Lodovico is a grown man; you can see how completely Shakespeare has sketched in the character. He has authority; he can appoint a new governor for Cyprus. He's Desdemona's kinsman and is jealous of her reputation; he isn't afraid to speak his mind to Othello. Are you following me?"

"Oh yes," I said. I was getting excited.

"We're having completely new costumes made for this production by Dickie Moon. I want you to make an appointment to see our designer, and I want something vice-regal for you, one of those tall hats such as you see in Piero della Francesca, to give you some height. Our Othello isn't a tall man; he's under six feet, but he's heavy, burly. Do you know David?"

"I've just seen him in Murray's and Diana Sweets. I know who he is, of course."

"With a jurist's cap, you'll be taller than he is. We might have you wear lifts. You should be half a head taller than David. You're much too slight and thin for the part, but we'll get you a big swirling robe and some kind of cloak to fatten you up. Here's the designer's phone number. Go and see her and ask her to show me a sketch. She'll know more or less what I want. And next week there'll be fittings at Sir Richard Moon's."

Dickie Moon, the costumier, was unaccountably an English baronet, one of two living in Toronto at that epoch.

We rehearsed *Othello* from the middle of February until the middle of April. By the time that the principals had mastered their lines and their blocking, it was clear that I was going to be really lousy as Lodovico. I couldn't move on stage with any grace, any accurate depiction of the way in which a human being actually moves. I can walk with perfect naturalness on any sidewalk as long as I know that nobody is looking at me in a dramatic context. The context is everything. Put me on a stage and I stop looking like a human being and begin to resemble some grotesque robot. I only had one gesture, a convulsive slamming of my left fist into my open right palm. I couldn't control my voice, which sank into my boots at times and in the next moment squeaked into the stratosphere. I had no talent of any kind for acting. None whatsoever.

People who aren't artists never understand this business or the presence or absence of talent. Everybody who has appeared in a high-school musical thinks he's an actor. Everybody who writes a good letter is a writer. A doctor who is a

Sunday painter looks at a Harold Town show and mutters, "Yes. He's further along than I am." These are the same people who wouldn't dream of performing brain surgery without any gift for it. Nor would they undertake to give a piano recital at the Roy Thomson Hall without years of arduous professional preparation. And their children's drawings . . . my God!

Several of the people who were in the cast of that production of *Othello* had real talent. The Moor was played by a man in the same course option as mine who afterwards had a long career on the stage. So did the Iago, a thin short saturnine geography student with great credibility onstage. Both men used to try to help me out with tips on how and where to stand, how to walk, pitch my voice, read the lines, gesture. Everybody helped, but all efforts were wasted. I hadn't the gift, wasn't an actor, never would be. Edie saw that production as a matter of fact, as a high-school girl.

"The best thing about your performance," she told me long after, "in fact the only thing that recommended it in the slightest, was that marvellous costume. Sexy!"

Mr. Gill did his best by me. He never reprimanded me or lost his temper because of my woodenness and compulsiveness. He got me a gorgeous costume, a plum-coloured robe with a cloak over it in a contrasting deep marine blue, a dark golden judge's hat, tall, highly visible. I wore a chain on my shoulders and breast. I think the conception came out of some art book. All wasted. We opened on a Friday night; there was a Saturday evening performance; reviews appeared in the Saturday papers and in *The Varsity* on Monday at noon. I wasn't mentioned in any of the dailies, although the play received distinct praise and careful accounts of the principal performances from both Cohen and Whittaker. On Monday, the review in the university daily signed R.D. said all that was necessary. "As Lodovico, Matthew Goderich let the play down with a dull thud."

I remembered that my predecessor in the part was called Roly Ducane. It seemed credible to identify him with the reviewer, a conjecture which afterwards proved correct. But there was no real malice in his observation, which was perfectly accurate. I did allow the final moment of *Othello* to fall flabbily to the ground out of sheer incapacity. These things happen.

And I'd had an excellent makeup too, damn' it, including a really professional false beard, fastened to my chin each night before the show by an attentive, and exceedingly proximate Adam Sinclair. I well remember how he would lean directly over me, patting my greasepaint-smeared cheeks lightly, his lips pursed in a near-kiss of concentration, as he applied the pungent adhesive, then attached carefully combed strands of false hair of a colour almost exactly that of my own. During the preparations for the first dress rehearsal, the first time he performed this chore, it seemed as though his countenance was about to be pressed to mine in an achieved kiss, a possibility which I could not at that time begin to understand. The tiny dressing-room, right at the end of the backstage corridor where the dressing-rooms were laid out in a long row, barely had space for two little tables backed by the traditional large mirrors framed with light bulbs; we were really crowded in together. There was a shallow closet, a washbasin, a hatstand, two chairs, and the dressing tables and that was all. As two of the male principals, we were entitled to dress privately, but not, I thought, quite this privately. The young man, whom I had at length identified as the Adam Sinclair of my childhood, had his face right up against my cheek. He hummed a popular love ballad of the hour as he smoothed the straggling long hair into place.

"It's going to be a kind of Vandyke effect, not quite period but devastating, my dear."

He finished applying the hair and started to comb it down.

"Hmmmmn," he murmured, taking a pair of small scissors from his makeup kit. "I'll give it some shape, and we'll leave the skin under your lower lip bare." Snip, snip, snip, snip, false hair fell on the floor and he kicked it into the corner. "There you are now, just grand." He handed me his mirror. "How do you like yourself?" I tried to see how it looked in profile. "See? Doesn't it look marvellous? It makes you look the right age, but you've got to be careful to deepen your voice much more, and speak very slowly. Your voice is the best part

# The Scenic Art

of your performance." He looked at my face very intently. "I think we'll build up your eyebrows a little, then we'll hollow the eye-sockets—you do that with this liner, and just a touch of the dark brown mascara, just rub it in lightly under the eyes. You'll look very handsome."

"Like James Mason," I said eagerly.

"No, not quite. I suppose we'd all look like James Mason when the lights are out if we could, wouldn't we? Do you think you could do this by yourself another time?"

I thought I could, and tried it on the night of the final dress rehearsal, but Bob Gill spotted my handiwork and commanded Adam to look after it himself for the opening performance on Friday night. I was able to do my own makeup by the middle of the run, and after that learned a great deal about stage makeup, a subject with its own fascinating lore. I used to store my makeup, a complete kit, in an old shoebox, with the names of all the shows I'd been in and their dates written around the top of the box in bright blue ink. From first to last I was in twenty-seven shows. I directed a couple of one-acters. I did makeup for other people who were just learning. In the end I knew as much about the theatre as you can acquire without talent for it. Talent. Talent. The artist's mode of Divine Grace. When I meditate upon talent I see how immediately and how necessarily life drives us towards theological questions about election and predestination. All would be saved if they could. All would have talent if they could. I don't mean to trivialise the question. The rationalist invariably finds the uneven distribution of talent unequitable. Why should not the writing or painting or acting of every citizen of a democracy (the most rational form of government and/or society) be as good as that of every other citizen's. It never is. There is no visible rational principle, no equity, no democracy, in the apportioning of talent.

Adam had talent. I had none. He was an elegant, handsome, persuasive Cassio, unforgettable-looking in the rôle; he made the most of what is unquestionably a "feed" part. You remembered him. If you were a woman, you thought that maybe that nice Cassio would have been a better choice than the Moor. When we were in our dressing-room together,

I could see in the adult Sinclair the same frightened child whom I used to protect on Saturday afternoons in the Beverly theatre so long ago. He of course had known who I was from the first day of our first term in university.

"I knew you at once. You were so kind to me. I've never forgotten you, Matthew. You must see that!"

"Oh sure."

"Not like that treacherous little brother of yours."

"Tony treacherous? What are you talking about?"

"He used to shout dreadful things at me as I went by on the street. Nicknames."

"Putty-face!" I said, rather impolitely.

"It might have been something like that."

I had to speak up in defense of my brother. "The fact is, you've turned into an expert on putty noses. And isn't that a piece of putty you've got in your hand?" Adam was growing famous in the profession, something like Olivier, for the variety of his noses; he was reputed never to have the same nose twice. As Cassio he gave himself a strongly aquiline profile by the application each night of just the smallest serpent-shaped piece of putty, formed so as to suggest that Cassio might at some time have broken his nose. This little touch made the character seem aristocratic and very masculine; it was a legitimate stroke of the actor's craft.

"Your little brother didn't know anything about that when he called me 'Putty-face.'"

"He must have been referring to the extreme mobility of your features, Adam."

"Horse manure," said Adam inelegantly. He went on working and rolling the piece of nose-putty and at length applied it just over the bridge of his nose. The effect was remarkable. I learned a lot from him that week.

We weren't exactly trapped in a long run, but we did get to give eight performances of *Othello* that season. We opened on a Friday night and gave a Saturday night performance, then took the Monday night off, and gave further performances on Tuesday, Wednesday, Thursday, Friday of the second week, and two performances on the closing Saturday, a matinée for schoolchildren at 2:00 PM and the regular evening show at

8:15. By Tuesday or Wednesday night we felt as though we'd been running for months; you really got a strong impression of what life in the professional theatre would be like. The rivalries, the professional jealousies and some unprofessional ones, the fleeting love-affairs, the jokes, modifications of costume, gradual strengthening of performance. By Thursday or Friday night I had lost almost all of my ugly, unbecoming, egotistical self-consciousness. The buffetings of fortune are sovereign medicine for egotism. The resultant relaxation and access of calm helped my acting immeasurably, not that it ever became professionally acceptable. But by Saturday noon I could walk into the theatre, make myself up, get into costume, wait to be called, with utter aplomb, then walk onstage in a credible gait and deliver my lines audibly, without hesitation, and with complete understanding of what I was saying, an element of Shakesperian acting not always found among veteran troupers. Mrs. Siddons never knew how *Macbeth* came out; when the sleepwalking scene was finished, she went home, probably giving no thought at all to the significance of any other speeches than her own. At Stratford, Ontario, actors and actresses very very often speak their lines in such a way as to persuade witnesses that they have no idea what the words mean.

In *Othello* I always knew what my words meant, and everybody else's too. I memorised that damn' text, and by the afternoon of the children's matinée, I could probably have recited the whole play. I might be able to do it even now. The children's matinée was a novelty at Hart House. Two previous Shakesperian productions had been received with such acclaim by press and public, that the management proposed to the Board of Syndics of Hart House that a matinée should be given on the second Saturday of the run, expressly for Toronto high-school children, tickets to be made available in blocks of around thirty to any high-school which cared to organise attendance. The idea proved amazingly popular; blocks of tickets were disposed of to several Toronto high-schools and a few schools in other cities and towns, Stoverville among them. This prospect was somewhat daunting to all those of us who were to be the first to stand up and be shot at, as it were. Nobody at that date had any idea of how nearly five hundred Ontario high-school kids would react to the experience of sitting packed together in a sold-out theatre, underground as it happens, for three hours on a Saturday afternoon, to watch a play by William Shakespeare. Robert Gill was uneasy. Jimmy Hozack betrayed anxiety. Marian Taylor preserved a poker face. Our Othello was, he freely confessed, terrified but ready for anything, thrown fruit, stinkbombs.

"They can't intimidate me," he kept saying.

Adam Sinclair said nothing on Thursday or Friday but I believe he was in an unexampled state of nerves. His hand shook as he applied lake liner and white stick to his laugh lines. "I don't want to look too beautiful on Saturday," he remarked once.

All of Saturday was shot, naturally. We had to be in the theatre by 1:00 PM at the very latest. Some of us were there, lounging around in the green room and the dressing-rooms at noon, in much the same way that Georgie-Balls Bannon used to appear at Maple Leaf Gardens three hours before the game. The matinée performance was to start at 2:00 PM precisely, and the first groups of students and teachers began to arrive in the theatre about one-thirty. They were not small children either; most of the males were nearly full-grown young men, the same size as us. "Bigger if anything," said Adam with glum relish, after peeking around the side of the curtain. "Huge, some of them."

"Did you see any brown-paper bags?"

"What for?"

"Oh, rotten eggs, tomatoes."

"Don't try to be funny!"

As the performance ran three hours, and the evening show began at 8:15, the management of the theatre decreed that the actors should remain in the theatre between the two shows; a buffet supper would be laid on in the green room, lavish, quite free, with beer and wine for those who could stop at one or two, to begin right after we got our makeup off. You could come in costume if you wished, but don't get any mayonnaise on the costume please, ladies and girls, or Dickie

Moon will be down our necks. He's coming tonight, bye the bye, so keep it clean for God's sake. Thus Robert Gill, who was dancing around backstage as excited as I ever saw him. Nobody knew what that afternoon audience would be like, but they were certainly making a different sound from out front than any of the adult audiences we had had during the rest of the run. It was exciting, electric, a very busy, taut, musical humming sound of many voices in a full auditorium. All the echoes were altered. There were no empty seats, a number of illicit standees, and some sort of strong and strange group feeling being generated among this intense crowd.

Well, they just loved it! They were bloody marvellous, that's all. They were dead quiet when Iago was whispering poison in Othello's ear; they laughed at poor Roderigo for being such a gull and a fop; they fell in love with Desdemona; they thought Cassio was really the right man for her. And by God they even listened to my twenty-six speeches with rapt attention, the best audience I've ever had. What a show that was! And afterwards they swarmed around to the dressing-rooms, dozens and dozens of cute high-school girls not much younger, if at all, than myself, and perhaps fewer dozens of high-school boys on the lookout for Desdemona, who was trapped in her dressing-room surrounded by masses of flowers. I found myself signing AUTOGRAPHS among clumps of kids who kept asking, "Which one were you?"

"I was the one who had the last lines. I had to make Othello a prisoner."

"Oh, that was you?" They weren't sure how they liked me.

Adam was in his element: gracious, gallant, handsome, approachable and forthcoming. After my admirers had receded—there weren't so many of them as all that—I sat in a corner of our little room and watched Adam to see how he dealt with his large crowd of petitioners. It was at this point that I realised finally that he really did have the special and necessary gift, the thing which makes the difference between the professional and the amateur. He knew precisely how to handle each of his fans. He was gentle with the timid, encouraging with the truly interested, distant with those who came to see for themselves that actors were just like everybody else. He was concerned to be not at all like everybody else. He felt those kids as an audience and a public. To me they were people just like me, only a year or two younger. There is more to this than I can explain.

That crowd of eager autograph-seekers in a dressing-room was a kind of Rubicon for Adam. I see that now. After that experience, which in certain ways unmanned him, there could be no acceptance of the ordinary or quotidian. Life must be intense, exotic in some sort, crowded, acted-out at a pitch near hysteria. He followed me up the stairs to the green room where our supper was displayed (and it truly was a lavish supper) babbling quite hysterically about what had just happened to him. I was a bit afraid for him. I thought he might be overwrought, and it was with trepidation that I saw that all the good actors in the production, the Othello, the Desdemona, the Iago, and a number of small-part actors with promise, all these people were in the same state of aboulia. They were way off somewhere out of themselves in a brilliant, elated state of almost religious experience, a species of ecstasy, and there was still this communal meal, a perfect love-feast, then the evening performance, and the cast party, to come. Saturday night would run well into Sunday afternoon.

The funeral baked meats in the green room formed the sort of meal I've always adored, an apparently inexhaustible spread of meats, salads, pickles, cheeses, hot breads. I'm not your heavy eater, I've stayed thin, but the idea of stuffing myself remains strangely attractive to me. I was seated beside our Othello, a region of exalted splendour for a small-part actor. He was for some reason being terribly kind and noticing to me. Adam sat on my left, and he too could not have been more attentive. Both men kept leaning forward and talking across me, but also about me, not about their own prospects. There was plenty of beer. I had a beer or two. And there was a profusion of terrible Canadian wine, Bright's Sherry, and some ghastly sort of red ink from Chateau-Gai of which, I noticed, Adam was ingurgitating copious draughts. I feared for his sobriety.

The meal lasted for about two hours; it was almost seven-thirty before the after-dinner addresses by Jimmy Hozack, Bob Gill (good old Bob, hooray, wow) and several other people whose faces tended to blur together, were wound up. I may have spoken briefly myself. It was close to a quarter to eight before the last of the actors lurched down the spiral stairs to the dressing-rooms. Makeup was hurriedly re-applied. I did my own beard that evening, and Adam kept pushing his flushed countenance into mine, licking his lips and praising my efforts, beardwise, in what seemed exaggerated terms.

"Go it, old lad," he kept mumbling, "comb that beard, tote that bale."

And then, naturally, the *Othello* company gave a stunning performance, by much our best show. I soared to heights of adequacy never before—and never afterwards—achieved. It was the last sizeable rôle with which I was ever entrusted, for very good reasons, and must remain in my heart as the pinnacle of my performing career. I might even have been good, in the final scene. I tell you, I had them in the hollow of my hand.

I used to come on with the actor who played Roderigo in the blocking of the curtain calls; we were the first principals to appear and we got a tremendous round of applause. As the Roderigo had been no better than ordinary that night, I must conclude that the applause was largely for my inspired, deeply stirred, reading of the closing speech. It was customary for quite brilliant audiences to assemble for the final night of a Hart House show, particularly for the Shakespeare play which closed the season. On that night we had in the audience the Chancellor and the President of the university, the Warden of Hart House, the Lieutenant-Governor of Ontario and his lady, the resident conductor of the Toronto Symphony, an American movie-star named Dane Clark who fought his way backstage, came into our dressing-room and congratulated Adam on his technique, and many other personages of greater or less celebrity. There were new masses of flowers for our leading lady, other lesser masses for our Bianca, and eight—eight—earned curtain calls at the end. It was past eleven-thirty when the curtain went down for the last time, getting on for twelve-thirty before the last well-wishers left the backstage area. On the record, so far, that might have been the most triumphant night of my entire life, my wedding night alone excepted.

There was still the cast party to come, a gathering which no well-advised person would have considered missing. Everybody came. People came who had no connection with this particular production but were unquestioned luminaries of the "the theatre crowd." Nathan was there, and Herbie, and Ron Evans and Pearl McCarthy and Dane Clark. Everybody was there. Bob Gill swept up to me in the hall, as I came into the huge house in Forest Hill where the party took place, shook me enthusiastically by the hand, by both hands, and said, "In another week you'd have been a star. Terrific, Matt. Simply wonderful." He passed on to Adam who was directly behind me, and kissed him ceremoniously on either cheek, like an old French general bestowing an award for gallantry. "The best-looking Cassio of a generation," roared Bob, and the American movie star gritted acknowledgement and approval of the judgment. "Bet your ass, kid!"

We passed into the throng, moving always in the direction of the bar. The house was absolutely enormous, one of those places on Old Forest Hill Road with walk-in fireplaces in which you could easily have roasted whole oxen. Adam and I managed to find drinks; he chose some villainous blend of liqueurs prepared by the daughter of the house: chartreuse, cherry brandy, Benedictine and Drambuie, topped with a slice of orange which instantly turned deep black. I had a shot of bar whisky and the first of several beers.

A good deal later I found myself seated, half-lying, inside the walk-in fireplace in the basement playroom. I knew I was in the fireplace because I was seated on the polished brass firedogs. No fire had burnt in this aperture for some years. If I tilted back my head I could gaze up a blackened flue at what appeared to be a single shining star. Perhaps it was an imaginary point of light. Adam lay at my feet, his face turned up to me beseechingly. The movie star slumbered peacefully, worn out by the cares that infest the night, in an adjacent corner of the fireplace. Other revellers were lodged in this or that nook. Dawn approached. Upstairs there was bedlam. I realised with a sudden shock that Adam was making some sort of declaration.

". . . and I've always loved you since that first afternoon in the Beverly when they ripped my trousers off, oh Matt, I felt so exposed and so shamed and at the same time so thrilled to think that you were looking at me and protecting me. I wanted to be exposed to you, my lover, I couldn't help it, you know. It was my mother that did it to me; she never guessed what she was doing, the damage she might cause. She used to handle me all the time when I was a baby; she used to give me enemas and hold me across her knee till I thought I'd burst, and I loved it. I used to tell her I hadn't been able to go, and then she'd march me to the bedroom and get out the enema bag, oh what a delight. Or she would spank me, but never so as to hurt me, just to make me warm. I love Mamma."

He produced a huge brandy snifter from some recess and went on.

"When I was held down tightly over her knee she'd handle my equipment; she'd kiss my little bottom and tickle me and squeeze me, and I can't tell you what a sensation it was. By the time I was going to the Saturday movies I just ached to have a friend who would do the same things. A boyfriend. And then you came along and were kind to me, and I hoped so much that you'd be the one . . ."

The form in the corner of the fireplace seemed to stir. Soon the room would begin to grow lighter. These reminiscences should now be brought to a close.

"But Adam," I whispered fiercely, "aren't you ashamed?"

"Why should I be ashamed?" he said muzzily. He seemed to try to rise. I heard the brandy snifter fall and break with a musical tinkle. "I tell you, I love Mamma."

"Can't you fight against it?"

"Don't want to fight against it. I love my cute little bum. Pearly pink."

I began to feel a wish to be in some other place as soon as possible. It must be nearly morning now, and it had been a long and trying day. I struggled to rise, but Adam clung to my hand and my balance was infirm. Fortunately a shadowy figure materialised at this juncture, framed in the light which found its way into the fireplace. This person prodded sharply at the small of Adam's back, hissing at him sibilantly, "Slimy Judas!" There was a sudden movement from each of us. Adam rolled out onto the floor and Roly Ducane—for it was he—poked him again, this time in the lower belly, with one of the fire irons. I was not greatly surprised to find Roly in this frame of mind at this stage of the proceedings. Only ill-luck on the slopes had cost him his part in the last week's great enterprise. And now here he was, self-cast in the rôle of avenging angel brandishing his weapon and threatening with it both Adam and myself. The scene had nuances, in conception and setting, of *Paradise Lost*. We had our Adam, and the name Ducane possessed appropriate associations. I fled from the room, looking over my shoulder only once to glimpse Roly and Adam locked in an embrace, shaking with either sobs or laughter. I realised all at once that I was nervously exhausted.

Persons unequipped for that febrile pace ought not to meddle with theatrical undertakings, and yet I found myself in for something closer to a pound than a penny. I turned over in my imagination all the subtle multiplicity of events and persons which the production of *Othello* had lodged, apparently forever, in my mind. It was months before I was able to persuade myself that I had mastered all their suggestions, years perhaps before their more riotous implications ceased to trouble my juvenile passions. I had been thrown into a situation for which my powers were at all levels of experience inadequate, and had felt the terrible exposedness of the poor artist, or the half-formed artist, thrust into a situation which demands more of him than his sensibility can furnish. I didn't like Roly Ducane, but I knew perfectly well that he would have made a much better Lodovico than I. There was the intensity of his relationship to other members of the company to be assessed. He had briefly courted the girl who had played Bianca; there were whole weeks when they never seemed to quit Murray's of a morning.

Yet Roly had some sort of passionate commitment to Adam Sinclair. There were emotions and hesitations in play

# The Scenic Art

with which I was simply unacquainted. Things kept happening during the production of *Othello* for which I was not ready, probably would never be ready. I don't have the stuff in me which issues in wild passionate tragic declarations. Behind Roly's nascent passion for Adam and his actual inclination for Bianca, "the white one," behind our Othello's graciousness to me, behind Robert Gill's kindness and ability as a teacher of dramatic technique, lay aptness for an art and the text of a great tragedy. At that time, I hadn't the capacity for real involvement in such matters, whether involvement of an acted-out and representational kind, or that of true passion. I have never understood the histrionic life.

But I have managed to resist its blandishments. I wanted desperately at twenty to be a person whose acquaintance with tragic experience was so fecund that I could give formed expression to it in the actor's art. First, I wanted to feel deeply, to see fully, to unite my destiny to the fates of others. Then I wanted to give voice to all this wealth of suggestion, suffering, passion. I was not a singer. I was not a poet. I was not my father. I resolved that I would go on doing what I had done in *Othello*, taking small parts which would give me at least the status of onlooker. I could speak clearly, though I couldn't project. I might be a radio actor, a movie actor. Much rehearsal and much time spent onstage might in the end make me able to perform as well consistently as I had on the last night of *Othello*. If I could reach that standard of adequacy consistently, I might reasonably look for some sort of a career as a small-part actor. *Not* an extra. A real actor whose specialty was parts like Lodovico or Casca, the villainous Casca. Dramatic literature abounds with parts like these, small meaty rôles of two or three scenes and perhaps thirty speeches, in which an actor of very moderate gifts can make his mark if he is able to maintain a recognisable and forceful presence. The star parts aren't for him; he must be content to lurk downstage left, half out of the stage picture except at the moments when he speaks his "feed" lines or mouths a crucial turn in the plot-line. Shakespeare is full of parts like that.

Soon after *Othello* closed, the plays for the next Hart House season were announced. *Julius Caesar* was the Shakesperian work to be given in April of 1950. It is a play with many many excellent parts for men, almost none for women, and was perhaps chosen because the three preceding plays that season were essentially vehicles for star actresses. I decided at once that I wanted to play Casca. I procured the best available text of the play and studied it closely. I got Casca's lines by heart almost at once. I practised them as I went to and fro on the campus, and tried to think of bits of business which would enlarge and give dimension to the character; at length I put my name down for an appointment with the director. I was not so lucky as before at my second private interview with Robert Gill. He heard me read and praised me for the thoroughness of my preparation for the audition, but the sad fact was that he had taken my measure. I wouldn't have been good enough in the part, which isn't important to the plot of the play, but is of immense importance poetically, in establishing the moral tone of the end of the Republic. You could argue that people like Casca were the reason why Octavius became Augustus. Casca's political cynicism is so profound as to be unmanning. I understood this, and even lectured Mr. Gill about it, with unbecoming pedantry. But I couldn't put it across. I would have provided an intelligent, clear, academic reading of the part, and I was not to be allowed by Robert Gill to soften the thrust of one of his Shakesperian productions a second time. He never again cast me in a part of more than half a dozen lines.

He cast in the part of Casca—played to great effect at Stratford a few years later by Douglas Campbell—the man who had played Iago in *Othello*. He was terrific. Casca's first big scene, Act I, Scene ii, is given in prose, words of that powerful, sinewy, expressive prose common to the poet's greatest political critics. Casca tells how Caesar was three times offered a kind of coronet by Antony, and thrice put it by, "but, to my thinking, he was very loath to lay his fingers off it." The lines are invested with Shakespeare's terrifying political clairvoyancy. I could see this, at twenty, but do you think that I could deliver it? Not a hope in hell. Mr. Gill cast me as Popilius Lena, a tiny part in the assassination scene, with only two lines, and some important silent business. I knew that this was the sort of casting I would receive in any major production, and I was disappointed and a little bitter, at the same time obliged to acknowledge how much better the production was with a strong actor playing Casca. I soon forgot my disappointment, began to take other small and medium-sized parts in less important college productions, and continued grateful to Robert Gill for the occasional opportunities he gave me. I became a kind of teacher's pet, or mascot, in the Hart House productions. I didn't get good parts, but I was in an awful lot of them, and there were other producers, other plays.

My shoebox full of makeup gradually evolved into a complete, very professional kit. I was pretty good at makeup, and sometimes was called in to a Gill production in which I wasn't cast, to help make up some of the crowd. I acquired a small library of books on the art of stage and screen makeup which I still possess, and I learnt by heart the texts of many great plays, and some that weren't so great.

In January of 1951, a couple of years after my venture as Lodovico, I was lounging in the back room at Diana Sweets on Bloor Street, having lunch with an army of hungry actors and one actress, all university players, some of them veterans of summer tours, or of the summer theatres which were beginning to dot Ontario vacationland, in Bracebridge and Jackson's Point and Peterborough, Kingston, Niagara-on-the-Lake. When you talked to these people, you sensed that the establishment of a full-time repertory theatre in Toronto could not be far away. There were starting to be sizeable groups of young actors and actresses available for regular work, the first wave of entrants to the commercial theatre after the war. Many of that generation had some war service, then returned to university a year or two before I got there, say in 1946 and 1947. There were plenty of them in their mid-twenties, not yet gainfully employed. A few directors and stage designers had emerged from college theatres and work at Hart House. Some of them were beginning to chafe under the tutelage of Mr. Gill. Various movements were launched at this time, towards the founding of professional and independent companies, the New Play Society, Jupiter Theatre, the Crest Theatre. The one thing wanting was the great playwright, the Yeats or Shaw or Synge or O'Casey who might provide dramatic expression for the currents in Canadian life then so powerful. We waited long in those days for such a voice. We are still waiting.

It may be—I often think that it is the case—that Canadians and Canadian life are deeply, fundamentally, hostile to plays, the theatre, histrionic life, the ability to see oneself in a dramatic light. This seems a hypothesis worth considering formally. Perhaps the closest allegiances in Canadian life, whether English or French, are to previous cultures which have been deeply hostile to the dramatic principle. We have had in our culture some excellent poetry, a little bit of worthy painting, and a surprisingly large collection of valuable prose fiction. But we haven't produced a single play worthy to find its way into the repertoire of the world's theatres.

Nothing like *The Seagull*. Over lunch at Diana Sweets, three or four excited young actors, the actress who was present, and an aspiring director, begged me to come in with them on a production of *The Seagull*. They said there was a part in it that might have been tailored for me, the schoolmaster Medvedenko.

I said, "Why do all the parts I get end in 'O'?"

"Because we all remember your Lodovico," said the actress.

There was a lot of laughter.

"All right now," I said, "I got quite good as Lodovico after a while."

"You did, you did, you certainly did!"

"I suppose this Medvedenko is a louse part?" I said. I'd never read *The Seagull*.

"It's a small part, but it has the opening lines."

"Just great! Now Roly Ducane can write, 'Matt Goderich let down the opening scene with a dull thud.'"

"Henry is going to work with you specially, and we've got Adam for the lead."

"Are you sure you aren't asking me just because of my father?"

They looked at one another scandalised. "We don't know what you mean."

The Nobel prize address had been all over the papers about two months earlier. I had found its heroic periods pretty damned hard to live up to. "The new state, the first modern society, the pacific country." The papers had taken up the phrase about the pacific country and connected it to the calendar and the mid-century. "Canada, the pacific country, at mid-century." You saw phrases like this at the head of political commentaries, and even at the bottom of travel posters. The notion was in danger of being totally vulgarised. Fame is highly corrosive, I find.

"There are a million Goderiches," said Henry, the aspiring director.

"Actually it's a rather uncommon name."

"Don't be such a baby, Matt. Forget your father for a minute," said Kate, apparently a prospective leading lady. "We want you for a small part because it's a small-part actor's part. We can't ask Eric or Don or Ted or David or Bill to do it. It's a part for an actor like you."

"A lousy actor. Why don't you get somebody who can act?"

"You'll be fine," said Kate. She fixed me with her huge and lustrous and velvety brown eyes. "I'll take you in hand."

"What are you playing?" I asked, determined to get at all the facts.

"Nina."

"The lead?"

"Since you ask me, yes."

Henry interrupted. "Not in my reading of the text, darling. I regard Madame Arkadin's rôle as of at least equal importance."

Kate impaled him with a swordlike regard; they began to quarrel bitterly, perhaps not the happiest point from which to begin. These talented young people had decided to form a company of their own to produce an entry in the central Ontario Regional Drama Festival of that year, which was to be held in Hart House in the forthcoming April. They had about three months in which to set the project on foot, choose a play and cast it, raise funds for the production costs, find a rehearsal hall, get the thing on. They wanted to do something wholly without assistance or direction from any existing university or professional authority. The girl who was to play Irina Arkadin—in whose vast home the *Othello* cast party had taken place—had raised enough money by the sale of two or three pieces of inherited jewellery to meet most of the expenses: design and construction of the handsome set, costume rental, Henry's far from nominal fee as director.

*The Seagull*—that exacting and extraordinarily subtle masterwork—was chosen for production on the grounds of its classic status and its situation in the public domain, no royalty being payable to the Chekov estate in the vexed state of world politics of the day. The company was to be called The Players' Studio. Anne Colindale—the jewellery vendor—was to produce and play Madame Treplev (Irina Arkadin). Henry would direct. Other members of the small cast were recruited from members of the growing acting community who wanted to do something on their own. Adam Sinclair was approached for the leading male rôle, Konstantin, because he had become one of the two or three most promising leading actors in the province, if not the country, a fact which I was only beginning to grasp. I wasn't sure that I should risk any further confrontations with Adam in Anne Colindale's recreation room in Forest Hill. I wasn't sure how much Adam might remember of our late-night passage through the fireplace. I remembered all of it, and I guessed that the recreation room of the Colindale mansion would be taken over as a convenient venue for rehearsal. In this, I wasn't wrong.

We began to rehearse *The Seagull* at the end of February, and presented it, for one night only as we thought, during the run of the CODF in mid-April. I sat on a rickety bench with my back against a papier-mâché treetrunk and solemnly intoned the doleful opening lines of the text. "Why do you always wear black?" I meant to convey by my intonation profound inclinations of the heart towards the young woman to whom I spoke, who took the part of Macha.

"I am in mourning for my life," she replied in the accents of the deepest depression, and the audience settled in to make it a night of unrelieved gloom. Henry treated the work like one of those immense Russian novels in which, as P.G.

Wodehouse observes, "nothing happens until page three hundred and eighty-six, when the moujik decides to commit suicide." I believe that this emphasis on despair and frustration was a mistake, and otherwise beyond the powers of the young company to deliver movingly. A more varied pace and emotional tonality seemed desirable. There is a notorious difference of opinion among Chekov's critics about this very point. Are the plays tragedies, comedies, or tragi-comedies, or something else altogether for which we don't yet have a name? I'd settle for the final option. I don't think the peculiar mixture of suffering and hilarity which we find in Chekov's plays, and especially at their most agonising moments, has been given its right name. Whatever it is, there was little of it to be detected in Henry's production of *The Seagull*. He wanted us to be gloomy, and boyoboy, were we gloomy! I have seldom seen an audience as depressed as the audience for our production.

We won the regional Festival competition. Best Production! Anne Colindale got the Best Actress award. Adam took Best Actor. Henry won the prize as Best Director. It was a clean sweep. It put the noses of the entire amateur theatre community of southern Ontario very much out of joint. All the other productions in the competition had been mounted by amateur groups who had been competing in the Drama Festival for years and years, ever since the then Governor-General, Lord Bessborough, had initiated the national competitions in the early 'thirties. They had, as they considered it, a lock on the competition and its kudos. Who were these college kids to come in with their heavy drama and walk away with all the honours?

Of course we felt that we were the younger generation knocking at the door, determined to brush away all the cobwebs of amateurism, the tatty Malabar costumes, the rank unweeded false beards. The adjudicator, an exceedingly distinguished British actor famous for his creation of the rôle of the Archbishop Thomas in *Murder in the Cathedral*, gave what we considered a very just résumé of events, on the Saturday evening which closed the competition. He had a low opinion of the merit of most of the other plays in the competition. Trained on Eliot, Yeats, and a friend of the then very popular Christopher Fry, he considered our choice of *The Seagull* to be the wisest selection of text of the week. And he was right.

At the same time, we did a poor job of the play. I was awful. Terrible. Every time I leant against that damn' tree it shook like a lily frond with the palsy. It hadn't been braced properly, and it weighed a ton. I used to hear it tottering behind me in rehearsal and the climactic performance, and I was sure that it was going to fall and destroy the production in some heavy, obviously symbolic, way. This would have been artistically appropriate to the tone of the production, in which heavy symbolism predominated. My father could never distinguish adequately between seagulls and wild ducks, and was certain that our play would seem ridiculous in performance because of an excess of wildly flapping wings.

"Isn't that the play with the duck in the attic?" he would ask innocently.

"You're thinking of Ibsen. There's a real duck in *The Wild Duck*. Chekov is too smart to bring any seagulls onstage."

"You're quite certain about this?"

"Of course I am."

"In that case, your text is probably fraught with second-level reference." How right he was!

Symbols, my God! We were up to our ass in symbols. Heavy, draggy, self-gratulatory, our version of *The Seagull* possessed no glint of comedy. Trigorin's speeches about his career as a writer, "not so good as Turgenev," have always seemed to me in re-reading to be painfully, exquisitely funny. Poor little Nina has always seemed foolishly imprisoned in self-regard, in ways that now seem an inspired commentary on one's own teens. Poor Nina, how I share her sufferings. Poor Konstantin, how is he to cope with them all, what is to be done with them? Henry never found the right note for our Nina; she never seemed a silly young girl much in need of a kick in the pants, an action which would have lightened proceedings immeasurably. She was long-winded and soppy, and it wasn't Kate's fault; that's how she was encouraged to play it.

Adam was our salvation. He was a perfect Konstantin, and has several times since played the rôle in London, New York, on television, and at least once in a film. In some respects it is one of the great classic rôles, a version of the ardent young lover of high intelligence and ambition, trapped in an unworthy environment, which sometimes makes me think of Romeo, sometimes of Ferdinand. Imagine what Shakespeare would have done with *The Seagull* . . . or for that matter what Chekov would have made of *Coriolanus*. I suppose my sympathies are clear. I think Chekov is the only dramatist who even begins to rival Shakespeare, and his great rôles are worthy to be undertaken by the greatest of actors and actresses, as Lear is, as Cleopatra and Gertrude, Cordelia and Ophelia are. In a few years Kate grew into a marvellous Cordelia, but as Nina she was insufferable. Adam went from his first Konstantin into rôles like Jack Worthing, Jack Tanner, Romeo, Edgar, Florizel. He had the goods. After some years in that sort of young actor's part, he began to play leading man's rôles without comic or ironic reservations, somewhat as the young Laurence Olivier played the second male part in *Private Lives* during its first production in 1931, light romantic leads (Gay Estabrook) in the West End and New York and in films during the remainder of the decade, emerging suddenly as a great Shakesperian actor, and almost without challenge the greatest actor of the English-speaking world, in the early nineteen-forties. It's possible for an actor to escape from romantic juvenile leads into the supreme parts. Inside every Jack Worthing lurks a Falstaff: inside every Romeo there's an Antony trying to get out. Not too many make it, but Adam made it. You could see him trying to fight his way out of cliché and misconception in our *Seagull*. He made Konstantin happy at certain times, suffused with an unjustifiable gaiety, even charm. At these moments you could catch glimpses of the delightful mannerly elegance which speakers of Russian assure us is to be found in Chekov. Konstantin's name is meant as an allegory; he is a fine loyal fellow. Trigorin rightly admires him. Doctor Dorn hopes a little desperately that Konstantin will win through. That is why the closing lines of the work are so heart-rending, though they are spoken so quietly, almost secretly. It is the indefinable mixture of delightful gaiety and insouciance, and terrifying emptiness, which is so persuasive. I have seen productions of *The Seagull* in which the audience didn't start to applaud for a full minute after the curtain fell, then wouldn't let the actors off the stage, so potent was the impression of quiet agony.

We didn't draw quite that reaction, but we won the Festival competition; there was a lot of stuff about us in the Toronto papers. I got into some photograhs in the *Globe and Mail* which my father noted with glee. "There's much more to you than to this Medvedenko," he remarked one morning, gazing at the drama section.

"I know that."

"Don't get any mistaken ideas from these people about your character and your powers."

"I'll certainly try not to."

I wasn't all that disappointed when we did *not* win the Dominion Drama Festival competition of that year, although missing out on the laurels infuriated Adam. We ran into an adjudicator who was very hard-headed, the chief critic of a newspaper in the north of England with all the tough and unromantic attitudes this implies, the critic in fact of *The Guardian*. He didn't like the unrelieved gloom of our show, and gave the top awards almost without exception to a production of the light American comedy *John Loves Mary* which had been produced in Hamilton. The actors from Hamilton got a great deal more out of their inferior play than we did from our masterpiece, according to the *Guardian*'s critic. He told us that we were pompous and stuffy in our approach, over-solemn, costive, remote from Chekov's true intentions, and a lot more to the same effect. It appeared that he read and spoke Russian with fluency. This was disconcerting. It left us without grounds for complaint or appeal; we lost the competition.

There was another peculiarity to the adjudication. This hard-headed and clear-sighted critic praised my performance as Medvedenko because, he said, "this young actor has precisely the gaucherie and lack of physical co-ordination, and the raw sexual hunger of the funny-looking man, that

Chekov wrote about so movingly, perhaps because he felt these torments so sharply himself." This observation annoyed the members of our cast because, as they said, I was being applauded for not acting at all, simply displaying my real emotional and physical state.

Henry said, "That's making a virtue out of total absence of technique."

"I'm not that hungry," I said humbly.

"Adam and Kate can act, and this idiot can't see it. You come on and fall over the furniture and he thinks you're great."

I tried to look modest and penitent.

"You were right for Medvedenko but you wouldn't be right for Treplev."

I bowed my head. "Anyway we all got to play the Royal Alex," I said. "I don't expect to appear there again in a hurry."

The Dominion Festival had taken place in Toronto that spring, and a good thing too, for otherwise we wouldn't have been able to take our production to some other regional centre. It was the custom during the existence of the Dominion Drama Festival to change the venue every year so that no single city had its home team favoured too often in competition. In fact, most of the time the production from the host city didn't win the top awards, as we discovered for ourselves rather painfully. But we couldn't have raised the money to send *The Seagull* out of town, so this condition was of questionable importance to us. The host production usually had to be distinctly superior to all the others in order to gain a nod from an adjudicator. Adam considered this a case of unjust leaning over backwards.

"It penalises the home town show. We were better than those ginks from Hamilton. That man from Liverpool . . ."

"Manchester."

". . . wherever . . . he wasn't competent to judge the Canadian scene. They should have had a Canadian adjudicator. He may know Russian, but does he know any French, for example? He didn't say a word about Les Compagnons. I don't think he enjoys the classics, that's all."

The Montréal entry had been a production of *Bérénice* by Les Compagnons de St.-Laurent which had been interminable, in the last degree tiresome. Adam claimed to have enjoyed it, and to have savoured every word of Racine's severe versification.

"The adjudicator said nothing whatsoever about Racine," he declared, with an air of injured virtue.

"Are you going to tell us that you enjoyed it?" asked Anne Colindale. A very good and honest girl, she had had no complaints about the unfavourable assessment of our work. Everybody loved Anne. She had achieved a remarkable performance as Irina Arkadin.

"It's a classic," said Adam sulkily.

"Be careful, Kostya, or Mamma spank," said Anne teasingly, but Adam was finished with jokes derived from the text of *The Seagull*.

"Anyway, Matt is right," he said, brightening up. "We all got to work at the Royal Alex, and that's such an honour. Maybe there'll be a resident company there, one of these days, and you won't find anybody from Hamilton playing rep in the Royal Alex. It'll be us."

This was in the late spring of 1951. Six months later the first proposals for the foundation of the Stratford, Ontario, Shakespeare Festival were aired in the Toronto papers. Enormous enthusiasm immediately sprang up among Toronto actors and actresses, from whose ranks the majority of the Festival players would have to be recruited. There were to be importations from Ottawa and from Montréal, and one or two from the west; but on the whole the first Stratford casts were drawn from the Toronto acting fraternity, for good or ill. The organisation of the Festival seemed to promise some sort of permanent company which would either tour in the winters or take up employment as a repertory company, and where else than in Toronto at the beautiful Royal Alexandra, one of the handsomest surviving theatres of the Edwardian era? Of course there would be full employment in rep for a number of actors. New companies would emerge to compete for the theatregoer's loyalties. There would be a renaissance—more exactly a *naissance*—of Canadian playwriting.

# The Scenic Art

All kinds of imaginable, and some unimaginable, consequences might flow from success at Stratford. The greater the success . . . the better all around for the tone of Canadian life.

This was our high argument. In the succeeding winter of 1952–1953, when the Festival undertaking, no longer a mere whisper of rumour among professionals, was launched on its snowballing descent of a precipitous slope, a company of about sixty actors and actresses had to be marshalled in support of the four leading players who were imported from England: Alec Guinness, Douglas Campbell, Michael Bates and Irene Worth. These sixty had to be found very quickly, and were in fact selected during auditions in Toronto, Ottawa, and Montréal. That sounds more representative than it really turned out to be. Much the largest part of the company came from Toronto, or in a few cases from smaller centres in central Ontario like Dan Slote, or the sweetly pretty Lynn Wilson, who came from what was really a suburb of Stratford, the small town of Saint Mary's.

Tyrone Guthrie and his associates saw all, or almost all of the actors and actresses who were hired, and picked out the forty-five or so who might be cast in speaking parts, in the *viva-voce* situation of an audition. A very few of the people who were to become extra ladies and gentlemen were as it were nominated by more senior associates, and hired by the Festival without having been seen by Guthrie. That was what happened to Adam. He had played big parts in university theatre and had a growing reputation in the semi-professional Toronto acting community. But he wasn't one of the people seen by Guthrie himself around Christmas of 1952. Most of those who were considered for leading rôles and substantial, though smaller, speaking parts, came from the CBC Radio world, like Lloyd Bochner, Robert Christie and Bill Needles, or in certain cases from special circumstances, like those of the renowned Montréal teacher of elocution and dramatic speech, Eleanor Stuart. Quite a number of small-part actors were from the Toronto university theatres: William Hutt, Eric House and Donald Harron, Harold Burke, Bruce Swerdfager, Beatrice Lennard—it is a long list. And the last few to be taken on were hired by small committees of very senior professionals who were asked by the Festival management to see and choose among a dozen or so promising aspirants who had been missed out of auditions.

Valerie Sherbourne of Stoverville, for example, was invited to meet one of these vigilante committees, but because she was about to go into rehearsal at Hart House Theatre as Perdita in *The Winter's Tale*, she felt unable to cope with both undertakings at the same time. Her Perdita was one of the very best Shakesperian performances during Robert Gill's long tenure at the threatre; it had immense consequences for the Stoverville region later on. But in the early spring of 1953 it seemed lost in the middle of preparations for renown at Stratford.

Adam was one of the last of these juniors to be invited to the feast, and he had not on a wedding-garment, I tell you. I vividly remember that terrible Friday night in the holiday season of that winter—it must have been not more than a week after New Year's Eve—when Adam Sinclair found himself so dizzied by the tormenting prospect of a forthcoming interview with one of these informal committees of visiting inspectors that he found himself going right off the rails.

"Right off the fucking rails," was exactly how one of his apartment-mates described the scene, speaking to me over the phone that night. This was a young musician, a composer from Newfoundland who was attending classes at the Conservatory. He had answered a want-ad for an apartment to let, and found himself invited to join in shared tenancy of this large seven-room apartment close to the corner of Avenue Road and Bloor Street, which Adam, Roly Ducane, and another chap who was still in university, not of any specific sexual persuasion, were sharing on a one-year lease. The musician, gifted, naïve, afterwards a composer of some celebrity, wasn't entirely prepared for the antics of his apartment-mates. On this particular drunken weekend, one of many, he had been deeply shaken by some of Adam's more desperate declarations, including an avowal of undying passionate love for the musician himself, whose name was Elwyn Bathgate.

"He just sits there and drinks his gin, and he won't leave me alone," Elwyn complained to me over the phone. "Can't you come over and damp him down a little?"

# The Scenic Art

I said, "He won't hurt you in any way."

"No, I know, but it's terribly tiresome. I'm trying to choose a tone-row for a work in the serial mode . . ."

"What?"

"Oh never mind. You wouldn't understand. But I can't have Adam at me all the time. I'm going to have to move out if this goes on. Come on over, will you?"

"Why me?"

"He keeps mumbling about you."

"Oh God!"

There seemed nothing for it but to comply with this request. I had known Elwyn for some months, and liked him a lot. He was a very interesting addition to the theatre crowd and their hangers-on, with whom I now found myself constantly involved, to my family's amusement and alarm. Tony had many smart observations to make on the nature of scenic representation, which seem more than ordinarily apt, and even prophetic in the light of things that happened long afterwards.

"You're not an actor, Matt. I don't know why you keep trying to do something you're totally unsuited to. You're too transparent."

"I know I'm not an actor. I'm simply enjoying myself innocently."

Amanda, still at that time resident in the bosom of the family, glowered at me. "It isn't innocent at all; those associations are disastrous for you. Just wait and see."

"I have no idea what you mean," I remember saying. They exchanged glances which I considered pretty smug. "You have no conception of what motivates a man like Adam Sinclair," I said stiffly, "somebody with real gifts."

"Well we all have gifts," said Tony.

"What are your gifts?" I asked.

"Never you mind about my gifts."

"Oh, you're just a kid. I don't know why I even bother to listen to you." This was when Tony was perhaps nineteen. I knew my words would cause him grievous annoyance. "And anyway," I said, "Adam Sinclair will make a mark in the theatre one of these days." I wiped my mouth and left the table feeling that I had scored a point for personal loyalties. I didn't know Adam really closely at that time, but two years later, when his state of near-desperation was described to me by Elwyn Bathgate, Tony's words and Amanda's obvious reservations about thespianism came back upon me vividly.

It seemed to me that they had been proposing a traditional view of the performing arts which holds that performance is corrosive to one's nature. That there is a certain truth in this is evident at once, and this truth can be shown by the words of the dozens of actors and actresses who have exlaimed to me at various times, "I've played so many parts I don't know who I am any more." Usually these plaints are overstated. I have noticed that most of these people, even though they may have changed their names several times, in the way that Brenda Schatzenberg saw herself as Brenda Conquest, then as Brenda Fitzalan, finally and definitively as Sadie MacNamara in public life, and for some years in the domestic situation as Sadie Sinclair, happy among her books and flowers, most of these people nevertheless retain a hard core sense of self-awareness.

She might have been born Brenda Schatzenberg, she used to say, but she perfectly plainly *wasn't* a Brenda Schatzenberg, nor was she quite a Brenda Conquest or Brenda Fitzalan. When she discovered herself to be the only genuine and original Sadie MacNamara it was like coming home, she said. We all took this to be nonsense, in the ordinary way of listening to Sadie.

To do him justice, Adam never thought of changing his name. Adam Sinclair is an interesting name for the stage, short, easy to remember, euphonious and fraught with suggestion. But his sense of himself was unquestionbly deeply fissured. When I arrived at the apartment at the corner of Avenue Road and Cumberland on the evening of Elwyn's anxious phone call, I received peculiar evidence of the actor's essential urge or need to reduce himself to the state of the blank page.

Elwyn met me at the door. "I think he's better now," he said in a hushed voice. "I haven't heard anything for almost an hour."

"What had you been hearing?"

He shuffled his carpet slippers on the hall runner. "Keening," he said.

"Keening?"

"Lamenting. Wailing. Ululation."

"I'd better go and see," I said. Elwyn followed me nervously down the hall. We threw open the double doors which separated the living-room from the hall and advanced onto the living-room rug.

"Well for Christ's sakes," exclaimed Elwyn in surprised disgust.

Adam lay stretched full length on the rug in front of the fireplace on his back, completely passed out and redolent—there is no better word—of gin. Apart from the necktie in rich plum-coloured silk which was knotted about his throat, not tightly, he wore nothing. His body was suffused with an interesting shade of pale green, which seemed very ghastly in the dim light. His legs were parted, the sexual members unduly evident.

"He has people coming to interview him in the morning," siad Elwyn in an awed undertone. "Actors."

"Would that be his Stratford interview?" I had heard the rumours which were circulating in the acting fraternity of how bands of seekers were scouring the town, looking for those last eight or ten walk-on ladies and gentlemen. I may even have heard that Lizzie Holcombe had been engaged, on what her peers considered inadequate grounds, then dismissed such gossip from my mind. I knew that these interviewing committees usually consisted of two actors and a critic, often the kind critic of the *Globe*. These would be people who would not take too kindly to the sight of the recumbent, nude, green, Sinclair. They would consider his behaviour frivolous and uncaring.

"What time are they due?" I asked.

"About ten in the morning. What do you think we ought to do?"

"I'll tell you what, we'll cover him up warmly and let him sleep it off. I'll stay here overnight if you've got room . . ."

"There's plenty of room," said Elwyn gloomily, "as long as you promise not to disturb me. I've got to compose, to compose. I feel it in me. Twelve-tone procedures."

"You won't hear a thing," I said. "I'll sleep over and set the alarm for seven-fifteen, and I'll get him on his feet first thing. Have you got coffee and aspirins?"

"Yes. We pretty well have to keep a stock on hand."

"Why don't you get back to work?" I said, "and I'll do my best for the cadaver."

"You don't think he's going to die?"

"I was speaking with a comic intention," I said reflectively.

"Oh, all right then. I'll show you the coffee and the aspirins and find you a bed. You can have Roly's room."

"Where is he?"

"Gone to Collingwood to spend the weekend with his mother. Roly's very close to his Mom." I let this pass. Soon Elwyn retreated to his quarters at the other end of the apartment and I was left gazing down at poor old Adam. Dorothy Parker's citation of Fitzgerald's own words, at the novelist's funeral, came into mind. "The poor son of a bitch." I covered the inert form and retired to rest.

When Adam woke up next morning, he was still green, a distinct viridian tint dwelling in the crawling skin, something like the virtuoso underglazes of Titian. I hustled him into the shower and kept him there for over forty minutes. I manipulated the taps cruelly, alternating between steaming hot water and intense cold. I made him shave in the shower stall, so that the steam would soften his whiskers and allow for a smoother, cleaner shave. I insisted that he shampoo copiously. I was thinking of the way the scent of drink hangs on from one day to the next during a bender. I didn't want poor Adam to stink of days-old alcohol fumes during the confrontation with the search committee. I found his cleanest shirt—none could be assessed as perfectly clean—and the same gorgeous plum-coloured foulard in which his neck had been swathed overnight. I smelled it. Uh-uh! He'd be wiser to face the interviewers with the strong brownish-green column of the throat bared. What the hell! Then I sat him down at the kitchen table and filled him with the dark, winy, deep-down goodness of Bokar blended coffee, the A&P's best. About nine o'clock he began to give evidence of recovery, and was able to totter into the front room and dress himself. When he returned to the kitchen to try to eat, he was in as good shape as anybody could reasonably expect.

"How do I look?"

"Pale and interesting."

"Not hung over?"

"Just enough to compel sympathy. Play up your background in Chekov."

"Oh shut up about that. Just because the adjudicator liked you as Medvedenko, though how he noticed you in that dinky little part I can't begin to imagine . . ."

"I'm not teasing you, Adam. You were good as Konstantin, really good. You'll be sure to get speaking parts at Stratford."

"If I ever get to give an adjudication, I'll make sure I know what I'm talking about. I won't simply barge in and shoot from the hip."

"I'm sure you won't. Do you have to read something for this group?"

"Why do you ask?"

"Because I can see them standing down on the corner; they'll be here in a minute."

"Dear God!"

"Now don't panic. If you have to read, read from *The Seagull*!"

"Will you shut up about *The Seagull* ? Where are my shoes?"

"You've got them on."

"Why so I have, that's strange. I can't seem to feel my feet."

"There's the doorbell."

He must have given them a sensational interview, because he got notice the following week that he was to be one of the Festival company; that was Adam's first professional contract on a salaried basis. He was engaged from mid-May through late August and actually drew pay for the whole time, and he had lines to speak. Popilius Lena parts, but lines are lines.

Inside a decade he was a renowned classic actor and a film star of considerable magnitude, the consort of a star of even greater magnitude than his own.

None of the romantic and highly public circumstances of Adam's courtship of Sadie MacNamara, their marriage in the UK at the turn of the sixties, and their triumphant return to this continent, need be rehearsed at this juncture. All that lay six or seven tumultuous years down the road, and none of it was directly witnessed by me. Those were the very years when Edie and I were getting our own marriage on foot, thinking about having kids, then actually having them and finding out what that had gotten us into. I had spent the closing week of 1952 in Stoverville, getting to know Earl and May-Beth Codrington. I remember helping Mrs. Codrington to carry her painting *The Stoverville Annual Regatta* up to her new painting room in the attic. And I recall that New Year's Eve with almost unwelcome vividness. For that was the night that Edie and I saw the green and gold and white ghost-ship in the ice at Brown's Bay, a delivery of reality so overwhelming to me that I found myself proposing marriage in the next instant. On New Year's Day of 1953 I found myself that novel kind of being, an engaged man.

So it must have been the week after that, the first week of 1953, when I sobered Adam up and prepared him for his appearance before the inquisitors. No more than a week separated the appearance before my eyes of the sunken vessel beneath the champagne-bottle ice, and the deathlike green cast of the moribund actor's skin. Green appears through many forms.

In the next few months Edie and I went along preparing for our wedding while the various Festival committees were hiring staff, arranging billeting services and making lists of available rental space, seeing about the tent, bringing the production chiefs of every department over from the UK, finding out about boots. Boots seemed very much on the collective Festival mind. There was a major difficulty about boots which was exceeded in disaster-potential only by the possible non-appearance of the tent.

While I was lollygagging around in Toronto and Stoverville, putting the finishing touches on my MA thesis and making various preparations for our wedding—for the groom too has certain small-scale preparations to make—I had the awesome disharmonious doubled green tones, champagne bottle and viridian, slurred together in my head. I think that I remembered our sighting of the frozen gunboat in the ice under moonlight, and its emotional consequences, better than the corpse-like glare of Adam's naked flesh under the dim lamps of the apartment on Avenue Road at Cumberland. Those were ill-sorted colours, whether in observable reality or in memory, elements of wonder and horror merged. I've never been able to bring them together. Poor Edie had different recollections of this period. While she was whizzing back and forth between Toronto, Stoverville, and Stratford that spring, she was taking a course of religious instruction which led to her reception into the Catholic Church on Easter Monday of that year, April 6th. I often wonder how much of her mixed remembrance of that time has affected her, as mine has me. I've got our shared vision of the ghostly ark, work on *Stone Dwellings of Loyalist Country*, a decision about further graduate study, and the dreadful form of Adam Sinclair, bubbling in my imagination. Edie has the ghost ark, the basic dogmas of Catholicism, half a year at the art college, and her first weeks at Stratford, glowing in her head. Which of us was given the superior imaginative endowment as a start on married life? I suspect that the deathly form of the actor was a counterweight to joy in my fantasy life. I never seemed able to expunge that dire blue-green tone from my remembrance of those days. Edie can have had no such sinister presence in her innocent recollections.

Nobody can share another's memories and imaginings. During the whole of our married life together we never thought to ask each other how much we remembered—and with what overtones—of the events leading up to our wedding. I don't suppose that I had Adam's dreadful naked body swimming in the very foreground of my fantasies just before the event. Edie had mentioned to me that we would have old friends in close proximity during our life together that summer. She can't have predicted how dismaying the realisation would be. If she and I were going to share a honeymoon suite in a smallish house in Stratford, Ontario, the very last neighbour I'd have wanted to encounter was A. Sinclair. Absolutely the very last! It was bad enough to find that Letty Millen would be living with us. Imagine coming upon a pair of spectral figures like Letty Millen and Adam Sinclair on the late evening of one's wedding day, rude shock! They were my east and west in infant imaginings. Letty had lived down at the east end of Summerhill Avenue, Adam up at the west end. They had been fixed like stars of the first magnitude in those locations during my earliest moments of understanding that I was I, myself, a person, not part of the grass and flowers, and two-legged forms that came and went above me. I woke up to Adam Sinclair and Letty Millen as soon as I stopped being an infant, and now here they bloody well were in an adult environment consisting of people like Alec Guinness, Irene Worth, Tyrone Guthrie, Sadie MacNamara, Lizzie Holcombe, Roly Ducane and Aila Strathdrummond. Only fancy the contrast and recurrence. Which way to look?

Edie can have had no inkling of this tissue of gossamer anxiety when she found her way to Stratford, causing me to follow. She happened to say, "Adam Sinclair is around all the time and Roly's going to be there. It'll be nice for you." This was late in May, wedding-date not ten days off. I quailed. And I wonder which of the revelations I made to her caused her to tremble inwardly and look pale. I use the Shakesperian phrase advisedly. I must have let things drop that surprised and traumatised her, sometime between New Year's Eve, 1952, and June fourth, 1953. I suppose one always traumatises a prospective spouse. How else explain what takes place in marriage? It is the terrible shock of the final encounter which causes all the divorces. Very difficult to take, to buffer the naked encounter. There we were, fish in a small aquarium.

While I was fiddling with that stupid MA thesis, Adam and Roly and Letty and Lizzie and Aila and Sadie (not yet Sadie) were assembling as though the fiery cross had blazed through

# The Scenic Art

their highlands and they came to represent the clans trooping down to Culloden. Think of the Strathdrummonds rising in the isles, the skirl of the Sinclair pipes. No, don't think of it. Try not to think of it. And I, even more innocent than Edie, thinking that I was truly taking possession of a share of her life, and she of mine, rode from Stoverville to Toronto in some stranger's car chauffered by my brother Tony, past traffic light after traffic light all the tiresome length of old Highway 2. Maybe those warning signals were trying to tell me something.

They might have been signalling some such absurd schema as this: Letty loves Roly who loves Adam who loves Matt who loves Edie who loves . . . there were Sadie and Lizzie and Aila to be fitted into this vortex too. Perhaps they would have to content themselves with peripheral whirlings at the edge of the pool. Somehow I didn't believe that they would remain contented with any such location. This terrible descending rotation had been prepared for me by the mere bare circumstance of growing up where I had, and when. The whirlpool spins at the bottom of Niagara and the powerless skiff is swept over the brink. I'd have been infinitely better off in a rubber barrel.

There were around us voyagers all the intimations of a terrifying storm about to break, roarings of mighty waters, unmanageable currents, precipitous fall, descent into the maelstrom. Niagara Falls is no distance at all from Stratford. Honeymooners might well take in both superb tourist attractions in the course of the same post-nuptial venture. I had not arrived in the Festival town with any formed intention of visiting Niagara Falls but the noise in the bedroom now suggested it. The heat-lightning of Friday and Saturday nights had now been superseded by bolts of the terrifying chain lightning of a southern Ontario June, greenish too in their approaching reflections. All four walls of the bedroom lit up at five-second intervals and the crashes came simultaneously. This electrical storm was directly overhead. The room flashed alive, went dark, crashings above, and simultaneously the rushing wash of torrents swept across the roof, wave on wave, driven cloudburst sweeping over brittle shingle, creaking and breaking pine, crash again and exploding brightness and through it all a new note, the note of the rest of that summer, a huge sonorous wholly embodied bass-baritone hum, very deep and full like the trombones of the Commendatore in *Don Giovanni*, other-worldly and retributive. The door to the bedroom burst open with a lesser slam and Edie rushed in with rain pouring down her face and body. Lightning flashed several times in a row very quickly and the thunder rolled without interruption. "They've just put it up," she shouted excitedly, "can't you hear it?" And then, "Who's that in bed with you, Matt?" She bolted across the room, through the other door towards the kitchen, returning immediately with our new broom which she brandished with a wide sweeping motion. She looked like the Queen of the Night. "Damn' you, Adam," she shouted vengefully, "I don't share my husband with anybody. Now get out of here, do you hear me? Scat. Scat!"

She took a full-armed backswing and poor old Adam vanished like a Demon King in a pantomine.

# 2

"Hey, I'm an uncle, did I tell you? My first nephew. Have I mentioned this before?"

"Three times in two blocks."

"It's a boy. Have a cigar!"

"Bleeeaahhh!"

"I'm sure it won't be the last."

"I'm sure you're right," said Adam with deep revulsion. "Must we discuss your philoprogenitive streak at length?"

"You'd be excited too, if it happened to you."

"I'd be more than excited, I'd be deeply alarmed. Possibly nauseated."

"I've often noticed how repelled you sissies are by the facts of generation. What is it Yeats tells us . . . 'honey of generation'?"

"Don't you dare to quote Yeats against me," ejaculated Adam. " 'What would they say, did their Catullus walk that way?' The devil can quote Scripture to serve his ends, you see. Yeats was no enemy of what poor Oscar used to call Uranian love. Why Uranian?"

"Because from the most exalted heavens. I'd have thought you'd know that."

"I think I did know it, but forgot. Poor Roly," added Adam with deliberate inconsequence.

"They're calling him Anthony Earl Goderich."

"Oh shut up."

"I will not shut up. Here, wait a minute," said Tony, putting his Pevsner in his pocket and taking out a crumpled letter. 'I'll only read the relevant bits."

"Your sense of relevancy, dear Tony, will not bear close

analysis . . . or even analysis from a distance. It is this lack of coherence in what you write that will at last bring down your efforts at playwriting in ruins around your feet. God help your producers."

"Here's a relevant bit."

"Oh God!"

". . . calling the child Anthony Earl Goderich to keep the names current in the family. The old Squire's been dead for quite a while, and you're the only living Anthony G. We thought of having you as godfather by proxy. Any small cash gift or silver mug will be put aside for the lad . . ."

"Why Earl?" said Adam, not really drawn into the heart of the matter.

"That was Edie's father's name."

"You are all so dynastic, my dear."

Tony went on reading to himself. He looked up suddenly and said, "Matt thinks his mother-in-law is going bonkers."

"The truly happy young husband will always imagine this."

"I expect so. He gives the symptoms. Mysterious withdrawals from society for long periods."

"There's nothing in the least irrational about that," said Adam huffily. "It's the most natural impulse available to us. How one longs for isolation . . . the quiet coolness of the tomb . . ."

"One does?"

"Why else does one come to London? Put that letter away this instant. You can read it over to me one day at teatime if you must. And explain to me what precisely has gone wrong with that demented pile of bricks and mortar in front of us. Who in his right mind can have conceived of it?"

"It's our local. You'll find the whole gang there night after night. Aila practically lives there."

"*Char*ming."

"Pevsner mentions the building in his perambulation of the west side of Tottenham Court Road. Here's the passage. 'Number 46. *Rising Sun,* in a fanciful Art Nouveau Gothic (1897 by Treadwell and Martin).' Worth a glance or more, he says. I never know what I think about that style. Fanciful Art Nouveau Gothic. Sounds a terrible mishmash."

"It *is* a terrible mishmash," said Adam, "and the whole of this part of London seems to be slimed over with it. Down in Oxford Street and Bond Street there are buildings in this— well I won't call it this style—this farrago of bits of ornament from three hundred years of architectural history, that have been blown up to nightmarish proportions, as though some- body had taken a Queen Anne cottage and inflated it to gigantic size."

"They sometimes call it Neo-Queen-Anne," said Tony, flipping the pages of his Pevsner. " 'So unlike any true Queen Anne,' according to the book. They seem to want to father the impulse on Norman Shaw, Webb, and Voysey, although I think Voysey had too much raw good sense to be implicated."

"One of the rare instances in which good sense supplied a saving grace."

"Those who possess good sense are seldom impelled to deplore it."

"You described me as a sissy," said Adam with heat. "If we are to cohabit—I use the expression in a purely neutral sense—for any length of time however brief, I must ask you to find language less wounding in which to describe my sexual preferences."

"Uranian?"

"Ooooh, I like the sound of that."

"Special tastes?"

"No, that means birchings in Saint John's Wood in the middle of the afternoon, or various ways of dressing up. Quite good fun in their way and perhaps special, but not my thing at all. There's nothing remotely special about my thing, is there, Tony?"

"I'm sure I don't know what you mean."

"Nor did your poor brother. I don't know when I've seen so expressive an attitude. Those shrinking buttocks. And then your *sister-in-law*, darling. Why are in-laws so terrifying, I wonder? Her broomstick and her air of a little witch on the brink of puberty."

"There's nothing of the in-law about Edie."

"She *is* your sister-in-law, the mother of your little nephew."

Tony made no rejoinder.

"Oh well then, come along, let's go and have a drink in this ghastly pub of yours, encrusted with mullions and oriels though it may be. Look, there's a date carved in stone, just by the roof. Look at the foliate forms, my goodness. 1897. Your guidebook is perfectly correct. All this Neo-Queen-Anne or whatever it seems to have been thrown up in the nineties like some horrible epidermal blight. How one longs for the boys from Dessau."

"*Style moderne* is simply this stuff turned inside out, d'you think?"

"It is the relationship of Walton to Elgar. But why 'Rising Sun' I wonder? Hardly Japanese."

"The name must pre-date possible Japanese influence," said Tony, "or then again, perhaps not. I don't think the English as a people would be much exercised to alter the name of a pub because of wartime differences. It was probably the Rising Sun from the start." He stepped suddenly off the kerb and made as if to cross Tottenham Court Road. Adam seized him sharply by the arm and pulled him back as a speeding automobile shot past. Currents of air stirred up by the vehicle made the skirt of Tony's jacket flap.

"That was close," said Adam. "Let's wait for the light." They moved up the east side of the road a few feet north of Store Street, and approached the button of the automatic stop signal. Adam punched at the button.

He said, "I enjoy these things. They give one a sense of power."

In a few moments the light changed, and in a subsidiary signal the words "Cross Now" appeared in clear white light against a dark background. They scuttled across the black and white stripes of the crosswalk, mounted a traffic island, stood there irresolutely for seconds, then proceeded across the final lanes in safety.

"Surprising amount of traffic for this time of night," said Adam. It was about eight-fifteen. "I'd have thought everybody would have gone home by now. Look at all those taxis. Empty too, most of them. Where are they all going, d'you think?"

Tony smiled with the intense self-satisfaction that the longtime resident of London feels, confronted by the defensive bewilderment of the visitor from home. "London never sleeps," he said. "Thanks for pulling me out of the way of that car. I might have bought it right there. You know, one of the most useful bits of advice anybody ever gave me when I came to Britain was something my father said just before I left. 'Always look to the right first,' he said."

"That almost got you killed just now."

"Well naturally he couldn't have predicted one-way traffic in specific locations. On the whole, his maxim was sound, and I advise you to act upon it."

"You damn' Goderiches are all the same under the skin. You just love handing out advice. I can remember when you were just a little squirt on Summerhill, and how you relished laying down the law."

"You're confusing me with Matt."

"He's not as bad. I'm thinking specifically of you. You used to boss the little kids around. You even used to try to tell me what to do, and I was much older." This was said with real resentment.

Tony halted at the corner of Windmill Street, and gave his companion his full attention. "Look here," he said slowly, "if I'm going to share my flat with you, even on a purely temporary basis, I think we may as well set a few matters straight. I'm very pleased to have you with me. It's always agreeable to have a friend from Toronto to stay. I think we may even be able to help each other professionally. But I'm quite grown up now, Adam. I'm not Matthew's little brother. I've got a life of my own over here and it's developing very nicely just now, thank you very much. I've got a publisher right round the corner in Great Russell Street, and access to the Museum in five minutes' walk from where I live. This is the most civilised community on earth, and I certainly don't intend to muck it about with a mess of tangled relationships from home. This is my home. I came here to get away from all that. I don't quite know why it is, but as soon as some artistic exile from Toronto arrives at the heart of the Empire, the first thing he or she does is to seek out Big T. and start complaining about my family. Now why is that? My father hasn't visited Britain for a decade and his name never meant very much to the British anyway, thank goodness. My brother is safe at home with his wife and child, hooray, hooray, and Amanda Louise, bless her, was never a problem for me. It isn't my family, it's my family's friends, who keep turning up to harass. Curse them." He paused for a moment and stood looking at Adam Sinclair, about whom he harboured secret misgivings. These reservations were not to be referred to Adam's now visibly defined sexual program. By 1958 a relaxed and kindly treatment of homosexuality was perfectly usual in British life, especially in the life of the theatre. Nobody minded and nobody cared what one did when the lights were out, thank goodness. It is true that a certain amount of wry comedy could still be generated by various pursings of the lips, hands placed firmly on deliberately protruded hips, phrases immemorially associated with campy joking.

"Oh don't touch it, luv, you don't know *where* it's been."

"Sweetie, you *are* a one."

This joky body of shared humour came from a large group's delighted awareness of an "us-them" situation widely prevalent in modern life, in which homosexual sensibility assumes that all of the really nice people are with us. The worthy and dull others who comprise the straight world are against us, and incapable of seeing these jokes. And on the whole, Tony felt in 1958, the gays have it over the straights. Almost all the nice people, the talented people, "us," *are* homosexual. Since his arrival in Britain five years before in the daunted state of a man who feels deeply excluded from somebody else's erotic happiness, Tony had gradually found that among his new friends homosexuality wasn't always, or even very often, a matter of conviction, passion, love; much more was it a matter of feeling as if one belonged to a very desirable and not very secret society. Old odium visited on the queens by the kings, visited on people like Wilde by people like Queensberry, was no longer supportable in British life. The closet door stood wide open, like the doors of the temple of Janus in exciting times, and people might go in or out as policy, conviction, momentary amusement, sometimes lifelong love, dictated. We had now reached the period when comedies about old queens in love began to be bandied about the West End, not always achieving production, yet often receiving sympathetic reading from management, especially the great controlling Management.

Small producers began to moot projects about sympathetic blackmail victims. Tony was himself contemplating two subjects which might be turned into plays, both of which had trendy homosexual overtones. Neither of his first two novels, both issued by the publisher in Great Russell Street to encouraging critical reception, had dealt with sexual matters in any way but the most conventional ways. He now felt ready to move in the direction of a more overt and approving treatment of these matters in a new work, not perhaps a novel. Contact with Adam might prove invaluable, since Adam had clearly transformed himself into a queer actor for motives of purest professional policy. In Tony's view of life—rather a layered view, to be sure—no person born and brought up on Summerhill Avenue in midtown Toronto prior to the mid-nineteen-fifties, could ever aspire to real, true, earned homosexuality, the way that certain celebrated Oxford dons or FO types could. You couldn't learn to be that queer, gay in that learned way, in a single generation; you had to be born into it, as you might be born into the upper classes, equally an impossiblity for a nice boy from Summerhill Avenue. Adam would never be *really* homosexual. He might learn to act it out (the histrionic laid over the dramatic), just as he was rapidly picking up London intonations. He'd gone through two new accents in the week he'd been staying in Tony's flat, rejecting both as undesirable, and was tonight employing a plummy, Soho costumier's tones which, Tony thought, he oughtn't to employ in the private bar of the Rising Sun. There might be interference if he did. It was an entirely spurious manner of speaking.

In fact Adam Sinclair and all his works and pomps were something of an enigma to Tony, who had seen virtually nothing of Toronto friends in the five years since he had arrived in the UK, asking little more of life than to be let alone and not asked stupid questions about Canada. His own reasons for getting out of the Dominion were mixed and private, certainly including a suspicion that any fiction likely to be written in the country at the top of North America at the time of his departure would be in a manner of which he could not approve. Sometimes in school he had been exposed to work by novelists such as Frederick Philip Grove and Murray Sansfoy, and these he had found to be fundamentally unsympathetic. He did not want to write or think in their manner, he was sure, but had no notion of how he ought to think about writing.

England, Britain, the UK, whatever the natives chose to call it, had if nothing else an enormous book-buying public, and an apparatus of bookshops of extraordinary proportions. Some large segment of the populace seemed prepared to support the production of books on a grand scale. Tony found his way instinctively, tracing the scent like a hound, to the place where the books were, the district near the Museum where the publishers congregated, in the exact sense of that word (Latin: *grex, gregis,* a herd) in an uneasy clump, each one trying to look over the shoulder of the next, a next-to-impossible physical feat, given their numbers and their close proximity. The lives of publishers in Bloomsbury were much like that of rugby players in the scrum, heads and knees bent in a tight protective ring, confidential and misleading information passed breathlessly from one to the next, legs working anxiously. His own publisher had for some years attempted to remain aloof from this professional cohabitation, maintaining an exiguous office in upper Soho. At length his self-willed exclusion from trade gossip began to wear upon this man, like all publishers deeply suspicious and mildly paranoiac by nature, and at about the time that Adam joined Tony in residence in the flat in Windmill Street, he moved house to Great Russell Street so as to be better able to survey his competitors, at the same time remaining alive to the apprehension, endemic to the trade, that his competitors were surveying him. The move from Soho to Bloomsbury made very little difference to Tony. He had enjoyed lying around in the tiny suite of offices in Carlisle Street, occasionally lending a hand in the packing department for no remuneration, out of sheer good will—an action which invariably confounded his publisher, as no British author would ever have undertaken any such gratuitous activity. The Carlisle Street rooms had been handy to two or three excellent restaurants and to Saint Patrick's Church on the other side of Soho Square, a building much admired by Tony Goderich, at various times frequented by him out of genuine religious conviction. There was an Irish pastor at Saint Patrick's RC Church. Soho Square, at that period, who was so perfectly representative of his kind that he demanded to be put into a book, a temptation which Tony was unable to resist. The character of Father Clare in *Down Off a Dirty Duck* is a pretty faithful rendering of this admirable priest, for years afterwards perhaps Tony's closest friend in London. In "real life" his name was Father Paddy Prout. He couldn't have been more Irish if he'd been dipped in a distilled extract of peat and potato. Father Paddy was enchanted with Adam as soon as they two met, and witnessed the Canadian actor's rise in the British theatre with entire satisfaction. Like Tony, he had small faith in Adam's professions of homosexual orthodoxy.

"He's only doing it to get on, the poor lad," Father Prout would say to Tony, "and be sure you bring him to the ten-thirty next Sunday. There'll be coffee after, and the lady from Broadcasting House. She may be able to help Adam to something."

A surprising circle of people connected with broadcasting, publishing and the theatre, used to meet for coffee after Mass at Saint Patrick's, in an upper room which always reminded Tony of the place where the apostles had concealed themselves on the first Whitsunday. Some of Adam's first useful contacts with television producers were made there, including one with a former Montréal man who was in process of becoming a big pot at Granada. In this and similar ways Tony, as longtime resident of London, was able to help Adam. He looked for favours in return at some future time when Adam should be in a position to do them. This happened sooner than either of them would have guessed as they sat drinking in the Rising Sun that night. The look of the pub made Adam uneasy.

He grumbled, "It's like living in an enormous stage set. What's all this curlicue and chimney-pot stuff, stuck all over the outside of the place like trim for a child's dolls house. It's like it was made of plasticene. Not, not plasticene, that other stuff, what do they call it?"

"Papier-mâché?"

"Exactly. How can you stand it? There's a building along Oxford Street just like this, only eight times the size. It's alarming."

"You'll get used to it. Drink up."

"Is this a free house or a tied house?"

"Where did you pick that up?"

"I heard about it today," said Adam proudly. "An actor's whole art consists in paying attention to personal styles. Now your poor brother would never learn that. He has no style."

"Listen Adam, I'm not paying any attention to anything you say about Matt. Or Edie either."

"Oho. Oho. So that's the way the wind blows, is it?"

"Never you bloody mind which way the wind blows. That's got nothing to do with you."

"So young Marster Tony . . ."

"Just you button up about that, see? Just drop it. Have another gin. What are you taking in it?"

"Orange."

"That's a whore's drink."

"*And* none the worse for all of that," said Adam in his plummy voice. A man at a neighbouring table eyed him anxiously.

Tony came back to the table with their drinks. Gin and orange for Adam and a half mild for himself.

"That beer is a strange colour," said Adam.

"Horse piss," said Tony comfortably; he drank very little.

"But a very sick horse. So tell me, what about these novels of yours, can you make a living from them? I never heard of them in Canada."

# The Scenic Art

"Nobody in Canada has ever heard of them, and they got a very good press in the UK. A Canadian publisher bought two hundred copies of the first one . . ."

"Which was?"

"It was called *Balancing Act*."

"I'll bet it was about a young Canadian who comes to Europe to escape from the stifling provincial atmosphere of life in his native land."

Tony burst out laughing. "A young Australian actually."

"Did it do well?"

"It did fairly well here. It was a Book Society alternate choice and was mentioned in a TLS fiction roundup. One hundred and three copies were sold in Canada. My second book was never issued over there."

"That's the one called *Down Off a Dirty Duck*?"

"That's it."

"Why is it called that?"

"Haven't you been keeping up with the American theatre?"

"I don't get it."

"There's this new Williams play, *Cat On a Hot Tin Roof*."

"I still don't see it."

"Titles come and go in families, you know. For a long time there were floods of titles that filled the frame, *The X and the Y*. You know, *The Bad and the Beautiful*, *The High and the Mighty*. I lay this vogue at the door of *The Naked and the Dead*. Bad artists always think that if they imitate just a teeny bit in a concealed way that they can pick up some of the merit of a previously successful work. So you get these families of descendants from the original success. But John Q. Public is never fooled for long; he knows when he is being fobbed off with an inferior article. And then satirists and comedians start monkeying around with these rhythms, and you begin to get television sketches called *The Short and the Fat*. *The Stupid and the Dull*. That's one of mine. It's an epic of Canadian life. It has Indians."

"But why imitate the Williams title? That play is still running, by the way."

"Certainly it's still running. I've seen the publicity shots of Barbara Bel Geddes in her underwear, and I know why it's still running. A deep-bosomed lass."

"You're very irreverent."

"I'm reverent about sacred matters, but about Tennessee Williams I am not reverent. Anyway when I began to hear publicity for *Cat On a Hot Tin Roof*, my ear started to play with alternate titles. *Shit From a Thin Grey Goose*. I thought about that for a long time. And then one day I exclaimed out loud, as I was walking to Fitzroy Square to meet a friend, *Down Off a Dirty Duck*, and then I knew that I had a title for my new novel."

"Are there any ducks in your novel?"

"Nary a duck."

"I still don't understand."

"You're simply not a literary person, and you don't have the technical means available."

"It just seems like a slightly silly joke."

"It's a very silly joke. That's what art consists of. Frivolous play. Performance. Why do you suppose actors call a play a play, and themselves players? Everything in art—this is much too solemn, like all generalisations—forms a second-level reference to things which have happened before, that aren't in themselves funny."

"That makes nonsense of tragedy."

"Quite so. And when tragedy is most fully itself it falls out of art and becomes merely laughable, like *Titus Andronicus*. What is our deepest impulse when we see Macbeth's head carried in on a stick, like some inspired popsicle? It is to laugh. Think of Robeson's Othello. Those rolling eyeballs. Shylock is never successful when he is played in the terms of sociological realism, as a suffering Jew. You have to play him as a stagy grotesque in an unconvincing false beard. Then you get your laughs."

"From Shylock you want laughs? *Oi weh*."

"You're going to get laughs, involuntary laughs, if you play him straight. Why not relax and enjoy, keep a happy thought? The play is a comedy. Who were the greatest British writers of # The Scenic Art

the nineteenth century, the most select geniusses? Dickens and Wilde."

Adam stared at Tony with dawning respect. "You're beginning to make sense. Dickens is my great personal hero."

"He can't be; that wouldn't be funny, in the way that Dickens is funny."

"This all sounds like a great camp."

"Close. Close. The best artists are those who are a great camp, without trying to sell the homosexual ideology. Dickens, for example, is evidently heterosexual—a homosexual Dickens would be unthinkable. He could never manage the double-mindedness, the ability to look back in on himself and laugh at his own attitudes, that Dickens has more than any other artist. Dickens is the greatest master of comedy in human history. He can cause Tattycoram to repudiate Miss Wade, while keeping the incident within the limits of the laughable, though only just. It was Wilde who said, very justly, that one must have a heart of stone not to laugh at the death of Little Nell. But Dickens knew that, as well as Wilde, and Wilde knew that Dickens had known it. It is the second funniest writer in the language paying tribute to the first."

"Salomé?"

"From first to last a hoot, a gay romp. I would lay it down that you cannot introduce a severed head into a work of art without making it comic. And the Crucifixion is a million laughs."

"Could we get back to *Down Off a Dirty Duck*?"

"If you wish. To those accustomed to this kind of silly cross-referencing, that title is an echo, an almost overt reference to the work of Williams, a writer of unbounded pretentiousness. Think how hard it is to choose whether to laugh or cry over Blanche Dubois, or those fey darlings in *The Glass Menagerie*. If Williams were able to come down hard on the side of the ridiculous and become what he really wants to be, a farceur, he might become a great playwright, a Feydeau. But he won't. He'll cling like the survivor of a sinking to his shreds and tatters of seriousness because he believes that this will aggrandise his own torments and make them 'meaningful.'

The curse of art is 'meaningfulness.' It produces the art of Samuel Goldwyn."

"Hmmmmn."

Tony pursued his line of thought. "Did you ever see Goldwyn's production of *The Adventures of Marco Polo* with Gary Cooper in the title rôle?"

Adam began to laugh. "I see what you mean. The shields and the shaggy ponies, and those beehive-shaped helmets."

"The art of the bad costume designer. As soon as Cooper came on you started to laugh. He looked so ridiculous. But if the rôle had been played by Groucho Marx, in precisely the same visual terms, we might have had a masterpiece of screen comedy. Come forward a generation, and consider John Wayne in *The Barbarians*, in the part of Genghis Khan, and you see what Cooper might have done with Marco Polo. The Wayne film is, in my judgment, intentionally ridiculous, walking a very thin edge. Kirk Douglas is the ridiculous, inartistic, version of Burt Lancaster, yet some people confuse them. This relationship is constant in art. The bad parodists of Beethoven are languishing in obscurity, but Berlioz has made something happily his own, and new, out of parodying Beethoven. He isn't a Kirk Douglas. All I'm trying to get at, Adam, is that I've heard you did something remarkable and original as Bassanio, which suggests that you may have something on the ball, like Berlioz."

"I wish your brother could listen to this, or that wife of his, a perfect Queen of the Night."

"What a compliment for Edie."

"Maybe. But the Queen of the Night fades out of the book halfway through. Sarastro has all the good lines, dreary old bore."

"Aha! How would you produce *The Magic Flute*?"

"As a knockabout laff-riot."

"Groucho as Sarastro?"

"Why not? It might be his greatest triumph."

Tony said thoughtfully, "I see you as the Countess in *Figaro*, all that dreamy summertime charm."

"With yourself as Susanna?"

"Cherubino if anything."

# The Scenic Art

"Bitch!"

"I'd love to sustain the homosexual attitude, but I can't, and it's a pity. One can do nothing in the West End without it."

"Is that really so? I've heard all the stories of course."

"I don't really know," said Tony. "There's nothing you can do with a boy, that I wouldn't sooner do with a girl. There have to be tits mixed into the stew, perhaps an occasional bum."

"I can show you bums of surpassing beauty which have nothing whatsoever—but not a thing—to do with the female sex."

"Girl bums have a distinctive texture, like *filet mignon*."

"Yeccchhh!"

"Adam, I want you to tell me something. I'm only going to ask this once, and it won't make the least difference in what I think of you, and it won't make me insist that you leave my flat. I simply have to know."

"Well, my darling?"

"Now cut that out."

"I couldn't help it."

"Yes you could've, if you wanted to try. It's that malformed sense of comedy that does the homosexual in. Anyway, tell me this. Are you really and truly a homosexual, a queer, a raging queen, a screaming faggot, a fruiter, any or all of those things? I just don't understand where you could have picked up the style. I mean, Firbank you ain't. Neither was anybody else in that awful logging-camp which was Toronto in the forties. I don't see how anybody could have graduated into legitimate queerdom in that place at that time. It must have exacted an extraordinary effort of talent, intelligence, discipline, and strength of will. Where would you learn? Who could instruct you? Swishing around, camping, these are acquired forms of behaviour after all. I'm not speaking about conventional perverts, you understand. Heavens, we've all met beery men who wanted to squeeze our genitals in some beer-parlour shithouse. In fact I think of that sort of encounter as the specific form of deviant sexuality in Toronto until very recent times. The grizzled stinking lout with the groping hands and the strangely liver-coloured penis. But I digress."

"No, no, no, this is all fascinating. What could have been your introduction to the love of men, my poor Tony?"

"I'm thinking of the beer-parlour shithouse in the old Rosedale Hotel, an extraordinary evocation of hell, the lighting, the stench, the hesitant mutable forms. Compare it, after all, with the delights of girls' bedrooms. Sachet. Pretty underthings. Feminine confidences exchanged in whispers. The frou-frou of the ball gown as it rustles to the floor, the naked tired seventeen-year-old body as it slips between satin sheets. Heady stuff."

"Don't you think it might be more fun to *be* that young girl and dream those darling dreams?"

"It might be, but that isn't what you want. Nobody desires an impossibility."

"Christine Jorgenson?"

"Come off it, Adam. Everybody knows that the sex-change operation leaves you just where you were before mentally. Christine Jorgenson will never carry a baby to term, poor thing."

"You think that the ability to give birth is what makes you a woman?"

"It certainly has something to do with it; biological organisation is fate. I don't say that childbearing is the sole focal point of woman's existence. But I do think that the physiological aspect is what distinguishes the sexes. No matter how deep an excavation some lunatic Swede has dug inside poor Jorgenson's body, no matter how securely some other living person's womb might be implanted—and that isn't how they do it anyway—it isn't going to transform poor Christine into a woman. You can't change your sexual identity because you can't change your identity."

"I agree with that," said Adam, "and I agree with something else. I'm a male. I don't want to be a woman, not really. I don't even want to take the woman's rôle in courtship. I don't want to be cuddled. I want to do the cuddling. A male homosexual may imagine the delights of being a pretty girl but he knows he can't be one. He's something quite different, a man with more subtle and deeply felt emotions than other men, more flexibility in his temperament, more ability to play rôles. To be what I am isn't a loss. It's an improvement in my life. I'm better off being what I am than being, say, your brother."

"Imagine Matt in drag," said Tony gleefully.

"You were the one who wouldn't listen to a word against him."

"That was a harmless joke."

"I wonder if there are such things."

"Perhaps there aren't. I'll withdraw that last remark. You see? I'm as flexible as the next sexually disoriented human. Do you fancy me at all, Adam?"

"Not a bit. I'm not in love with you and I never could be. You're not a type that I find attractive."

"Is that so? I've had my share of proposals, you know."

"Everybody has those proposals. I'd been the object of dozens of attempted seductions before I was sixteen."

"Something like your attempt on poor Matt?"

"I wish I hadn't mentioned that."

"Yes, you'd have been wiser not to but I won't hold it against you, not indefinitely anyway. And you aren't in love with me, that's reassuring, I need my sleep. But you still haven't answered my question. How did you learn to be queer? You must have had some instructions. I can never remember your father, for instance."

"I never knew my father; he went back to England not long after I was born. He'd come out after the war looking for work, and the depression sent him packing. He was always going to write and fetch us back to the old country, but he never did, and then there was the second war and all that. He was a valet. A gentleman's gentleman. That was his profession."

"Have you seen him since you came over?"

"Oh I expect he's dead long since; all that was nearly thirty years ago. And besides, I hate him. He was very cruel to my mother, just buggered off from one day to the next. I don't know how he managed to make his way back to Britain."

"Was he Scotch?"

"Scottish? Well he had a Scots name, but if you're thinking of the accent, it was my mother's and came from her side of the family. They hadn't been in Canada all that long. I lost my trace of an accent by the time I reached high-school."

"Deliberately?"

"More or less. I can still do various Scots accents for stage purposes. It wasn't my delinquent father who revealed my homosexual feelings to me. It was your brother, if you really have to know. I suppose I was a bit of a Mamma's boy because of our being left alone together, and the boys on our street used to treat me like a sissy, which I suppose I was. But I never loved a boy, I mean really loved him, until your brother took me in hand."

"An unfortunate turn of phrase."

"Until your brother started to take care of me. God but he was heaven, such a serious little boy. He used to stick up for me when the other boys mistreated me."

"What sort of mistreatment?"

"The usual sexual indignities. What we all have to put up with from the straight world. They used to sit on my head and pull my pants down and tweak my genitals. They used to put pencils up my rear end."

"What?"

"And then old Matt would tell them to leave me alone. We used to walk home together, and I can't tell you what a joy it was. Such a sturdy fighter against injustice. I used to long to have him put his arms around me and hug me, and then let me hug him. But he always left me in front of our house in the gloaming and trotted off to your place down the street. My first great love."

"I'm sure there have been others."

"But not like that," said Adam disconcertingly.

"And you can't get off with girls, not at all?"

"All that mess every month, you can't do this, you can't do that, not tonight dear, I've a headache, not tonight dear, I'm not in the mood. Women are such a bore with their special rules to suit themselves and their dreary unending emotional blackmail and their fat rumps."

"All I can say is I'd sooner have the ugliest conceivable female gorilla than the most beautiful boy alive. It's just a thing about me."

"You ought to have it seen to. What about another drink?"

"Will you pay?"

"It's my round, isn't it?"

"Yes, and you'll have to pay for Aila as well."

"Oh Lord, is she here? Is she coming over?"

"Hello Aila," said Tony. "Are you joining us?"

"Yes please, if I may. Can I get you anything? I'll pay."

"Gin and orange, and a half, no a pint, for me. I'll nurse it."

Aila crossed to the bar and ordered drinks. She had the same blowsy, large-scale endowment of energy and the same inaccurately judged movements as always. Coming back to the table she upset a neighbouring drinker's ale, and there was the usual business of apologies, moppings-up, offers to replace the spilled glass; this occupied quite a quarter of an hour, but at length Aila was seated next to Adam, gazing at him adoringly as he fidgeted, crossing and uncrossing his legs, apparently unable to find a comfortable position for the lower part of his body. The chairs in the Rising Sun are notoriously uncomfortable, have been for years. There seemed more, to Tony, than the ordinary level of discomfort in Adam's new attitudes. He seemed greatly dismayed by Aila's proximity. The young woman, now in her late twenties and full-blown in her womanliness, to say the very least, hovered caressingly next Adam, hung on his words.

"Of course I'm only a humble member of the crew," she said at one point. She had somehow or other wangled a job as wardrobe mistress in a West End long run; this might have been because of her energy, her kind heart, or her competence, which was genuine. It might have been because of all three. Aila claimed to detest the production standards and ethos of the West End. She had only accepted this job so as to be able to hold on to her modest savings for eighteen months, while she looked for a permanent position with a firm of designers. She and Letty Millen were living together a few minutes away from the Rising Sun. (A *ménage*, do you think?

Adam's comment). They spent their free time working up a portfolio of costume sketches for every imaginable sort of play, a collection of swatches of available fabrics, a library of references to costumiers and museums of costume. They were doing the thing in a big way. They were calling themselves Milldrummond. They were having a brochure produced by a friend of theirs who was employed in the offices of a firm which specialised in designing pamphlets and brochures for business and industry. She spoke largely of her plans.

"Milldrummond," said Adam, relaxing somewhat as the evening wore along. "I like the name. It's catchy, original, easy to remember."

"We're only waiting until the brochure is ready. It's going to be in four colours and black and white. We're going to send it to every management that isn't part of the system."

"The system?" inquired Adam delicately. This was a recognised means of setting Aila off.

"You know perfectly well who I mean," said Aila tightly. "The theatre in this country simply will not survive unless the monopolistic situation of West End management is broken by independently minded managers. The monopoly has its hands on every theatre, on every important director. Why, even Doctor Guthrie has to clear it through them if he wants to direct in the West End."

"There's always the Old Vic."

"Canonised by now and not in the West End and deadly dull."

This opinion, neither novel nor especially penetrating, was nevertheless surprising on Aila's lips. She went on. "Adam, now, Adam can't get invited to join the Old Vic, no matter how good he is. They aren't interested at all in new talent. They're an establishment body and that's all."

"My dear good Aila," said Tony, "somebody's been getting at you. This sounds almost inflammatory coming from a sweet girl like you. Are these Letty's opinions?"

"Letty thinks that, but she's not alone. Everybody at the RADA thinks the same way. We see them all the time. We may even design a production for the Vanbrugh."

"Really, darling? We're coming up in the world."

"I won't be wardrobe mistress in some tatty comedy at the Globe for the rest of my life, Tony," said Aila, tossing her splendid head. Masses of heavy black hair flopped around as she threw out this statement. Adam winced. The truth was, Aila exuded such an attar of the female that it overcharged the corner where they sat. Access of self-assurance had altered her greatly.

"You're near the RADA?" asked Adam politely.

"Just along Gower Street. We're at number four, in the old servants' quarters next to the areaway. We've a dumbwaiter in our bedroom, Letty and me. You'll have to come round and pay us a visit."

"I should enjoy it above all things," said Adam, glancing at his wristwatch.

"What it is," said Aila, "is that we're beginning to get answers from provincial managements."

"Oh, provincial managements," said Adam with hauteur.

"No, but do listen. There are new theatres going up all over Britain and new plays being written for them. I really do think that the next wave in British theatre is going to come from the provinces. *Look Back in Anger* was just the beginning. You'll find in the next few years that the best acting in the country is being done in Cardiff and Nottingham and Coventry and on the telly."

"The telly," said Adam, as if Aila had pronounced an especially dirty word.

"Best acting in the UK on the independent network, mate," said a solitary drinker at the adjoining table, a burly middle-aged man who had been eyeing Adam for some minutes. "Actor yourself, isn't it?"

"That's right."

"Classical line perhaps. Bit of Shakespeare, occasional Chekov, Shaw and Congreve."

"You've hit it."

"Come along and see me any time," said this man. He rose, handed Adam a business card and left the pub. Aila and Tony and Adam sat back in their chairs and looked at each other.

"And that's how one makes a start in the show business," said Tony. "If I wrote that down, nobody would believe it."

"I'll go and see him tomorrow," said Adam, putting the card away carefully. Later in the year he was cast in two television plays and a radio series by this casual pub acquaintance.

"Word gets around," said Tony. "I hear of nothing but your triumph as Bassanio. It's an unlikely part in which to make a great success. I mean, isn't he your usual Shakesperian young man, a bit of a ninny? Shylock has good scenes, and Antonio has good scenes, and even Lorenzo has that 'sit, Jessica' bit that we were all tired out with in high-school. Gratiano has one good speech. Gobbo gets off a few funny lines."

"Old Gobbo or young Gobbo?" Aila asked. Tony and Adam stared at her and she blushed and stuck her nose in her drink.

"Any flipping Gobbo you like. But Bassanio? He's down the cast list with the Prince of Aragon, making exclaiming noises over the casket. And all he really does is entangle Antonio in debt and mishap, because he's crazy about Portia. Why is he so eager to get off with Portia anyway? A mannish piece, I should have thought. Who wants to marry a lawyer?"

"She isn't exactly a lawyer," said Adam slowly.

"A Daniel come to judgment. Doesn't somebody say that?"

"Shylock, and then Gratiano," said Aila helpfully.

"Shut up Aila," said Adam in a not unfriendly voice. She shivered, and looked at him with intense pleasure.

"I don't see Portia as a full-time pleader. It's true she has some skill in the law. Ellen Terry used to play her in an advocate's gown and one of those continental lawyer's hats, a kind of larger pillbox. I remember seeing photographs of her as Portia; it was perhaps her greatest rôle."

"Beatrice," murmured Aila, but the men ignored her.

"Portia may have served as the model for some of those witty young women in Restoration comedy like Millamant."

"They all talk about Millamant," said Tony. "Name me another heroine of Restoration comedy if you can."

"Olivia in *The Plain Dealer*," said Adam smartly.

"Miss Hoyden," said Aila.

"I'll Hoyden you, Strathdrummond, will you be quiet?"

"Boo hoo."

"Let the poor child alone, Tony. No need to be so fierce."

Aila gave Adam another adoring look and Tony allowed himself a silent chuckle. "Why not let our lady companion tell us about your Bassanio?"

"Why not indeed."

Aila said, "The thing that was so marvellous about it was the way he played against the grain of the whole casting and direction. They'd got the idea that Antonio was in love with Bassanio . . ."

"Dear Jesus," said Tony, scandalised.

". . . and they cast Orlo Vosper in the part."

"A Brit," said Adam, meaning to enlighten.

"I don't know his work."

"Wispy," said Adam, "one of those actors who wants to play everything in a minor key to the accompaniment of wistful lute music. When he grows older he'll play Lear the way one ought to play Lear's Fool."

"This can't have been one of Guthrie's productions."

"No, no, no, Doctor Guthrie had left by this time," said Aila.

"He's given me a lot of introductions," said Adam. "I may have something next month at the Bristol Old Vic."

"And Orlo Vosper played Antonio in this languishing bittersweet series of attitudes," said Aila. "It was simply ridiculous."

"But it was simply marvellous to play off," said Adam. "It gave me a chance to give Bassanio a lot of dimension that he doesn't usually have. I played him dead straight, very young, very manly, a warrior Bassanio. I wore a sword and a dagger, and I made the designer give my costume a military air. I discarded the lovesick idea of Bassanio. I made him a man of great good sense, but not a bluff buffoon. In the casket scene, I took the lines so that you could see him working out the poetic and symbolic implications of the clues. He was almost like an intellectual there, and the wonderful thing is that the lines allow this. I walked around the casket room like a philosopher working the thing out. I took very long pauses, then let drop a few more words as though I were squeezing them out of a finished tube of toothpaste. My makeup made me look lean, hungry. Imagine a Bassanio played something like Cassius. I often thought about that during the production, a saturnine Bassanio. That way he became a worthy opponent for Shylock, don't you see?"

"And his reviews," said Aila, "the reviews were such as you wouldn't believe. I saw them all, all the important ones anyway, and they were unanimous. 'Sinclair saves misguided *Merchant*.' 'Bassanio redeems director's misbegotten Venice.' And much much more, all to the same tune."

"I think I may have achieved a unique quadruple-first," said Adam with becoming modesty. "I got absolute raves from four major critics, in Toronto, London and New York. Herbie Whittaker loved what I did. I couldn't have had a better notice. It was hard to believe. And then Nate Cohen gave me a wonderful plug on his radio show and in his column. Now you know, Tony, nobody or almost nobody ever got simultaneous approval from Whittaker and Cohen."

"Tell him about the *Herald-Tribune*," said Aila excitedly.

"I've got that clipping here somewhere," said Adam. "I always carry it for luck. The first rave review I ever got in New York. I was the only thing he talked about."

"Who was that?"

"Walter Kerr, their regular man. He comes to Stratford every summer, usually with his wife."

"Isn't she the one . . ."

". . . the one who writes the farces? Just so. They're both in love with the new building at Stratford . . . Ontario, that is. Jean told me that if she ever wrote a play that wasn't a farce there would be a part in it for me, so you see I live in hopes. Walter's column was worth a mint to me. I got my TV series out of it."

"Who was the London critic?"

"Tynan. He said he'd never seen Bassanio treated in that manner but from a re-reading of the text my version seemed obviously what Shakespeare had had in mind all along. Well, I mean to say, you can't say any fairer than that, can you?"

"I should say not. I had no idea you were getting notices like that. Will you be getting in touch with Tynan, now you're here?"

"I've got an invite from 'im, I have, to write or call at any time. He has some grand project in view, I believe. He's not much older than any of us, I don't think, and he's the coming man among the critics."

"He's exactly my age," said Tony succinctly, "almost to the day. We've met once or twice at South Ken parties."

"Where's that?"

"You'll find out in due course."

"Bloomsbury. South Ken. Where are we right now?"

"We're just on the border of Bloomsbury and a district that has no name, just a reputation; it's been writers' and artists' country for decades. Windmill Street. Charlotte Street from Rathbone Place north to where it turns into Fitzroy Street, just at Fitzroy Square. Whitfield Street, Goodge Street."

"Where the tube station is?"

"Right. There are about a million good cheap restaurants around here, and over every restaurant there are a couple of flats. My place is an exception; there's no restaurant downstairs. I don't know exactly what to call the streets around here; they have no definite occupational character like Wigmore Street or Harley Street. Somebody will give the quarter a name one of these days, like Belgravia, but just now it's simply a random collection of streets and shops gradually developing into a recognisable district. You can live a very satisfying life round here without ever going more than half a mile away. You only have to cross Tottenham Court Road to find a flock of publishers, or walk down through Soho to the theatre district. And there's the BBC half a mile northwest of here. If you were to say that we live in the middle of the theatre, the Museum, Broadasting House, and the railway stations, you'd have us placed. There's probably some profound significance to that, but I don't know what it is."

"The railway stations?"

"Euston, St. Pancras, King's Cross, all up along what used to be called the New Road. And I suppose you could count Paddington in too. I don't want to go on about London. I'm not really a Londoner and I never will be, and I don't really know the least little bit about the place. I just happened to find my way here, and honestly, Adam, you couldn't choose a better district for your purposes. You can walk almost anywhere you might need to go, and the busses are marvellous too."

"The twenty-four is the most heavenly bus," said Aila. "It bisects London from Pimlico to Hampstead, from the Tate to Kenwood House. Naturally we like the other side of Tottenham Court Road better. Bloomsbury is so nice and quiet; the three of us live there for practically nothing."

"Three?"

"We've got a new roommate. Sadie MacNamara is at the RADA, you know, and she's moved in to share expenses."

"Is that the same person that used to live at Mrs. Roop's?"

"The same! Only you should see her now."

"I don't want to see her now. She was a spoiled untalented brat at Stratford, on the make, and pushy, and no more a Sadie MacNamara than I am. She's at bottom a Judy Gluttz stuffed into a foundation garment two sizes too small for her. That woman spent the first three seasons at Stratford bothering me. Oh God, and to think that at one time I was more interested in her than in you and your roommates, except for Matt, of course. Is the other one with her, that Lizzie Holcombe?"

"Lizzie's given up the theatre, and gone into education. She's a don at one of the women's residences at Varsity."

"I hope that she's found her niche," said Adam peaceably, "and so young Sadie's at the RADA. She's such a faker, that girl. She's far too old for drama school. She must be thirty."

"Oh she is not," said Aila. "She got started in the theatre very young. She was just barely eighteen that first year at Stratford. I think she's still in her early twenties, perhaps twenty-three."

"You're too good to live."

# The Scenic Art

"You must come and see us soon, just as soon as we've fitted in Sadie's things. Talk of publishers, my goodness, there's a big publisher two doors down from us, and another at the end of the block, and two or three more on the other side of Bedford Square and more on Great Russell Street. Isn't your man there, Tony?"

"Alas, yes."

"Why alas?"

"Oh, no reason," said Tony hastily. He had no wish to offend Aila, and indeed rather liked her. "We'll have to dine with them in their servants' quarters, Adam. They must be like three little Victorian housemaids left to their own devices while the butler is on holiday."

"Sexy!" ejaculated Adam glumly. "It sounds like an absurdist comedy, something by N.F. Simpson."

"Or the new man, what's-his-name, chap who wrote that revue sketch we saw last night. 'The Last to Go.'"

"I don't know who you're talking about, but I remember the actor, a tiny man with huge nostrils and extremely talented, I thought."

"Oh you've been to see *Pieces of Eight*," said Aila woefully, "and you never let us know you were going. We've got costumes in one of the numbers, 'True Blue Love Song.' Only two, but there'll be more to come. Didn't you just love that little man? 'Arthuritis, suffered bad, 'e did.'"

"And then the other chap says, ''E never 'ad no arthuritis, not when I knew 'im.'"

"That's good dialogue," said Adam.

"It reminded me of *Salad Days*," said Tony.

"No," said Aila. "That was at the Vaudeville, I think."

"Not the theatre, Aila. I mean the quality of some of the numbers. Not that arthuritis number though, that's something rather special."

"'Suffered bad, 'e did,'" quoted Adam with approval. "I wouldn't mind playing in something by this fellow."

"We've got costumes in one of the numbers, we can easily find out who he is. Come to dinner tomorrow night and we'll give you his name. Is that a date?"

"Will you all three be there?"

"Yes."

"Should we bring an extra man?"

"No," said Aila comfortably. "Let's keep this a professional conference. Ta, then."

She rose and made her way to the door.

"There's a nice girl."

"There's about two nice girls, or at least a girl-and-a-half."

"Don't be catty, Adam."

"No I won't. I'll rise above it. I suppose the third girl will be that MacNamara person."

"I fear so."

The next night Aila told them that the chap who had written the revue sketch, "The Last to Go" was a new writer called Pinter, who had had a couple of short plays on the telly and a full-length work called *The Birthday Party* produced in London earlier in the year. He was said to be John Osborne turned inside out, terse where Osborne was talky, obscure and elliptical where Osborne was blunt and explicit, in short one of those reversed images who recur in literature and drama, the artist who completes and rounds off the work of a contemporary: Haydn and Mozart, Wordsworth and Coleridge, Fellini and Antonioni, Bonnard and Picasso, Pinter and Osborne, Larkin and Hughes, Tennyson and Browning. It does however seem that there are certain singular artists who give birth to no image of this kind. Shakespeare. Dickens.

Emily Dickinson clearly requires Walt Whitman—her spiritual opposite *and* double—in order to make her full effect. Hopkins and Swinburne. Spender and Auden. Ravel and Debussy. Hemingway and Faulkner.

The late 1950s will likely be written up in histories of the British theatre as the age of Pinter and Osborne, who were the two most produced, most discussed, perhaps most admired new dramatists of their time, coming as they did when the management and traditions of the theatre were undergoing drastic revision, the hegemony of the West End being undermined, eventually destroyed. In the late 1950s most managements did not take television seriously, and

# The Scenic Art

weren't much interested in an actor's TV credits, which would seldom be listed under his name in the program of a stage production in which he appeared. John Osborne's work, which had clear affiliations with preceding stage traditions—Osborne himself an aspirant actor with a deep emotional commitment to the music hall and provincial rep—was precisely work *about* the stage, for the stage, especially plays like *The Entertainer*.

*The Entertainer*, an enormous success as play and film at just this time, was a work about the relation of the stage and the music hall to British society, and could not be understood in any other way. It was when the play was filmed that its intense theatricality became clearest. The great central performance was the work of an actor who remains the actor above all others who embodies stagecraft in his performances on the screen.

It is impossible to decide about Olivier whether he is a stage actor who has incidentally given some great screen performances, or a movie star with a great voice and wonderful eyes, or simply a great actor whose gift expands and recreates the artistic possibilities of both media. Most actors who appear on both stage and screen, Richardson, Gielgud, Adam Sinclair, show a clear inclincation towards one or other medium. Richardson was clearly a stage actor, an artist who preferred to work on the stage than the screen. Alec Guinness, late in his career, in his performances as George Smiley, the hero of John LeCarré's tales of espionage, seems to have discovered his true medium. With his beautiful voice and subtle intonation, and his minimal use of facial movement, Guinness has become the greatest and most expressive of television actors. Adam Sinclair was never destined to be a film star, although he has at different times appeared successfully in big-budget films.

Olivier is the enigma, the test-case, an actor with film star looks like James Mason, and the immensely stageworthy dramatic presence which Mason never commanded. So it remains unclear whether Olivier is a movie star or a magnificent stage actor, or both, or something more than either. Whatever he has been, he hasn't done it like anybody else. In

*The Entertainer* in those years, he was unequalled and unexampled on the stage, and on the screen too, giving in the film an entirely different reading of the rôle than his stage version, a reading which reinterpreted Archie Rice for the cameras. No other actor has done anything quite like it, and it is perhaps Olivier's single most extraordinary achievement. After seeing the film of *The Entertainer* everyone was certain that when Olivier finally appeared on television, he would give the definitive performance as a television actor. When the opportunity finally presented itself, twenty years later, the artist was worthy of the challenge, in a death-scene in which he spoke no dialogue, merely indicating the state of his heart and conscience by tracing the sign of the cross and then lying perfectly still. Only Guinness as Smiley has excelled him in the medium.

In late 1958, Pinter and Osborne functioned like Auden and Spender in the thirties, drawing the imaginations and ambitions of a whole generation of young artists behind their chariot wheels, with Adam, Aila, Sadie, in the dusty ranks towards the rear of the column. A crowd of new playwrights marched with them: John Arden, John Mortimer, Arnold Wesker. Half-hour and one-hour television plays began to provide dozens of opportunities for young actors and actresses to get work. New directors, new designers, new managements not wedded to the methods of the existing West End, began to emerge in London and the provinces. The Royal Court was by now well launched on its controversial and splendid career. A little later Bernard Miles founded the Mermaid. Later still came the National Theatre and the Royal Shakespeare Company, and throughout the period new provincial theatres opened and began to mount plays by unknown playwrights whose works formed a new repertory.

When Tony and Adam went over to Gower Street to dine with Letty, Aila and Sadie, they did so with no particular expectation of any professional good accruing to them because of a kind action directed towards friends. Playwrights and actors are apt to consider young actresses a dime a dozen, and people who work on costumes or props as of scant importance: this is simply a traditional professional attitude,

# The Scenic Art

a mode of the infinitely complex caste system which obtains in the arts. They arrived bearing grocery-store plonk, a couple of copies of Tony's pair of novels, flowers snatched up at the last moment on Tottenham Court Road, with little notion of doing themselves good by these harmless kindnesses. It was one of those infrequent instances in contemporary artistic life where a bit of a jolly-up for three girls adrift in Bloomsbury issued in valuable and delightful collaboration for longer or shorter periods.

Adam and Tony liked the area steps, the smell of cookery drifting out of the open area doorway and up past the iron railings. It was a pretty sight to see passersby on this crowded metropolitan street pause and smile at the mouth-watering suggestions of *boeuf bourguignon* which floated out to greet the evening's guests. Hardbitten Socialists from Birkbeck, disillusioned medical students, assistant curators of Bronze Age artifacts, the denizens of Montague Place and Bloomsbury Street, paused, inhaled, perhaps felt proudly concealed hunger pangs, eyed the blooming Aila as she stood at the top of the steps swinging the area gate back and forth, waiting for Adam. He and Tony arrived at seven, descended to the kitchen and were shown through the dim basement recesses by Aila and the slinky, torpedo-like anonymous form which turned out to be that of Sadie MacNamara advancing upon them from behind the door of the lavatory from whose cavernous deep a sound of moving waters emerged in Wordsworthian strain.

"That toilet is a loo unto itself," said Sadie.

A good entrance line, thought Adam.

"Come and look at it," she insisted, "it has painted flowers round the bowl. Daisies and hepaticas." She switched on the inadequate overhead bulb and below them, sure enough, lay a great expanse of porcelainware, creamy, crazed with a myriad of tiny lines, like something mystical out of *Idylls of the King*, Tennysonian, the manufacturer's device perfectly clear after a century: Armitage Ware, the legend supported by an arm in chain mail bearing a mace. Around the bowl were delightful floral patterns reminiscent of illustrations in children's books of the eighties, distinct reminiscence of the Arts and Crafts movement delivered in their delicate line, and the soft yellows and purples of the petals.

"England, my England," breathed Sadie solemnly as the group tranquilly contemplated the object.

"Another good line," Adam said aloud. He saw that Sadie was no sweet and blushing twenty-three; she was much closer to his own age, probably nearing thirty. An actress's fortune is hard, he told himself, with an agreeable and rare sense of solidarity with his own sex. They age so fast, poor darlings. After forty there's nothing much to be done with most of them while a man, in his fifth decade, may have thirty years of vigorous appearance left to him, if he takes care of himself. He stood aside and let Sadie pass him on their way to the outlying parts of the flat. There were two bedrooms where the wine cellars and the butler's pantry had been, and a staircase at the very back of the building which led up to an enclosed garden behind the terrace, of impressive size, the property of London University and open to tenants of the house who cared to use it for evening strolling. Aila and Letty had placed two or three seats out in the garden, and they directed the boy chums in that direction with their drinks, while dinner matured in the guise of an extremely palatable stew with wine sauce. The food and the drink were surprisingly impressive; talk continued well past midnight. The five young people gradually began to share a special sense of adventure, of having found their way at last to a place that was civilised. Five Canadians under thirty in a terrace house catty-corner from Bedford Square, two minutes from the Museum, bursting with professional chat about the newest aspects of the British theatre. All of them remembered the evening for many years as the point in their lives at which everything serious really began.

Tony began to get flashes of the idea which was to turn into *Claude and Gertie*, as he sat back and stared muzzily at Sadie and Adam.

Letty and Aila told how they had begun to receive very encouraging letters from new theatres in Nottingham and especially Coventry.

Adam revealed the hitherto closely guarded secret of his contract with the Bristol Old Vic, and recited the serio-comic misadventures of his appearance during the previous year in the pilot for a TV series, made at extravagant cost in Los Angeles and offered to CBC executives over most of a year, only to die unscheduled in production limbo.

"It was after my Bassanio," he told his eager listeners. "Lemme see, it must have been July 57. I know it was about two weeks after Walter's piece in the *Herald Tribune*. I still think Jean put my name up for the series, even though she's always denied it. A baseball series. There never has been a really successful treatment of baseball in the movies or on television. I wasted most of last year developing that pilot."

"What happened?" demanded Sadie, hanging on his words.

"It's so obvious you'd think everybody would see it at once. It's just the same with movies about boxing. They never succeed either."

"What exactly is the problem?" said Tony, taking a cigar from his breast pocket and looking at it speculatively. Letty and Aila shied away from him, viewing the tarry stogie with visible repulsion.

"I hope you don't mind," said Tony suavely. The girls shuddered but said nothing. Tony was a man with a future, they knew, and they would do nothing to jeopardise the friendship. He lit the cigar and a fearful stench filled the dining room.

"To make a film about baseball players you have to have actors who can move like baseball players. I never gave it any thought until I was cast as a pitcher. Then I went to see some games at the Hollywood ball park. They have a team in Hollywood called the Hollywood Stars, wouldn't you know? Ballplayers can do amazing things; things that no other people can do. You see them making these lazy, easy, motions with their arms, like this." He stood up and made a throwing motion, and Tony sat up alertly. He had known that Adam was talented, but hadn't realised that his talent might be very considerable. The way he moved his throwing arm was revelatory. He had clearly studied the ballplayer's characteristic professional attitudes with extreme care. The motion he made was precisely the highly idiosyncratic, subtly skillful physical action of somebody who has been playing organised baseball at increasingly demanding levels of skill for twenty years. It was a beautifully soothing and releasing piece of artistic notation.

"And then," said Adam, "they wave their arms in this funny way and the ball will travel a hundred and fifty feet in a dead straight line about six feet above the ground, and seem to be *speeding up*. None of us could throw a ball that far without taking a run and a jump and hurling it with all our might, and then it would dribble off along the ground. When the throw gets to the glove it makes a sharp spanking noise. POCK. And they do this in play between the innings or before the game; they have funny little jokes they do, throwing three balls at each other, or flipping the ball up behind their backs. They have all these little rituals. Some painter should do something about baseball."

Letty, who had been silent all evening, now remarked, "There are no good baseball paintings, and practically no good paintings of boxers."

"Bellows?"

"Yes, but nobody else."

"The reason isn't far to seek," said Adam. "They move in such specialised ways that actors and painters don't anticipate the problem and can't recognise it. I found that I could not make myself look like a ballplayer. I couldn't get the uniform to sit on me the right way, I couldn't walk or swing a bat like a ballplayer, and I threw like a girl, pushing the ball in a funny sidearm motion. Watch sometimes. The difference between the way a man and a girl throw from the shoulder. I don't see any reason why they shouldn't throw in exactly the same way; the arm is fitted into the shoulder with the same sort of socket joint."

"Girls don't run like boys," said Sadie demurely, lowering her eyes.

Letty took up the question of costume with real interest. "A baseball uniform is cut in quite a special way, with extra material under the arms and at the crotch, in a heavy flannel which folds and gets worn in a special way. It takes the creases that a distinct kind of movement gives it. The uniforms made for you were probably cut to fit like an ordinary suit, and didn't break down in the right places."

"That was part of it," said Adam, "and I didn't stand in the right way or run or throw or move properly. You might say, who not hire real players for the long shots and do a lot of doubling and trick editing. And they did this, but the real ballplayers were so self-conscious that they gave the trick away. They couldn't move like actors. Anyway that was only one of the problems. There are a couple of boxers who have done well in the movies, playing themselves, but no ballplayers."

"Gary Cooper looked ridiculous in *Pride of the Yankees*," said Tony. "I remember it well, poor Cooper. Early in his career he possessed a great, faintly bisexual, beauty; he really was a wonderful-looking man. But at some point he got identified as the strong silent American hero, and after that his personality grew infinitely less interesting. Now all he's allowed to say on the screen is 'Yep' and 'Nope.' He didn't look at all like Lou Gehrig. Gehrig was known as The Iron Horse by some sports fans, but insiders called him Old Biscuit-Pants. He had an enormous rump. Most power hitters have enormous rumps. Babe Ruth had a rear end of truly mastodontic scope. Gary Cooper did not look like a baseball player. He looked like a very elegant, well-educated, society figure, with a proper marriage and an occasional discreet affair. He wore evening clothes well, but you can't say 'Yep' or 'Nope' while sporting a white waistcoat and a silk hat. Fred Astaire never said 'Yep' or 'Nope.'"

"The most elegant public figure," said Letty, and there was a moment of silent reverent contemplation of the image of Astaire.

"The man makes the clothes," said Letty. "I think that Aila has told you that we have two costumes in a popular revue of the moment."

"We long to see it again," said Tony, and Adam nodded polite agreement.

"We have plenty of tickets if you'd like to escort us," said Sadie.

"Oh but couldn't we go all five in a clump one night, and you could point out your work?"

"That would be better," said Letty, rather mournfully. Now well into her thirties, thinner than during earlier Toronto and Stratford days, Letty had just begun to recover from a disastrous affair with Roly Ducane which had dragged on for the length of some deep, fairyland attachment, close to seven years in fact, since long before the first Stratford season. In her mid-twenties she had spotted Roly Ducane in a tiny rôle in a semi-professional production of *In Good King Charles's Golden Days*. She had been desperately, hopelessly entangled with Roly since that time, an epoch almost unimaginable now, buried in the mists of Toronto theatrical pre-history. She had tormented herself during the first Stratford season with the sight of the weak-minded Roly writhing in the toils of purely professional attachment, she had thought, to Adam Sinclair. In fact it had not been Adam who was the object of Roly's ambiguous affections but another, far more celebrated actor, whose world-renowned good looks and uncompromisingly heterosexual nature had reduced Roly to a state of grovelling emotional disarray.

In this state of frustrated longing he had not been amenable to the comforts of feminine sweetness. Roly liked Letty in the way you might like a kindly boring sister. He could find no sexual use or good in her, and went one hundred percent gay not long after their relationship failed. He was by now sunk without trace in the lower depths of the CBC. Letty had come to London in a state of distraction after the débâcle, and had worked so hard, and had exacted so much hard work from Aila (not a ménage at all; the two women were acutely interested in the buccaneering male sex in every way) that their little enterprise Milldrummond looked like becoming a serious professional undertaking.

"A man from the provinces came to see our show—well I shouldn't say 'our show' as we've only got the hint of a connection with a single number—but he liked our costumes. They were supposed to be too terribly Pont Street, and they were. It's a funny song. Anyway he got in touch with us, and asked if we could find clothes that were as East End as these were West End. Dockers, fish merchants, shopkeepers from the late nineteen-forties. He's got hold of a new playwright who writes about that, and they're doing two of his plays, and perhaps three, in the new theatre in Coventry."

"He's called Bryan something, our chap."

"The writer?"

"No, the director. The one who came to our show. He knew Ken Williams when he worked in Birmingham; they're old friends. Now this Bryan chap has got his hands on a completely new theatre and a completely new play or two, or three. It's called the Belgrade, Coventry."

"Why Belgrade? Belgrade is the capital of some Countess Maritza sort of country with a grand hotel and terrible red wine. Yugoslavia? Hungary?" said Adam, concealing genuine interest.

Aila said, "Let me tell this part, Letty. Belgrade is the capital of Yugoslavia. It used to be the capital of Serbia, before the first war."

"They also Serb who only stand and wait," said Tony drowsily.

Aila ignored him. "Belgrade and Stalingrad were twinned with Coventry after V-E Day. The three cities have some sort of formal association because they were all badly damaged during the air raids and all that. Well everybody knows about Coventry and Stalingrad. I'm not sure what happened to Belgrade."

"Marshal Tito is what happened to Belgrade."

"Shut up, Tony."

"Anyway," said Aila, "after the war the people of Belgrade made contact with Coventry City Council and offered them a gift of wood. Trees. Timber, like. From the forests of Serbia, for a new building in the city centre. Coventry had to be completely rebuilt after the war, like Rotterdam or Dresden."

"Or Hiroshima," said Tony muzzily.

"Shut up, Tony."

"At the end of the forties, the civic administration of Belgrade made this offer of enough of their local wood to build a wonderful new theatre as part of the rebuilding of the city, something to go along with the plans for the cathedral and the new shops. But it turned out that the Coventry building regulations wouldn't allow an entirely wooden structure, so they accepted the timber and used it for the theatre-interior, the cladding, interior roofing, flooring for the performance areas, dressing rooms, staircases, everywhere that the fire regulations would permit. Wait a bit, I've got something written down here."

She put a hand down the front of her dress, to everybody's delight, and withdrew from some recess a small flat pocketbook or wallet.

"I wrote these down; they're inscriptions on two wall plaques."

> This stone commemorates the gift of timber by the people of Belgrade to the citizens of Coventry for a civic theatre and was laid on the occasion of the visit to this city of representatives of Belgrade and Sarajevo. May 19th, 1953.
>
> This building was opened by Her Royal Highness the Duchess of Kent, 27th March 1958, in the presence of the Right Worshipful the Lord Mayor of Coventry Alderman Mrs. Pearl N. Hyde, MBE, JP. Director: Bryan Bailey.

"And this Bryan Bailey is your man?"

"That's him," said Letty, becoming more animated. "He's got his hands on this beautiful new building. Not a toy. A full-sized theatre, seats about a thousand, wonderful equipment, and now he's found a new writer. I should think that might make you sit up and take thought, young Tony. A theatre can't operate with just one writer, can it?"

"Building an audience takes more than one writer," said Tony, "because variety is the life of show business. *Variety* is the Bible of show business. Stix nix hix pix."

"Doesn't he ever shut up?" said Sadie, who now began to give increasing signs of acute interest in both men. "Something could be worked up from this connection," she said with shrewdness. "I mean what we have with us tonight is a complete tiny production unit or almost. An actor, an actress, a writer—and I'm sure dear Tony has a script concealed somewhere in his pockets."

# The Scenic Art

"As a matter of bald fact," said Tony, "I just happen to have here the first draft of a new work for the stage."

"... which he intends to try to read to us tonight. But we won't allow that, will we? We won't spoil our first night?" Sadie looked at Adam with terrible meaningfulness as she said this. "We've got two production people who, I'm sure, do other things besides just costumes."

"Just costumes?"

"More important things," said Sadie, exerting her charm on Letty and Aila, "like stage managing, or even direction. It seems to me that we might all find things to do in a place like Coventry. Where is it?"

"It's about ninety minutes from London by train. You take it on your way to Birmingham and the north. I've been there," said Aila. "I was there last week. It isn't at all a commercial theatre. They get a lot of state assistance and they want to do new regional plays. Not just plays from the Midlands. Plays from the north of England. Scots writers. Welsh nationalists."

"Fuck regionalism!" said Tony under his breath. Nobody noticed.

"I don't at all see why they might not think of doing a Canadian play," said Sadie, "treating it as a regional work. As it would be. They want to keep themselves apart from West End standards. There couldn't be anything less West End than a new production of a Canadian play . . ."

"Proust the Parisian regionalist," said Tony, "Shakespeare the Warwickshire kid."

". . . I mean they won't even touch Canadian plays in Canada, and in New York producers barf on sight when a Canadian script comes into the office."

"Barf?" said Adam. He had never heard this word before.

"Perhaps I should have said, 'Crap in their drawers,' " said Sadie coarsely. She giggled.

"Please don't be vulgar, Sadie," said Letty.

"Oh do, please, I love it when girls talk dirty," said Adam.

"You old softie," said Sadie. "If anybody in the world might be willing to do a new Canadian play by an unknown novelist. Better make that little-known novelist . . ."

"That's more like it," said Tony.

". . . it would be a regional playhouse in the Midlands on a subsidy. We should all go up there and talk to this Bryan Bailey, and we will. What's the play about, Tony? Is there anything in it for me?"

"God, yes," said Tony. "There'd be two marvellous parts in it for you, if you were a little older."

"I'm older than I look."

"I thought so. I'd have figured you for around twenty-eight. Do they know about that at the RADA?"

"What they don't know at the RADA won't ruin any careers. I'm not twenty-eight though. What's the play called?"

"*Claude and Gertie.*"

"Oh, like *George and Margaret.*"

"No, not like *George and Margaret*, although in a way you're right. There really isn't much wrong with the plays of Gerald Savory or Ben Travers or Dodie Smith or Terry Rattigan."

"Terry already?"

"At the same time, the Aldwych farces and *French Without Tears, Thark,* and *George and Margaret*, are in for a very rocky time for the next couple of decades," said Tony. "We're in for a long period of fake-revolutionary garbage where people will speak with regional accents and throw things and try to smell like miners and rugby players. There's a total reversal of social values coming in this country. In a little while a play like *George and Margaret* will seem as quaint as a Dion Boucicault burlesque. Young women living at home on an allowance from Daddy, doing the flowers and running up to town to buy clothes because there's nothing else to do. Mother wandering in and out of the French windows from the garden. People are going to think that they hate all that, and that it's part of a vanished past. Mind you it isn't; it isn't at all. People will be behaving like that for a long time to come, but it won't be an acceptable subject for a serious play. The only way you'll be able to get around the kitchen sink and lavatory seat school of the theatre will be to come at it from the angle of sly savage parody. So you're right when you ask if *Claude and Gertie* takes off from *George and Margaret*. Of course it does, and so does *Waiting for Godot.*"

# The Scenic Art

"Because in these plays the title characters never appear?" asked Sadie.

"Clever little girl," said Adam.

"Something like that," said Tony, "because you see my play is a special kind of intellectual farce, a work that depends for its meaning on something that's absent. In this case, the text of another work of immense celebrity. My play is written in the spaces between the lines of *Hamlet*."

"What does that mean?" said Aila.

"Imagine a production of *Hamlet* in modern dress on a bare stage or in a smart apartment building, a block of service flats in Belgravia or in Sutton Place, some contemporary version of Elsinore."

"I've never seen *Hamlet* done like that," protested Aila.

"Maybe not, but the thing isn't inconceivable. They've done *Hamlet*, poor old play, in a hundred versions, in Victorian costume, in rehearsal clothes, as a dramatic reading, as an anti-Nazi sermon. A text like that can be read any way you like. Shakespeare was working with at least three earlier versions of the story when he wrote his play, and just think how his text was buggered about by the actors. OK then, it's taking place in some fancy, *style moderne*, hotel deluxe or apartment building. Then try to guess what the characters were doing before the play started, and what they're up to when we don't see them onstage. What sort of guy is Horatio really? He can't always be as dull and as square as Shakespeare makes him. Maybe he digs rock and roll. Is Claudius a prize bastard or a decent human being? And how old is he? Suppose Gertrude and Ophelia were played by the same woman in these 'offstage' scenes? You can think of all kinds of variations. The idea is so rich that you have to keep a tight rein on yourself to keep from writing a Marx brothers script. Just suppose you cast Groucho as Claudius, Chico as Polonius, and Harpo as your Hamlet, with Zeppo as Laertes and Margaret Dumont playing both Gertrude and Ophelia, and none of their scenes was in Shakespeare's version, but could have been if Shakespeare hadn't cut them. What does that give you?"

"*A Night at the Castle*," said Sadie promptly.

"*Danish Pastry*," said Adam.

"*Great Danes*," said Letty, smiling faintly.

"*You Can't Trust an Old Cold Ghost*," said Aila.

Adam said, "Now we're starting to act silly. Are you going to read us some portion of this work?"

"Not tonight. We've all had too much to drink, and we're not in the right mood. Adam and I will just take ourselves off, ladies, but we'll all go and pay court to your friends in Coventry, won't we? Soon."

"Jack Benny starred in *To Be or Not To Be*," said Aila as the boys tottered up the area steps. "It isn't such a dumb idea at all."

Tony and Adam walked the three or four blocks from Gower Street to Windmill Street in close and intense conversation about the structure and meaning of *Claude and Gertie*, while Letty and Aila gathered materials around them and began to make sketches for costumes appropriate to dockside life, which they put together in a portfolio a few days later, together with two large suitcases crammed with sample suits and dresses. These objects they transported to Euston where they caught the eight-thirty for Coventry and Birmingham. They were in Coventry by ten-ten.

This quick rail-run, almost a commuter trip, became habitual with the staff of Milldrummond through the winter of 1958/59, as programming and production at the new Belgrade grew more and more vigorous and exciting. The first works of a promising playwright are always highly stimulating theatrical ventures, sometimes abundantly rewarded by transfer to the metropolis and subsequent international repute.

The early plays of Arnold Wesker, which were first produced at the Belgrade, the celebrated *Roots* trilogy, were only the first of a type of production which was to dominate British drama for close to twenty years. Writer after writer surfaced in places like Nottingham and Scarborough, Coventry and Glasgow and Cardiff, and in the universities and in little, left-wing, portable theatres: signals of a profound shock, a vast seismic disturbance under the superficial strata of British society.

The new actors, the new directors, writers, technicians, might come from anywhere, even so far away as the misty, rockbound coasts of Canada. All the time that Letty and Aila were commuting to Coventry they kept preaching to the Belgrade production staff the virtues of the young Canadian dramatist, Tony Goderich, promising novelist, the author of *Balancing Act* and the brilliantly funny *Down Off a Dirty Duck*, at this very moment at work on a new play which wasn't simply a new *play* but a totally new *kind* of thing, a play in the holes of another play, lines between the lines, scenes that ought to be in the other play but weren't. The cuts from *Hamlet*.

"That wouldn't be a bad title," said the director at the Belgrade, over lunch one day in the theatre restaurant. "*The Cuts From Hamlet*. I've just read *Down Off a Dirty Duck* on your recommendation. He's got a very good publisher, your friend. Not very many young authors from Canada acquire a Bloomsbury luminary for their publisher at the start. I liked *Dirty Duck* a lot; there's a funny priest in it, Father Clare, handled with great tact and generosity. And this fellow's writing a play, is he? I don't quite know how a play by a Canadian would go down with my board and with the Arts Council. I could take a proposal to them, of course."

Aila said, "Would you consider reading through the script?"

"I read dozens of scripts, luv, hundreds. One more won't break my back. Just you bring it in with you the next time you come, and we'll see what's to be done."

That was early in 1959. Mid-March. A season when Coventry could be desperately bleak, when the wind blew along Corporation Street between the shells of bombed-out buildings which still hadn't been demolished and replaced, more than a decade after the war. The centre of the city around the cathedral was by now almost entirely rebuilt, the department stores, the under-the-roadway pedestrian crossings, the new theatre. But here and there lay monuments to the blitz, through which a March wind might pass with deadly penetrative chill.

Walking west along Corporation Street towards the theatre one morning, Bryan Bailey motioned towards one of these towering shells as they passed. "That's where old stagehands go when they die. That's the old Rex Theatre, that is. Sad, when you think of it. A legitimate theatre most of its life, a picture palace in the thirties, and suddenly a tomb. Destroyed during the blitz, you know, in the same raid that hit the cathedral. November 4th, 1940. The most famous date in Coventry. I suppose the citizens of Hiroshima have their own special date. I wasn't in Coventry in those days, but everybody here remembers the Rex. We've a wardrobe mistress on staff—well, you know Marge—who was in the theatre the night it was hit. They were showing *Gone With the Wind*. She told me that she and the other ladies who survived tore up their knickers into strips for bandages."

Letty and Aila kept their heads down, facing into the whipping wind. "We never had anything like that in Toronto," said Letty.

"When you say it like that," said the director, "'Toronto,' the place sounds wildly exotic like Bloemfontein or Calgoorlie. Perhaps there's something in the idea of a Canadian play. I've read *Claude and Gertie*, and it certainly isn't what I expected. It's terribly witty and it doesn't mention Toronto once."

"It couldn't be less like Arnold's work," said Aila in an insinuating tone.

They arrived in front of the Belgrade.

"I see what you mean," said Bailey. "The *Roots* plays seem provincial, and Goderich's writing seems highly sophisticated and original. I mean, not what you'd expect from a Canadian."

"That's the conventional wisdom," said Letty.

"You'd better ask Goderich to come up here and talk to me. I'm making a sounding with the board this afternoon."

"Oh, Mr. Bailey," said Aila, "you are kind."

"It's true," said Bryan Bailey, "I am kind. I have everyone else's interests at heart. Have Tony Goderich write to me, and we'll arrange an appointment."

Preliminary talks about a Coventry production of *Claude and Gertie* began in April. The script was gone over in the last detail; there were numberless long arguments about what sort of a thing this thing was. Would it play? Would Midlands audiences be familiar enough with the text of Hamlet, and the

# The Scenic Art

critical literature on Shakespeare's play, to grasp the references and the jokes?

"I don't see that this matters," Tony always said. "To my sense, this is just a play about a man who wants to winkle his older brother's wife away from him, by fair means or foul. That's a motive that's always dramatic, and always farcical, ridiculous. The man who cuckolds his brother will always be a ready butt, especially if the brother is much older. People sense uneasily that there are farcical situations immediately underneath *Hamlet*. 'Well said, old mole, can'st work i' the earth so fast?' 'I'll lug the guts into the next room.' Those are funny lines; people invariably laugh at them, and foolish critics say that it's 'nervous laughter.' But it isn't anything of the sort; it's a natural response to a very funny remark. 'I am but mad north by northwest.' There is no such point of the compass."

"There isn't?" said Bailey.

"Of course there isn't. Why do you suppose Hitchcock called his film by that title? It's a very Hitchcockian joke. North by northwest is exactly nowhere. It's right off the map. You can't get there from here."

"You're a very clever Torontonian."

"Well there you go, you see? You take it for granted that because I come from Toronto I'm totally uncivilised, and you're surprised that I can write a witty, funny play that works in a way that Arden and Wesker and Pinter and Osborne and Shaffer and Mortimer don't. I never wanted to write like them. I mean, you've had plenty of Wesker here. I imagine you took me on because you wanted something fresh. And you've got it, haven't you? *Claude and Gertie* works off an original conception, so far as I'm aware. Mind you, I'm not saying that there won't be other plays like it in the nineteen-sixties, because there will. I think this play is going to be a success, perhaps not in the West End, but certainly here."

"Now you're implying that we're provincial."

"You *are* provincial. I thought that was the point. You don't want the Belgrade, Coventry, to turn into another West End, do you? I'm not saying piss on the West End. I hope that *Claude and Gertie* has a long run there, but only after it's been tested and proved at the Belgrade."

"We're simply a proving ground for Tennent's Limited?"

"The days of the monopolistic management are over. The theatre clubs and the regional and university theatres will see to that. I don't intent to have anything to do with H.M. Tennent."

"In short, you're using us for your own ends."

"Quite right. Isn't that awful? All the same, you get the first go at my play, and if it does as well as *Chicken Soup With Barley* you'll have another success to your credit, and the first thing you know, you'll be moving to Shaftesbury Avenue."

"How cynical you Canadians are."

"Letty and Aila aren't cynical."

"No," said Bailey. "They're two of the nicest young women I know. Are all Canadian young women like them?"

"Wait till you meet Sadie," said Tony. "Sadie and Edie."

"I know about Sadie and I'm terrified of her. Who is Edie?"

"Just a friend. A girl back home."

"Not somebody I'm likely to have to deal with in rehearsal?"

"No."

"Sadie will be enough of a handful by all accounts. When do I get to see her?"

"Any time you like. I do very much hope that you'll think seriously about Adam and Sadie. They were in on the play almost from the first sketches last September. I didn't have anything on paper, the first time I talked to them about it."

"Not even an outline?"

"A few scraps of paper with ideas noted on them. I thought of the play originally as a kind of essay on what a text is. Then I got the notion of writing something around something else. Every work, and especially every famous work, has a limitless series of alternate versions open *around* it."

"I'm not certain what you mean by 'around it.'"

"It's a question of what the characters are doing between the scenes of the basic text. Take the narrative of the life of Christ. We are told that He was born, that He made a trip to

# The Scenic Art

the temple with His parents, and that His public life began at the age of thirty. The various events of His public life don't seem to fill three years, yet His age when He dies is traditionally given as thirty-three. Every attentive reader of this story asks himself or herself a number of questions at once. What did the Holy Family do in Egypt? Did Joseph find work there as a carpenter? What made them decide to return? I'm taking the narrative at the most literal level, you see. What schooling did Jesus have in Nazareth? How was He treated after He astonished the doctors in the temple? What was He doing at the age of twenty-one or twenty-nine? Don't you see how beguiling the problem is? Any very rich source offers an infinity of possibilities inside itself, all or any of which may illuminate the known narrative in a number of ways. Now let's take *Hamlet*. There's a lot been left out of the play. The minor characters bristle with possibilities, especially the six young men: Horatio, Laertes, Rosencrantz, Guildenstern, Osric, Fortinbras. There's a suspicious over-supply of men in that play, given the number of girls available, only two, really, Gertrude and Ophelia. Put the case, for example, that Osric is not a homosexual. I know he's usually acted as a swish, but that isn't in the lines. Suppose he's in love with Ophelia. Suppose he hates Hamlet, and admires him at the same time. You might write a play all about Osric, Laertes and Horatio. Or again, suppose you decide to have Gertrude and Ophelia played by the same woman . . ."

"Can't be done. They're onstage together."

"Not absolutely necessarily . . . not more than twice anyway. Take another look at the text. Treat them as alternative possibilities of female love, the woman who's emotionally older than oneself, and the woman who wants to be your little girl, but have them played by the same actress. Sadie will be marvellous."

"I think you're making this up as you go along. All the same," said Bryan Bailey, "there's a play in *Laertes and Osric*."

"Sure there is. *Claude and Gertie* is simply a play about envy. You hate to see your brother settled down with somebody he can fuck every night, while you're young and alone. 'Oh beware of jealousy, my lord, it is the green-eyed monster.'"

"That's not from *Hamlet*."

"I know that, but the point is that Shakespeare knew all about jealousy. How much older is Claudius than young Hamlet?"

"I can't say. It isn't established in the text."

"You bet it isn't. Suppose that Claudius is one of those in-between uncles, younger than his married brother, nearly the same age as his nephew. Has anybody ever played it as though Claudius and young Hamlet were of the same generation?"

"Not that I know of."

"It's a possibility. The whole discussion turns on what we mean by 'character' in dramatic writing, and on how we select a limited number of events from a given story for our specific treatment of it. It's the distinction between fable and subject."

"I haven't the least idea what you're talking about."

"I haven't either and I don't want my play to be submerged in a sea of concepts. It has to be a good exciting amusing story first."

"It's all of that, on its own terms."

"Does it stand up if you know nothing about *Hamlet*?"

"I think it does. I've tried reading it that way, and then it reminds me very much of Beckett."

"Oh dear."

"I shouldn't worry. We're very fond of Beckett in Coventry."

"Thomas?"

"No, Sam."

"Ah."

They went along to a conference with the theatre board and got good news. A production of *Claude and Gertie* would form part of the 1959–1960 season, probably early in 1960. Casting would of course be in the hands of the director, and suggestions made by the author would be allowed consultative force. This exact phrase was used in a letter from the board of the Belgrade to Tony Goderich, which he received at the Windmill Street flat in early summer. He and Adam, who was between engagements but had something pretty nifty looming up on the horizon, and Letty, Aila and Sadie, used to spend four or five hours of every day going over revisions of

*Claude and Gertie,* usually around a picnic table in Russell Square, quaffing innumerable cups of lukewarm tea and munching those peculiarly British sausage rolls, found as a rule only in railway stations but exceptionally in the Russell Square tea kiosk.

Those sausage rolls came to have a special emotional association for Tony, just in his mid-twenties, all by himself in London, celebrity beginning to rise seductively over the horizon. It became a summer of crucial developments in his career. *Balancing Act* and *Down Off a Dirty Duck* were picked up by Penguin Books for worldwide distribution, in which format they sold in huge numbers for many years, successive changes of cover art veering more and more towards misrepresentation of contents. At length the covers grew suggestive, then explicit, in their evocation of the sexual theme, itself never more than a minor element in Tony's art.

"People like to hear about an occasional tit or bum," he used to say, "and who is Tony Goderich to say them nay?"

"But you do more, far more, than present an occasional tit or bum. Actions are evoked which your ordinary good citizen in the street hasn't entertained."

"Bad luck to him," Tony would reply with insouciance and savoir faire. The Penguin editions continued to move briskly in all retail situations in Barbados, New Zealand, in Scandinavia, where the satirical element in modern fiction is much canvassed, but seldom in Canada. It was another twenty-five years before Canadians grasped that the notorious Tony Goderich was one of their own. *That* Tony Goderich, the outrageous one? The flouter of convention?

There were beginning to be film and TV offers too, as the little cenacle of five lolled around joyously in Russell Square, soaking up the sunshine, sensing the heady onset of fame. Fame certainly for Adam, who had been cast as Claude in the forthcoming production, for Sadie, who was to undertake the dual rôle of Gertie and Feely, for Tony, who had a third novel—the breakthrough novel—coming along behind his play, and a mitigated but genuine fame in their profession for Letty and Aila. The Milldrummond credit appeared in the Belgrade Theatre program four or five times that season, and when *Claude and Gertie* transferred to the West End their name was attached to it. The summer of 1959 went by in this delightful way, all five of them deeply involved in tinkering with the jokes in the script, altering an emphasis here or there, bringing out nuances and trimming what seemed superfluous.

Aila was for some reason unpersuaded of the truly heterosexual nature of Claude's actions.

"It doesn't matter," Tony would protest. "Aila, can't you see that the whole damn' thing is a philosophical farce?"

"Maybe it is, but you shouldn't admit it publicly. If you say that in public, people will stay away from the theatre in their thousands. Philosophical farce is what closes Saturday."

"What else is *Waiting for Godôt?*"

"Did you write this play with *Godôt* in mind?" demanded Adam.

"I wouldn't admit it. Beckett goes well in the UK though."

"Not in the West End. You don't want to spend your whole life as a playwright in regional theatres and theatre clubs in Hampstead."

"Why is everybody so pissed off with Hampstead? It was good enough for Keats."

"Yes, but look what happend to Keats," said Letty. They all laughed a trifle nervously. Adam thumped his chest. "Sound as a pound," he muttered.

"Oh bugger," said Tony, "let's make the play as funny as we can, and let the audience worry about what it means. Now tell me, what makes a man go after his brother's girlfriend, just as the two of them are getting married?"

"There's an obvious psychoanalytic explanation."

Tony mused, "It's interesting that the word 'anal' is buried in the longer words 'psychoanalytic' and 'psychoanalysis.' I mean, it isn't as though it was 'psychoralitic,' or 'psychoralysis.' You'd expect it to be 'psychoralysis' because if there's one thing they do it's talk." He took out a piece of paper and scribbled a note on it. As if rehearsed, a pigeon flying nearby released a dropping which narrowly missed the piece of paper and splattered on the picnic table where they sat.

"Nature's critics," said Adam.

"It just means that psychoanalysts are a bunch of assholes," said Aila emphatically. The others stared at her; it wasn't generally known that Aila had passed some time in analysis in Montréal before embarking on a life in the theatre. "I see Claude as a deeply unhappy man," she said. "His brother is much older than he is, with a new young wife. You hint in the play that the brother has been married before. I think you should change the brother's name, by the way. Frank Bacon is the wrong name; the reference is too obscure. Why not simply Bacon?"

"Bryan made the same suggestion. I think we're on the right track."

Aila continued, "A man who deeply desires his brother's wife is necessarily in a farcical and absurd position. He is professing that he can't find a wife of his own, that he is terrified of women. He secretly wishes that his older brother would agree to hand over his wife, as he has handed down articles of apparel and the forms of experience. A younger brother comes to expect this sort of indulgence, unless he makes his way through the hazards of youth towards maturity with some good fortune, and alone. Think of Richard the Lion-hearted and Bad King John. 'King John was not a good king/he had his little ways.'"

"Stick to the point," said Adam.

"That gives me another idea," said Tony.

"Watch out for the pigeon," said the prudent Letty.

"I've been shit on by bigger and better birds than that," said Tony. He jotted down a note about royal brothers, then took up the defence of his script. "The position of the younger son and brother is an anomaly in all societies like that of Britain, where primogeniture so long obtained, and indeed still does in many instances. A peerage passes to the oldest male heir, with the exception of a very few cases of descent in the female line by royal prescription. Baroness Fauconberg and Conyers holds her patent in this way."

"That's enough," said Sadie, rising and making as if to quit the park. "Whenever Tony gets started on the peerage the fun is over, and the snobby little games get started."

"You wound me deeply, Sadie," said Tony, "and you'd do better to stick around and listen to what I have to say. You and Adam have been definitely cast in the parts. You get the real plum, the double rôle, and the production is going to launch you on an unsuspecting and wholly unprepared public. So sit still and listen."

"You're a great man," exclaimed the joyful actress.

"Fucking right," said Tony. "Now let me sum up what I meant about brothers and wives. The young and wifeless brother feels jealousy, inadequacy, a tendency to see his sister-in-law as his mum. He feels a reluctant dependence on her; she makes him feel like a little boy. Claude—this is you, Adam—may even be subject to the torments of a latent homosexual impulse. The attraction towards a brother's wife is after all a denial of responsibility for finding a mate of one's own. The older brother, necessarily a father-surrogate, has already blazed a trail through the forest. Excuse the metaphor. Has already shown a man's understanding of womankind and the secrets of the marriage bed. The subject can hardly be discussed without banality, hence the requisite recourse to the methods of intellectual farce, parody, elaborate tease. I predict that critics of *Claude and Gertie* will often discuss it in these terms, as an allegory of homosexual anxiety, latent or overt, and of the fear of women. They will say that having a single actress play both a mature woman, Gertie, and an adolescent, Feely, will show how divided Claude's sexual impulses are. And goddamn' it, for once, for once, they'll be right. And now I want you to take hands, Adam and Sadie, and kiss each other, because you'll have to do it onstage a lot, and if you can't manage it on a beautiful summer afternoon in Russell Square, you won't be able to manage it onstage in midwinter, I promise you."

"Who the hell do you think you are, Prospero?" said Adam.

"Oh brave new world," said Aila.

"Kiss her, Adam, I dare you," said Letty.

Spurred and challenged, pricked on to action, as 'twere, Adam assumed his soldierly-Bassanio stance, took hold of the squirming Sadie, and kissed her lingeringly. There was applause from people seated on neighbouring benches and

# The Scenic Art

from passersby; the whole scene had a balletic, poised balance. Later they all five dined hilariously at one of those enormous hotels on the other side of Woburn Place. A week or two later, Adam, Tony and Sadie went up to Coventry to have a talk with Bryan Bailey and a look around the theatre, now just a year old, beginning to shake down into an established production routine. There were now some signs of wear on the carpeting of the promenades and the staircase treads, just that little deposit of grit and dust and faint footprints and fingermarks on blonde wood that takes off the raw newness of a recently-completed building. It seemed a very comfortable theatre, on which much time had been expended by the architects and designers in the anticipation of playgoers' wishes. Adam was surprised and impressed by the front elevation of the structure, as they approached it along Corporation Street.

"Oh God how marvellous," he exclaimed, "pure essence of the middle nineteen-fifties, a building which couldn't have been conceived or executed at any other time. Do you know what you've got here? It's a shrunk-down half-sized version of the O'Keefe Centre. They might have been designed by the same man. The glass fronting outside the promenades and the parterre. The colour of the wood. The grey surfaces of the exterior walls, a general intimation of cement. The whole shape of the thing. It's precisely the O'Keefe Centre."

"The man's no fool, Tony," said Sadie. She was clinging to Adam's hand, swinging their arms vigorously, exuding an air of possession. "They might as well be twin theatres."

"This building's much smaller," said Tony in his rôle of proud Torontonian. "I guess it seats just under a thousand. I've never seen the O'Keefe Centre myself. I understand it's rather an awkward place to mount a show in. Too big, no proper orchestra pit, something like that?"

"Oh my gosh," said Adam, disengaging his right hand from Sadie's left, and making a broad gesture with it, "utter hell, my dear. It's too big for theatre, and the acoustics are awful for music, very woody and dead. It seats around twenty-five hundred, I think. But these two buildings are enough alike to make me feel bewildered. I didn't come to

Britain to play in theatres which are little sisters of those I left at home."

They turned in at the main entrance and went upstairs to the restaurant, where they ordered coffee.

"Now this, this is cosy," said Adam, cradling his cup between his palms. "The wonderful English simulation of coffee. How do you suppose they prepare it, and is it intentional?"

Bryan Bailey joined them at this point. Talk about the forthcoming production began at once and continued for the rest of that day and most of the remainder of the week. The director took them over the theatre installations, explained the method of production he had in mind, an abandonment of the box-set and proscenium frame then considered novel and liberating, much influenced by Tyrone Guthrie's use of the thrust stage at Stratford, Ontario, a stage widely discussed by theatre critics of the day.

"We don't quite have the audience on three sides of us at the Belgrade," said Bailey, "and I'm not certain that I could direct in that mise-en-scène without a few years' apprenticeship to Guthrie or one of his assistants, maybe in Minneapolis. You have to learn to re-route all your actors along arcs of the great circle, if you see what I mean. The playing area ceases to be flat and rectangular and becomes like the surface of a network of arcs of an enormous sphere . . . if that's clear."

"We've both played at Stratford," said Sadie, "under Guthrie and Langham. Of course I never had parts like Adam did, but I've often worked on a thrust stage, and in arena theatre."

"Well, at the Belgrade we've opened out our playing area; no flats, nothing pinned, no cloths flown in. We're seeking flow, movement, clarity in the stage picture, a feeling of continual circulation. We'll have the curtain up as the audience comes in."

"How is that going to work?" breathed Sadie, amazed.

In 1959 and 1960 it was considered venturesome, even daring, to do this. Abstract settings made of piping or scaffolding or unpainted lumber were *le dernier cri*. Later on they became conventional, too easily identifiable with a particular social and political use of the theatre, and finally achieved, about 1984 or 1985, the status of period clichés, a degeneration which overtakes all but the greatest artistic forms.

"The incoming audience will find the actors already onstage, some struggling into their clothes, some calling to each other like lonely birds . . ."

"Goodness!" said Sadie.

". . . and the speeches of the play will gradually assume coherence once the audience is in the house; this will be achieved by the use of filler dialogue, some improvisation, some use of signals and cues."

"This might be hard to organise," said Adam.

"Oh certainly, it will be fiendishly difficult to rehearse. It will have to look completely unrehearsed and arbitrary, and at the same time it will have to be perfectly precise, like a jazz concert."

Sadie said, "We can do it. It's a fascinating idea. Of course you'll build the patterns of movement around Adam."

"It's the only way," said Bailey.

"Then we'll all concentrate on Adam and take our lead from him, like he was Oscar Peterson or something," said Sadie, all innocent compliance and girlish spontaneity. "I've learned so much from Adam while working on a thrust stage."

"You have?" said Adam. "Where was that?"

"At Stratford, darling. I used to follow you around like a puppy when we were at Stratford."

"I don't remember any of that," said Adam, "but I'll try to live up to it." He smiled cordially at Bryan Bailey, and one or two other actors, who had found their way into the conference room. "No actor ever objects to being the centre of attention. I suppose it's a bad habit."

"We'll just have to make the best of it, won't we?" said Sadie in a snuggly voice.

She certainly had the right idea about the staging, as Bryan Bailey realised at once, when he considered her remarks. When *Claude and Gertie* finally opened at the Belgrade, it was after a much longer period of rehearsal than was customary in the Coventry theatre. The opening had to be postponed twice, other elements of the season rearranged to fill in. The work was eventually brought onstage in late March of 1960, when it enjoyed a much longer run than was customary in the subsidised regional theatres of the time, the run continuing down to the end of the season in late June. The management of the Belgrade made a good deal of money out of the sold-out houses during the long run, and a number of important and influential critics, directors, and managers of other theatres travelled up from London and from places like Nottingham and Liverpool and Chichester to see what was happening on the Belgrade stage; by and large they were probably over-impressed with what they saw.

When the audience came into the auditorium—which is a high-ceilinged, roomy space, with a beautifully-designed seating plan, a very gentle rake to the seats, and superb acoustical properties—they found the bare stage in full view and the house lights and stage lighting full up. There seemed no shadows anywhere in the space. You had an impression of pipes overhead, and the sound of toilets being flushed in the dressing-room area. This was actually cunningly rehearsed. Bryan Bailey had one of the apprentices moving from loo to loo, flushing each one as she came to it, such that the audience had no notion that the performance had begun before they were admitted. A number of people were seated or moving about slowly onstage, some conferring, others moving heavy objects around, chairs and footstools. Then there was an imperceptible softening of the lighting, which brought it down from full as the chatter of the people onstage began to exhibit some patterning.

One brilliant bit of staging was the way in which, after perhaps four to five minutes of random chat, everybody but Adam and Sadie left the stage. For some moments only the two of them were visible from the auditorium, and they appeared to take no notice of one another. They might have been in separate rooms. An extraordinary impression of furtive intimacy was evoked. Without a word's being spoken, they created a complete set of implications about their relations in the way they stood and moved. Sadie used one inspired bit of business as a cue for the others to return to the playing area. Apparently unaware of Adam's presence, she would lift the hem of her perfectly modest and well-fitted skirt, and adjust the fit of one of those rubber button and metal loop fasteners that in those distant days used to be attached to pantie-girdles as stocking suspenders. As she did this, a tiny area of plump pink thigh was visible, not to Adam but to the audience. Adam was instructed by the director to take no notice of her action. The effect of immodesty and invitation achieved by this business was extraordinary. The audience, not yet perfectly certain that the play had started, feeling that Sadie might have forgotten that they were present, always used to give a rippling collective sigh at this point.

Some writers on the history of the recent British theatre have claimed that this gesture assured Sadie MacNamara's future stardom.

The audience's sigh of sensual stimulation was used by Bryan Bailey as the main cue for the actors to start to 'play' their lines rather than delivering them off-handedly in the manner of unrehearsed conversation. Names, Claude, Feely, Bacon, Gertie, began to surface in the lines. By now the audience had realised that the show had started; this process of easing them into it, without their being aware of what was happening, was completely novel at this date, and made a great impression. Bryan Bailey was always being written up in the Sundays as a tremendous technical innovator. There began to be brisk talk of a London production in the Fall 1960 season; more than one overture was received by both author and director. Fortunately no contractual obligation existed on either side which might have buggered up such negotiations. It was always the Belgrade's policy to leave their new writers as free of legal and contractual encumbrances as possible, in order to assist their progress towards national and international recognition. A commercial management might sometimes tie up a promising dramatist with option clauses and assistance in the form of advance payments against future work which implied permanent association. This sort of strategy was specifically rejected by the Belgrade's production committee.

When the London offers began to materialise, with famous faces turning up night after night in the front rows at the Belgrade, Tony found himself in the enviable position of a new dramatist with a proven success under his total control. There were feelers from the Royal Court, and from the Royal Shakespeare Company, which was just then in process of completing a move to London and the Aldwych. There was serious talk for quite some time about mounting a production of *Claude and Gertie* as the opener for the RSC tenure of the Aldwych. In the end, Tony turned the offer down.

"I think I'd be wiser to take a chance on a commercial production," he remarked to Bryan Bailey. "I mean, I'm marvellously pleased with the chance you've given me here. Look at the notices we've had. I'll always be grateful—and by 'always' I don't mean until next Tuesday—but I've had one subsidised production of this piece, and now I think I'd like to see how it would go in a Shaftesbury Avenue house."

"Or in Piccadilly Circus," said Bailey cheerfully. "When might you have another play for us?"

"Oh God, I'm hatching out another novel right now. I still don't know whether I'm a novelist or a playwright or a screenwriter, or all three, which would be terrific, super. But nobody is all three. Almost nobody. I'm tied up with this novel *Hungry Generations* but I ought to have it out of my system by next spring. I've got a good idea for a new play. I can't tell you much about it but the idea is there in the back of my head, and it's solid."

"And you think of bringing it to the Belgrade?"

"You can count on it."

"Then I'd advise you to take the Piccadilly offer. It is the Criterion that we're speaking of, isn't it?"

"Bathroom tiling and all," said Tony, "it's a hell of a theatre."

The tiles he was referring to are still to be seen in the tiny foyer of the Criterion Theatre, tucked away on the south side of Piccadilly Circus, looking more like a highly histrionic public convenience, perhaps, than a West End theatre. The foyer is one of the curiosities of the West End, a space not much larger than a small drawing room, made to seem much more spacious by carefully juxtaposed mirrors and a delicately coloured high ceiling which just misses being erotic.

This mitigated subtle eroticism, keenly evocative of a specific late nineteenth-century English exercise of sexual energy, is carried forward in the tiled and painted panels on either side of the staircase as you descend from the foyer to the auditorium. Negligently draped ladies and equivocal masks smile or grimace at you as you pass. The theatre possesses a disturbing atmosphere of liveliness, of the presence of spirits, but not those of stuffy angels or Grecian muses viewing-with-alarm. The presences evoked are those of the young Graces who, during dusty sunny late-Victorian afternoons, might undertake faintly questionable games in secluded gentlemens' chambers not far from the site of the theatre. Lightly clad, rosy, not long perhaps from country town or situation as housemaid, these dainty creatures might lightly birch a stockbroker on all fours beneath them, or themselves agree to be ridden in ribboned harness around the study, might afterwards softly recite a lewd lyric or perform a variation of ordinary lovemaking which at that epoch possessed only a Latin name.

As you go lower and find your way into the theatre itself, this atmosphere of the delicately indelicate is reinforced by the charm of the décor. In the Criterion there is no heavy scarlet, no opulent gold. When the management undertook to redecorate the theatre, just at the time when *Claude and Gertie* moved to the West End from Coventry, it was decided to eschew this conventional *luxure* and select instead colours that would have adorned the house at the time of its opening in the early 'eighties. The new costume and décor consultants, Milldrummond, were engaged to do the necessary research, and on their advice the entire house, stalls, dress circle and upper circle, were repainted in soft, muted airy tones of azure, turquoise, very restrained feathery old rose, suggestive of the plumage of the small birds. The gilding was rather pale than rich, in the kind of broken-down gold that suggests a young girl's first little ring, a signet ring perhaps, gift of a proud parent.

These choices of tone, whether consciously or not, support the whispering, almost voiced, liveliness, the haunted hushed echoings, intimations of presences, which give the Criterion its unique theatricality. The first time Adam Sinclair ever saw the auditorium, as *Claude and Gertie* was being re-staged in the late fall of 1960, he exclaimed at this ghostly evanescence.

"It's as haunted as Hart House," said Adam. He began to walk up and down the rows of seats, remarking as he went on this or that resemblance to the small underground theatre at the University of Toronto where so many actors began their careers.

"Everywhere I go in this country I'm confronted by copies of Canadian theatres."

"What are you talking about?" demanded the director of the play, a man of few words and those, for the most part, foully abusive.

"This damn' place has just been redecorated by Milldrummond," said Adam.

"Yes, yes, I know all that. They've done a splendid job too. The house looks just as it did when my old grandfather played here before the first war. I've got pictures of him appearing at the Criterion in some ghastly verse play in 1908. *La belle époque*."

"Do you know who Milldrummond are?"

"Isn't it a trade name, like Motley?"

"It's two friends of mine, Canadian girls both," said Adam. This was almost the first time in his adult life that he had spoken of women as his friends. Perhaps his heart was softening. Sadie, listening to this discourse, hoped that this might be so.

The director sighed, "And you're Canadian and this young woman here is Canadian and our author is Canadian. Is this some sort of horrible blight, spreading over the English theatre like fungus or bacillic spores?"

"It may be," said Adam. Sadie came over and sat right next to him. He smiled at her, not entirely disregardfully. She moved closer. "I was speaking to a man the other night who's going to be working at Chichester next year, with Olivier." Adam brought the famous name out like the ace of spades. "Olivier. And this fellow showed me some rough sketches for the new theatre at Chichester, and guess what?"

"I know all about that, I'm going to be there too, you fool. The theatre is going to be 'open stage' with the audience on three sides of the playing area. Who were you talking to? Was it Dexter?"

"I don't like to say."

"Of course it was."

"Perhaps it was. What of it?"

"Just give your little all to *Claude and Gertie* as of present date, won't you? We can't have you haring off on some new trail of your own while we're busy here, can we?"

Dissension, thought Sadie comfortably. She had plans of her own, and had no wish to be trapped in a long run of *Claude and Gertie*. There was this man, who called upon her agent constantly with information about a TV series which would run to six instalments, and very likely more, on independent TV. Sadie's nose wrinkled prettily when she thought of it.

"All I mean to say," said Adam heatedly, "is that the Chichester Festival Theatre is a copy of the Stratford Festival Theatre in Ontario."

"We know all about that, dear," said the director acidly. "Tony Guthrie was perambulating London for years trying to find somebody to build a theatre like that."

"It took Canadians to do it," said Adam, "and when I come in here what do I find but an underground theatre just like Hart House in Toronto. I expect this one is older than the one in Toronto, but it has all the same production problems. It must be hell installing scenery, and I'll bet it's very stuffy. Where's the air to come from?"

"That is a cogent objection," said the director, "but our play has no scenery to speak of. That's why it's a hit, or at least a provincial success."

"Don't you think it will be a success in London?"

"I think it'll be a critical success. It's already a critical success because of the things that were written about the Belgrade performances. Tynan, Hope-Wallace, they've all praised the staging. Which, I may say, I intend to follow as closely as possible, given the difference in theatres. I wanted to work on the play because I think it will be remembered as one of those plays that people wish they'd seen. But I don't think it will have a run here."

"Why ever not?" said Sadie.

"What does this place seat?" said Adam, looking about him with care. The auditorium in the Criterion is sufficiently far below ground that no daylight can penetrate there; this circumstance confers a quality of unmediated histrionic artifice on any conversation held in the place. Adam and Sadie and their director, and Tony, who now joined the colloquy, shared an impression of unreality, of being caught in a rehearsal of life. Futurity seemed to have become part of the texture of the event.

"It seats six hundred and fifty and there isn't a really bad seat anywhere in the house," said Tony. "You're perfectly right, Adam. The feeling of this theatre is just like Hart House, even though Hart House has no dress circle or upper circle. I think the stalls here will take the same number as at Hart House. The air is the same, stuffy, and much in need of better circulation. The stage machinery is more professional here, but the wing space is about the same. And I will say that I agree with our director. I don't believe we'll get a run, but we'll be glad to have been here."

Sadie said to the director, "What did you mean by saying that this was a play you wanted to be associated with?"

"Oh, well, there have been three or four of them in the last few years. *Look Back in Anger*, of course. *The Birthday Party*, and the new one by Pinter. *Birthday Party* didn't have a run; it came off almost at once, but everybody wishes they'd seen it. I don't mean plays like *The Hostage* or *A Taste of Honey*. They're curiosities, but they're not very interesting as plays. But *Claude and Gertie* is an interesting dramatic structure in itself, and it will have its influence and its following, but it isn't likely to last long in the West End. Now shall we go to work?"

Sadie and Adam mounted the stage with the director, and Tony settled down to watch. The Criterion is a charmingly intimate small theatre, very characteristic in its architecture of the proscenium theatres of the nineteenth and twentieth centuries. It proved next to impossible to adapt *Claude and Gertie* to its tight, small space. The frame of the proscenium seemed to close off the action and separate it irredeemably from the audience. It was like seeing Tony's text on television, a medium in which this play has never made much of an impression. It seems to be one of those plays which is permanently wedded to the playing area in which it was first given. It has now and then been revived, in Chichester and in Stratford, Ontario, but on the whole is best described as one of those plays which made its mark on the history of the contemporary British theatre without entering the standard repertory, like *The Birthday Party*, *Live Like Pigs*, *The Kitchen* and *Armstrong's Last Goodnight*. It achieved a moderately respectable run of thirty-five performances at the Criterion, coming off in October. In a two-column roundup of the season to that moment, in the *Observer*, Ronald Bryden spoke kindly and accurately about the play, predicting that his young compatriot would write other plays which would be less inventive dramaturgically (a favourite Bryden word) but perhaps more adaptable to varied production techniques. He hoped that this talented novelist and highly promising dramatist would choose to remain in Britain, where greater scope was offered to his indisputable talents than in his native Ontario. This last observation greatly annoyed Tony, who was nevertheless obliged to concede its force. He had *Hungry Generations* ready for publication in the spring of 1961, and the *succès d'estime* of his first play would certainly do the novel no harm.

None of the Canadians involved with *Claude and Gertie* found that it did their careers serious harm. Towards the end of the run, when they were playing to audiences of a hundred to a hundred and fifty, mostly young men in duffle coats who carried notepads and took copious notes on the staging, everybody felt that the people who really counted were coming to see the play. It might have gone better at the Royal Court or the Mermaid, but they had done wisely to try it on the general theatregoing public.

Adam, never slow to determine where his next engagement was to come from, chose the final night of the run to inform Tony and Sadie of his latest piece of good luck or good management of himself. It appeared that the other really serious new play of that year was about to lose a key member of its cast and he, Adam, was to replace him in the long-running West End production. This was an enormous step forward for Adam. It placed him immediately in the position of appearing before the large theatregoing public in a famous success, as the successor to a young actor now widely acknowledged to be the most important new leading man to have appeared in the theatre since the first productions at the Royal Court and Theatre Workshop. This was Alan Bates, whose part as Mick, in *The Caretaker*, now devolved upon Adam.

The three actors in the original cast of Pinter's great success had created an almost biological life in its organism. How introduce a new, strongly personal style? Many of the critics were interested enough in this aspect of a long-running success to come and take a look at what Adam Sinclair could do with the part of Mick. It was his enormous tact, his flexible response to the problem of how to ease himself into the run without destroying the structure of the organism that first made the London critics fully aware of the range of Adam's gifts. He was greatly praised by the whole gang for not trying to be Alan Bates, for finding a vocal music different from his predecessor's but not too Canadian, for his ability to listen and to be silent while remaining vital, pulsing with menace. The opportunity to take over this part was probably more advantageous to Adam than an original creation of it would have been, and he took full advantage of it.

He became known with startling rapidity as one of the two or three most important new actors of the rising decade, with Albert Finney, Alan Bates, and in films Michael Caine. Adam was now spoken of in the profession as an actor who could listen and respond to dialogue as few leading men could. He could 'feed' and play in ensemble with other members of a cast, and at the same time bring a leading man's necessary prominence and ascendancy to any part which demanded it. These are qualities which make it easy for an actor to work in films as well as on the stage. In a couple of television appearances from the period he showed that he could scale down his performances to the dimensions required by the little box. In short, he was now widely

# The Scenic Art

recognised as a star actor who could with ease and comfort make his way in any of the three media. This is an exceedingly rare accomplishment; there are many actors who can do films and television, or films and theatre, not many can do all three.

Sadie, for example, was to achieve her first great success on television, then to become an international star name, in the first half of the sixties, in the movies. Just as Adam was establishing himself in the work of Pinter, Sadie showed British television viewers, in the 1961–62 season, and again in the two following seasons, that she could be as deft a television comedienne as any of the big American stars, Lucille Ball, Loretta Young.

Sadie in fact pioneered in a kind of television comedy which was to dominate British production for another twenty-five years, the six-part series which could be renewed and developed in further segments if its popularity demanded it. British TV never adopted the American format of the series intended to run for several years, with from twenty-six to thirty-nine original episodes required annually. Instead the major British production units, Granada, London Weekend, and the BBC, have concentrated on short series, normally about six episodes, which can be dropped into a season's schedule at almost any point, to run long enough to develop the characters, then disappear. If such a series recruited a following, a further number of episodes might be put in work at a later time. In 1961, not long after *Claude and Gertie* came off, Sadie accepted an offer to appear as the female lead in a series of six segments called *Bed Sitters*. This became the funniest and most celebrated comedy series on British TV during the first half of the sixties.

The setting for the show, and several of the recurring minor characters, as well as its ridiculous premise, established the format for similar shows which were afterwards produced in many parts of the English-speaking world. As the title indicated, *Bed Sitters* was set in one of those parts of central London where young men and women rent furnished rooms, sometimes with breakfast included, most often single rooms, although it isn't unheard-of for two men or two women to share a large room. A bed-sitter has a bit of a living area containing a table and chairs, perhaps a washstand, a place to hang one's clothes, as well as a sleeping area. The bed is often disguised or concealed, perhaps as a divan or couch with a throw over it, latterly as a foldaway bed, or 'hide-a-bed.' Such accommodation is found everywhere in central London, in Pimlico and Marylebone and behind Paddington. *Bed Sitters*, as it happens, was shot on location in Earl's Court, a district then not at all fashionable. Later on Earl's Court rose in social esteem, very largely because of the success of the TV show.

Many of the streets in the district are called 'Gardens.' Bolton Gardens. Wetherby Gardens. Bramham Gardens. Lines of dialogue, almost always delivered by Sadie, about going out and playing in the gardens, became catchwords in Britain at that time, like other lines which became catchwords in North America. "Sorry about that, chief," or "What you see is what you get."

Sadie used to grin mournfully, when queried about the whereabouts of the girl who lived in the adjoining room, making some such remark as, "Down the gardens, sweetie." She would grimace like a small, engaging monkey. She had some of that quality sometimes characterised as *beauté de singe* more reminiscent of certain French stars than of British or North American players.

"She've gone up the exhibition," Sadie would profess with a qualified leer, and the viewers would howl with delight. Or else she would claim that her friend was "watering her geraniums, like." Watering one's geramiums became a favourite mid-sixties euphemism for a certain range of mild sexual misbehaviour among young women in cities.

If you were to say to somebody from the UK, "She's down the gardens, ducks, watering her geraniums," you could reasonably well guess that person's age from his or her reactions. If they should laugh, they were grown up by 1964, but only just. Much of the humour of *Bed Sitters* was vested in joyful feelings of independence and escape from the authoritative intervention of parents. The character played by Sadie, young Mavis Carthew, was several years younger than Sadie herself, but the huge audience never seemed to understand

# The Scenic Art

this. Sadie was into her thirties by now, and Mavis Carthew was supposed to be about twenty-one. Sadie had everybody convinced. She got one of those cap cuts and did her front hair in ragged bangs which gave her an agreeably waiflike appearance, a kind of less expensive Audrey Hepburn quality, though Sadie was never as thin as Hepburn. There was something of Hepburn too in the cut of her eyelids, and she played up the resemblance unobtrusively. It made quite a subtle point in the characterisation.

Mavis Carthew and the girl in the next room, Charmian Windrush, are living in this Earl's Court lodging house, each ostensibly dwelling alone in a room of modest size. The comedy premise of the show is that both girls, unknown to each other and to the elderly couple who own the house and live in the former servant's quarters below stairs, are letting their boyfriends sleep over almost every night. The boyfriends in fact are living in the building rent free, and must never be identified by the lodging house proprietors as anything more than occasional visitors.

The landlady and her husband were the principal comedy types in the series, Mr. and Mrs. Puckerton, physical specimens with their roots in the music hall. Elsie Puckerton was a tiny little woman under five feet tall, terribly thin to the point of emaciation, with an absurd accent reminiscent of Irene Handl. Mr. Puckerton, a retired butcher, was an enormous man, crooked as only a butcher can be crooked, with exceedingly heavy thumbs and a manner oozing spurious bonhomie. A lot of the funny lines in the show contained references to those cheaper cuts of meat dear to the heart of the great British public: scrag end, sweetbreads, pigs' trotters, lambs' fries. Alf Puckerton wasn't above suddenly producing a string of sausages from under his waistcoat from time to time, to get a laugh. The charm of the obvious was at no time underestimated, and the show had an abandoned, absurd quality at times, which anticipated some of the comedy of the mid-seventies.

Then there were the two comic lodgers who eventually became regulars on the show. One was a professional burglar called Tiny Coddle, whose odd comings and goings were only gradually shown to depend on his peculiar employment. And there was Maisie—she had no other name—who lived in the top floor back and who resembled a totally potty songbird, with frizzy feathered hair and a weird cooing voice. And there were the two boyfriends of course, Ronnie and Herbert. Gosh but it was a good show!

There were so many funny ideas that swarmed readily out of the premise. Ronnie and Herbert, for example, were nice young men of widely different appearance and accomplishments, nicely matched with their girls. Mavis Carthew, as Sadie played her, was the quick, funny, scheming girl, witty and quite a beauty in her way. It always came as a distinct shock to the viewers, who were encouraged to see her as perhaps just slightly mousy behind her harlequin glasses, to be reminded that Sadie had—and has—a superb body.

According to a set rhythm in the series, she began to undress in the last few moments of every second show, ostensibly secure in the knowledge that nobody could see her—except about twenty million television watchers. She was never allowed to get her slip off, but the glorious deep MacNamara bosom and the strong legs were partly visible and fully guess-at-able. These fake strip-shows came around so regularly in the first six segments of the series that you could have set your watch by them, an instance of an artistic convention in process of formation. When further sets of episodes were made in later seasons, the production company and the writers discovered that Mavis had to appear in her slip. If she didn't, there would be thousands of angry letters in the post the following day. Mavis was supposed to be a theatre attendant, an usherette, with dramatic ambitions. The character wasn't all that far removed from the reality of Sadie's early life, though there were wide factual divergences. Most viewers were persuaded that Sadie was Irish, because of her name. Irish, but brought up in Britain. She used to affect the merest hint of a lilt or brogue in her speech, which made an exceedingly charming music. Plenty of people—not all males—were in love with the character and the actress. Mavis was always getting into comic scrapes connected with the problem of getting Herbert out of the house before Mrs. Puckerton rose

# The Scenic Art

in the small hours. There was plenty of farcical nipping in and out of bedroom doors and closets, and up and down stairs. Herbert was always pretending to pay an early-morning call, whereas in fact he was leaving the house after an overnight stay. Some of the dialogue in these situations verged on the suggestive, if never the indecent. Alf Puckerton invariably greeted Herbert with the line, "Keeping it up, are we, Herb?" Herbert was supposed to be a promising young musician, a clarinetist, one of those denizens of the sandwich shops about Wigmore Hall. He was always in and out of work, often wore a seedy dinner jacket which made him resemble a waiter in a trattoria. Many witticisms in the scripts turned on the long, thin, stiff, form of his instrument, and its colour, a sombre black. He was a long, thin lad of a lanky melancholy cut, and when engaging in fisticuffs which he sometimes did, always shouting, "Watch out for me fingering; it's me livelihood," he strangely resembled an angry stork or heron. His hair stuck up like the feathers of a marshland bird.

As time passed, and the series acquired additional dimensions, Charmian Windrush became the best-loved character in the narrative. She was at first presented as a completely empty-headed blonde, with the customary ample physical endowment of the stereotype. But the actress who was cast in the part, the adorable Linnet Olcott, an extremely gifted newcomer from the Nottingham Playhouse, took an unexpected approach to the conception which gave her character an effective human reality. She used to hesitate over her lines, give the throaty little pauses, seem to be trying to think over what she was saying. People liked her. In later sequences of the series her part grew larger. She was able to communicate a suspicion that she was much wiser than her words suggested, that the character had limited means of expression but a formidable depth of perception and feeling, a rather unusual development in a TV series of that date.

Charmian's boyfriend, Ronnie, was played by Ronnie Corbett, so there is nothing much more to be said about that, except that he was alleged to be a scoutmaster in Ealing Broadway or some such place, and a solicitor's clerk in chambers somewhere near the Temple by day. Much was made of the supposed necessity to get him safely off home on the District Line before eleven PM. Elsie Puckerton always used to greet him on the staircase with, "Just getting off, then, dearie?" which convulsed the fans. The take which Ronnie Corbett used to do on this line was in itself an education in the best traditions of British comedy—straight from Dickens.

The burglar in the third floor front, Tiny Coddle, was only gradually revealed to be a member of that interesting profession. He spoke in an accent of heavy East End rectitude and working-class gentility, and he was enormous, bigger by far than Alf Puckerton. He might have been six feet nine. He filled the screen. You couldn't see around him. Graham da Costa, the actor who played Tiny Coddle, later found himself in the position of a performer who has become identified in the minds of millions with a single part, somewhat as Peter Sellers became identified with Inspector Clouseau. Da Costa has been playing Tiny Coddle in spinoffs and guest appearances for more than twenty years on the strength of this identification. His little black valise and its clinking contents have become inseparable from the character.

The first time da Costa appeared on *Bed Sitters* he got some of the biggest laughs in the history of British show business. Mavis and Herbert are locked in each other's arms along about four AM. Mavis is wearing a nightdress. Herbert is probably wearing nothing though he contrives to conceal this in the darkness, and then in the bedclothes. Suddenly there is a noise at the window; we see the gleam of one of those old bullseye lanterns much favoured by burglars in British films. An enormous form blots out all illumination from the window. We hear the clinking of metal instruments which became Tiny Coddle's trademark. It is important that he doesn't turn on the light, and that he behaves with polished sophistication. The gigantic silhouette moves across the frame towards the left, where the door might be located. And a surprisingly genteel voice says, "I begs your indulgence, Miss or Madam, indeed I do."

Long pause. Fumblings at the door. Then he makes his exit in nearly total darkness, just looking back once, with his head around the door, to say, "I believe I chose the wrong means of entry."

The door closes. Mavis and Herbert clutch each other in terror. Then from outside the room there is a tremendous crash and the sound of people shouting and squeaking and running about on the stairs. Mavis is stuffing the bedclothes into her mouth to keep from bursting into hysterical laughter.

"Who was that?" inquires Herb.

"Third floor front."

"What does he do when he's at home then?"

"He's a sexton."

"Go on!"

"No, he's a sexton, God's truth. A gravedigger like. He has to work nights."

"Why can't he come in at the front door like a Christian, then?"

"Perhaps he forgot something. You never know, do you?"

"I think somebody just fell downstairs."

"Time for you to go, lovey. They'll be knocking me up in two shakes."

"Oh Mavis!"

"Oh 'Erb. I do love you."

There were hundreds of implications to be worked off this input. In the next episode, Mavis had to find a way to hand back to Tiny Coddle a large metal implement which he accidentally left on the floor of her room.

"Cold chisel, that is, Missy," says Tiny, to a very big audience reaction.

Then there was the famous scene in which Elsie Puckerton made her way into Mr. Coddle's room on the top floor front—perhaps to do some cleaning and dusting, perhaps from sheer nosiness—to find a number of curious little bottles, and several smallish crates lying around the room, which upon inspection seemed to contain various kinds of explosives. The little bottles were nitroglycerine naturally, what else? Or at least they were so labelled, and frantic comedy ensued when Elsie burst out of the room and ran down three flights of stairs holding one of the bottles in her apron. When she gained the basement and her husband asked her what was wrong she replied that she was holding enough explosive in her apron to blow all of Earl's Court to hell.

Alf Puckerton found this a disquieting rejoinder.

"Na then, Else," he said. He always called her Else. "What dost want to go muckin' round wi' that stoof, then?" The accent varied from West Riding to London shopkeeper. Audiences never seemed to notice, or if they noticed, to care about linguistic accuracy. Alf Puckerton got many laughs by relapsing into incomprehensible guttural chokings which might have represented any of half a dozen northern dialects. One thing he never talked was Geordie. The actor apparently didn't know about it, or hadn't developed it in the course of his provincial wanderings.

"Take it away from me!" screamed Elsie.

"I'll have no truck wi' it. It's none of mine, lass. Chuck it down the closet."

"Alf, Alf, have some sense, do. This lot would blow your backside through the roof and never notice."

"Take it outside and give it to one of them coppers, lass. They've got little enough to do as it is."

Terrified moans from Elsie. Mavis and Charmian appear behind her. Neither wears more than the minimum demanded by public decency—and a public decency of a broadminded, liberal tendency.

| | |
|---|---|
| CHARMIAN: | Wotcher got there then, Missus? |
| MAVIS: | At this time of night, I mean, really. |
| ALF: | That's nitroglycerine, that is, property of Mr. Coddle. |
| CHARMIAN: | Just fancy! |
| MAVIS: | I'm off down the gardens, water me geraniums. (*Laughter.*) |
| CODDLE: | (*Enters from rear.*) Now then, now then, what's all this? |
| ALF: | Here you, Coddle, where's your bleedin' sense of what's right and what's wrong, mate? I mean ter |

|           |                                                                                                                                                   |
|-----------|---------------------------------------------------------------------------------------------------------------------------------------------------|
|           | say, bringing the means of destruction into an honest retired butcher's respectable home. (*Laughter.*)                                           |
| MAVIS:    | So that's what it is.                                                                                                                             |
| RONNIE:   | I say, is anybody down below? (*Enters wearing Boy Scout costume including shorts and hiking stave. Laughter.*)                                   |

The scene went on like this, with hysterical interruptions from poor Maisie, requests from passing constables to be a little less noisy down there, please. Finally Mr. Coddle seizes the bottle from Elsie.

|           |                                                                                                                                        |
|-----------|----------------------------------------------------------------------------------------------------------------------------------------|
| CODDLE:   | That's me nighttime cordial. For the chest, like.                                                                                      |
| CHARMIAN: | Do you take it in bed, Mr. Coddle?                                                                                                     |
| CODDLE:   | I takes it wherever I finds it, Miss. (*Laughter.*)                                                                                    |
| MAVIS:    | What's in it then?                                                                                                                     |
| CODDLE:   | I don't know about that so much. I gets it from me old Mum.                                                                            |
| ALF:      | Let's see you swallow a dollop then, just to set our minds at ease.                                                                    |
| CODDLE:   | Easy as winking. (*He drains the bottle in one swallow. Pause. He gives a tremendous belch.*)                                          |
| MAVIS:    | That's nitroglycerine, that was. (*Laughter.*)                                                                                         |

That scene was from one of the later series of *Bed Sitters*, made early in 1963 when the show was at the height of its popularity. For several episodes thereafter, whenever she saw Coddle, Mavis would say, "Nitroglycerine, that is," contributing largely to the amusement of viewers. Eventually the characters and the situation became so familiar to their audience that laughter could be squeezed—sometimes unquenchable and painful laughter—from mere repetition of one of these recurrent phrases. When Ronnie referred to knot-tying instruction, the sheepshank, the sheet-bend, clove hitch, round turn with two half-hitches, anything like that, all the aficionados remembered one mercilessly funny episode in which he had been supposed to give a demonstration of tying things up, for the edification of the Chief Scout, Ealing Region, without any prior knowledge of the subject whatsoever. The night before this ordeal he turns up in Charmian's room and spends a loony half hour tying her to the bedpost in various positions.

Linnet Olcott and Ronnie Corbett made this one of the most unforgettable comic moments in the history of television. It was a comedy idea which implied much more than the writers had imagined. The small capering rotund koala-like figure of Ronnie Corbett, running around and around the bed with a length of lariat whirling behind him, and the innocent compliance of Charmian, devoid of salacity or suggestiveness, made the scene an oddly tender one.

RONNIE: I think this end goes through here like that. (*His tongue between his teeth.*) There, that ought to hold you.

CHARMIAN: Oooooohhh Ronnie, you're so clever. I can't move a muscle. (*He has her attached to the end of the bed in a posture of ardent submission.*)

RONNIE: I hope I haven't made it a granny knot. Can you move anything at all?

CHARMIAN: Not above the waist. (*Laughter.*)

RONNIE: I say, what luck! (*Loud laughter.*)

CHARMIAN: You *are* good at it. (*Hysteria.*)

RONNIE: (*Timing the curve of the laugh.*) Now I think I'll attempt a sheet-bend. (*And we fade.*)

One of the cleverest elements of *Bed Sitters* was its introduction of a number of recurring characters, none of them appearing frequently enough to be considered regular members of the cast, but visible often enough to give viewers a sense of the ongoing world outside the lodging-house set. Mavis, for example, was visited two or three times in her room by her boss, a smooth cad type, the manager of the theatre in which she is an attendant. This fellow, usually dressed in impressively tailored evening clothes, with a full, bushy moustache, a flower in full bloom in his lapel, and correspondingly full figure, was called Monty Beaulieu (pronounced Bewly) and was played with grand effect by Adam Sinclair, in his only television appearances of the period.

By now, mid-1963, Adam was enormously in demand in the West End, and committed for the next season to Tony

# The Scenic Art

Goderich's new play. He found time to appear in the three Monty Beaulieu episodes of *Bed Sitters* in response to heartfelt pleas from Sadie, who was convinced that he, and only he, could give the rôle the vocal definition it required. Monty always spoke in a fruity Edwardian accent found only in West End theatrical figures, and Adam was a great master of its modulations. When you heard Adam doing Monty Beaulieu, you were reminded of about a hundred and fifty years of the history of the London stage. He made you think of George Alexander and Charles Hawtrey and Seymour Hicks and Bram Stoker, and all the glorious stew of theatrical reminiscence associated with Piccadilly, Leicester Square, Shaftesbury Avenue. The character was an unqualified success with the TV audience, giving Adam a mass recognition he could have obtained in no other way. It brought Sadie and Adam together in the public mind, and in their own imaginations, in a way that appearances together onstage never had, although their joint début in *Claude and Gertie* formed part of their myth. Already in 1963 Tony's play had begun to take on the status of 'a classic of the contemporary British theatre,' which it has continued to maintain. *Look Back in Anger*, *The Entertainer*, *The Caretaker*, *Royal Hunt of the Sun*, the *Roots* trilogy, *Armstrong's Last Goodnight*, *Entertaining Mr. Sloane*, *Loot*, *Rosencrantz and Guildenstern are Dead*, and a few others, belong in the same position as *Claude and Gertie*, and receive much the same treatment in the standard handbooks of the period. In 1963, Adam and Sadie were a popular pair of theatrical personalities because of their apparently effortless ability to move from serious and even modestly experimental work in the theatre into highly popular and entertaining television comedy. Critics and public saw them as tightly linked, a tendency which their appearances in *Bed Sitters* intensified. Their lives together were described in more than one of the Sundays, in idyllic terms. It seemed clear that their union in one kind or another, personal or professional, could not long be postponed. When they saw Adam doing his Monty Beaulieu number on the show, people realised that Monty was the man for Mavis, that Herbert was at best a wet smack, a back number, and a poor bet for success. Monty would see that Mavis made it to the

West End. Herbert would fade into the background; the fusion of Adam and Sadie as a popular acting team would be accomplished. It began to look as though they must marry, more because of this pressure from the great public than from anything else.

"It would be great PR," said Sadie to Adam one afternoon in a Charlotte Street coffee bar. They were due in Portland Place in an hour's time, for a first read-through of a TV script for BBC-2. "You're getting a public figure, Adam. You need a wife the way a politician needs a wife. And I need a protector."

"You'll need more than a protector, if CBS takes up that option."

"Do you think there's any chance?"

"I should say I do. I think *Bed Sitters* would be a smash on an American net. Funny *and* vulgar, can't miss."

"Oh God, I hope they take it."

"That's not a bad idea of yours," said Adam, eyeing Sadie with misgivings. "I mean, think of Olivier and Vivian Leigh."

"Or Myrna Loy and William Powell."

"They were never actually married."

"Perhaps we wouldn't have to be legally married," said Sadie lingeringly, "but the Lunts were married."

"Is that who you have in mind? I always hated the Lunts. I wouldn't want to be like the Lunts. I see us as more like Noel and Gertie or Fred and Ginger."

"Fred and Ginger, that I'll accept. Adam and Sadie."

"Or Sadie and Adam, if you like it better that way," said Adam. It was his one romantic gesture, and it did him in.

"We'll be late for rehearsal. I hate this play," said Sadie. She stored what Adam had said in her memory. He would come round, she felt, particularly if *Bed Sitters* moved to America.

Not much more than a week after that conversation, Jim Aubrey of CBS authorised production of a pilot for a series to be produced in New York, and later in LA, under the working title *Out By Midnight*. His emissaries flew to Britain and signed Sadie to a contract covering production of the

# The Scenic Art

pilot, with options and provisions for production of up to thirty-eight additional episodes, should the series be a success. Her agents saw to it that Sadie would be free to accept film and stage offers from time to time, and she left for New York in July 1963, for meetings concerned with the new show, which wasn't really a new show at all, but an Americanised version of *Bed Sitters*.

The producers decided to junk the title *Bed Sitters* because it had no audience-recognition factor in the U.S. Of the British cast they only hired one member, Sadie, around whom the new show was supposed to be built. But as often happens when a development of this kind takes place, surprising new aspects of the basic narrative line and the characters changed the emphasis of the show out of all recognition. An English visitor to the States, exposed to an episode of *Out By Midnight*, would never have guessed that he was watching warmed-over *Bed Sitters*, even though he might have been able to spot Sadie in her rôle as Bubbles McCoy. And even that feat of recognition would have been difficult, because American residence, enormous commercial success, an incredibly expanded income (very capably handled by Sadie herself) and some years of marriage, altered Sadie enormously. By its second full season on CBS, *Out By Midnight* had become a vehicle for the skilful and subtle actor who played the part which had been Alf Puckerton's. In the new show, the lodging-house owner was called Vito D'Angelo, and as might be expected he was an Italian-American of the strictest sexual morals. He and his wife are running a boarding house way downtown in Manhattan, somewhere around Twenty-third Street and Eighth Avenue, while he puts in his time until retirement from the Post Office.

*Out By Midnight* came on the air midway through the 1963–64 season as a mid-year replacement for a program which had been axed because of low ratings, opposite a long-running NBC entry in the viewer sweepstakes, a one-hour Western series about a matriarch and her three feisty daughters. The first time viewers saw Vito D'Angelo holler up the stairs, "I said out by midnight, you little goombah, do you hear me? Out, out, out!!!" they fell in love with him for mysterious but telling reasons. After four or five episodes had been shown, negotiations began between the agents for the actor who played Vito, and the producers, looking towards an adjustment of salary, billing, and residual earnings.

This actor, veteran of dozens of movies and Broadway appearances, wasn't Italian, and he wasn't a New Yorker either. He was Jewish, from Chicago, and his name—if anybody needs to be told—was Abe Sonnenschein. One of the major audience preoccupations, in their collective love-affair with *Out By Midnight*, was the singular way in which this actor, plainly and proudly Jewish, managed to suggest an Italian, redneck, postal worker, who could not have lived elsewhere than in New York. Articles were always being written about how Abe Sonnenschein was college-bred, how he had studied sociology under George Herbert Mead, how he was hand in glove with people like Saul Bellow. And here he was acting the part of Vito D'Angelo and convincing everybody of the reality of the character.

"Out by midnight, sleazebag! Out!!! Do I hafta come up them stairs? Bubbles, do you hear me? Are you gonna' throw that bum out or am I gonna' do it for you?"

*Out By Midnight* was the Vito D'Angelo show from the start, and it carried Abe Sonnenschein—and Sadie MacNamara—to worldwide celebrity.

For those were the days when it was finally clear that stardom in a hit TV series could bring to an actor or actress a kind of mass response unparalleled by that of any other medium. An actor might appear on the stage for forty years in a series of critical and popular successes; he might make a number of films of greater or less popularity, and in all that time achieve a twentieth part of the exposure that a single season's appearances in a popular TV series could bring. Abe Sonnenschein couldn't go out on the streets of Naples or Tokyo or Tashkent without being mobbed by the friends of Vito D'Angelo, and it was the same for Sadie. *Out By Midnight* was an instantaneous smash hit in half a season, between January and April of 1964. Those first episodes are now part of anybody's TV Hall of Fame. They were the establishing scenes in which Abe and Sadie functioned in a televisically (new word) perfect relationship. The dialogue written for

# The Scenic Art

them, that first season, was as nearly pure TV as possible, simple, repetitive, in two different but easily identifiable accents, in a syntax derived from that of the vaudeville comedian, readily translated onto the small blurred screen. In the seasons which followed, 1964–65, 1965–66, 1966–67, the players in *Out By Midnight* enjoyed a kind and degree of fame that cannot be duplicated in any other medium.

In those three or four years, the careers of Sadie and Adam brought them both to international repute, but there was never any question about which of them was more widely known. As Bubbles McCoy in *Out By Midnight* Sadie was by far the more famous of the two, a fact which didn't help to keep them together. At the same time, Adam's successes were infinitely more prestigious than Sadie's. He had the leading rôle in Tony Goderich's new hit, *Cross Now*, at first in the West End, where the play was the biggest success of the 1963–64 season, then on Broadway for eighteen months, finally in the film of the play, for which Tony wrote his first screenplay, with enthusiastic help from Linnet Olcott who got a writer's credit on the film. During the summers of 1965 and 1966, Adam took two vacations from the run of *Cross Now* in New York, which allowed him to appear at the Stratford (Ontario) Festival, establishing him in the minds of people like Valerie Essex as "the star from Stratford," which is how she described him to me, as we stood and chatted in front of Stage Stoverville, on King William Street in late June of 1966. "The star from Stratford" would naturally mean more to Valerie and George Essex and their friends in the Players' Guild, than would the star of *Out By Midnight*. At the same time, Valerie and George and their friends would welcome the presence of Sadie Mac-Namara at the proposed Centennial Year Drama Festival in Stoverville quite as much, though for wholly different reasons, as that of the star from Stratford, and from *Cross Now*.

*Cross Now* had its sources in an image which had lodged in Tony's imagination from his earliest days in the flat on Windmill Street, just off the Tottenham Court Road. About fifty yards north of the corner where Store Street and Windmill Street run into Tottenham Court Road, there stood one of those automatic traffic lights controlled by a pedestrian's pushbutton which allowed people to interrupt the heavy northbound flow of traffic. When they first shared the flat, Tony and Adam always used to wonder why the traffic flow was so heavy until very late at night. The answer to the conundrum lay in the circumstance that three major railway stations lie just on the other side of the Euston Road: King's Cross, St. Pancras, and Euston itself. Cabs and private automobiles conducting passengers to their trains flow endlessly up Tottenham Court Road towards the railway stations, and a great fleet of empty cabs passes by the corner where Store Street and Windmill Street meet. Tony used to stand in front of the Trattoria Alpina and contemplate the unending stream of cabs. Something about their beetle-like black shapes impressed him mightily. He made this black insectoidal (another new word) form a brooding presence in *Cross Now*. The famous title, best remembered in connection with the celebrated film, which still shows up constantly on late-night TV, derives from the illuminated message on the traffic-light standard. You stand at the kerb, press the button and wait, watching the traffic press on towards the north. Sometimes a vehicle will brush so close to you as to frighten you severely. You wait and wait, and then after what seems an intolerable length of time, the traffic will halt and the printed message, "Cross Now" appears, illuminated and unambiguous in well-formed letters, in the "Go" signal. These terse words, and the shadowy constant river of insectoidal cabs, are the literary sources of the play and the filmscript.

They tell the story of a youngish middle-aged Liberal MP for a West Country constituency, called Rex Benedict. He is very close to the leadership of the small Liberal contingent in the House. The next party policy review may bring him to that post. As the play opens, Benedict is reading a blackmailing letter, the first of several, which proposes to expose him as the homosexual lover of a groom living on the Benedict estate in Dorset. Photographs—perhaps faked—are enclosed with the letter, and other documentary evidence follows. We are not made certain of the quality of this evidence, nor do we ever realise exactly what Benedict's sexual orientation is. If he's a homosexual, he sure doesn't look it. As the scenes

# The Scenic Art

progress, we are introduced to the blackmailer, a person of whom it is impossible to approve. He is gross, menacing, and is very cunningly made to aim at the secret weaknesses of audiences. He says things like, "Every man can be cut to ribbons, you take him on his worst side." Every night in the theatre when this line was first spoken, audiences would react strongly in a wide variety of ways. Sometimes most of them would catch their breath; sometimes the whole audience would break into fearful laughter.

Towards the end of the play, this character is shown standing at a traffic-light control in the Tottenham Court Road. He presses the button and there is the usual long interval. Then we see the traffic-signal light up, and the words of invitation appear. The blackmailer steps off the kerb and is run down and instantly killed by an empty northbound cab which doesn't stop. We never see it; we only hear its growling motor and exhaust, but it must be identical in appearance with the thousands of cabs which pass this spot day and night. Just before the blackmailer steps off the kerb we hear the sound of a screeching, braking turn, as if the oncoming cab had turned out of Store Street from some place of concealment. The death-vehicle has been waiting around the corner for a special target.

After the death there's a lot of played-down menacing dialogue between police officers and Rex Benedict, MP, but the case is never explicitly connected to him, and there is no prosecution. The audience is left wondering whether or not Benedict conspired to murder his blackmailer. His constituency agent is given the curtain line, which invariably drew loud ironic laughter and tumultuous applause.

"Unfortunate for the victim, I do see that, but Rex, it's been the most incredible stroke of luck for you, for all of us. Cheers, dear boy."

On this line, Adam, who created the rôle onstage and in films and has made it peculiarly his own, pirouettes in a campy dance-step and makes a ballet dancer's low bow to his agent, as the curtain falls. The critics who managed not to call the play Pinteresque always called it Goderichian. Which it was.

As between world renown as Bubbles McCoy and slightly lesser fame in the rôle of Rex Benedict, MP, there can't be much to choose. It was perfectly clear, when these rôles had been settled in the public mind, that Sadie and Adam enjoyed the extraordinary vicarious power which came in the 1960s to be called charisma, and in the full plenitude and exercise of this power, Sadie flew over from New York for a two-day visit while Adam was still running in *Cross Now* at the Globe, Shaftesbury Avenue, playing to sellouts and working on the film in the daytime. This was just when *Out By Midnight* had been picked up by CBS and scheduled definitely for insertion into the network schedule right after New Year's, 1964.

Sadie knew, and Adam knew, that a crisis in their affairs was at hand. The CBS series looked like being an enormous success, though nobody even guessed at its final immense, outrageous popularity. Adam's film of *Cross Now* was likewise widely talked over in the industry as the feature film most expressive of life in contemporary Britain, the age of Pinter and Orton and Bond and Carnaby Street, the miniskirt, of "Long Tall Sally" and "Roll Over Beethoven" and "Can't Buy Me Love," the age of the Beatles.

Power lay in front of them, Sadie knew and Adam saw, a reciprocal relationship which now existed between them, binding them in a death-struggle interrupted by passages of heated love, in the course of which one party's popularity might vary with, or in opposition to, the other's. They might be the darlings of the world together. They might act out the fated deathly love story of the epoch now rising with them. They must begin it together. They got married in a Registry Office in Westminster on the afternoon of December eighth, 1964.

Only the concentrated devotion of the theatre management and the London representatives of CBS permitted them to make their way from Westminster to Beauchamp Place, a tiny thoroughfare off the Brompton Road, behind Harrod's, where their pursuers were temporarily distracted by the sight of a Daimler posted outside the store. The breathless couple were protected by the serried ranks of their guards. They were shoved in the front door of the little house in Beauchamp

# The Scenic Art

Place, the property of a retired actress, now in her eighties and very poor, who had rented it to the network for a week, at an enormous charge, for this very use. The house, which smelt of chill and plastered walls, was a single room and a staircase wide, the counterpart—as it seemed to Adam, mounting the stairs—of multitudes of houses in Toronto, inescapable destined city. There was a refrigerator full of costly food and wine in the basement, and a heated bedroom at the top of the house, the only chamber with any warmth in it in the old actress's dwelling. She, poor woman, passed the next few days in a luxurious hotel room not far off, while Adam and Sadie rejoiced in the warmth of her bedchamber. Dazed and unable to plan or control what was about to happen to them, they sat on either side of the old woman's silken bower and tried to get a fix on where they were now. Adam trembled violently with nervous exhaustion; he had a performance to deliver in two hours. Perhaps nervous exhaustion would provide an extra dimension in his reading of the rôle. Sadie now approached him with a gesture of arresting erotic explicitness.

"Come here, Adam," she begged. "I'm not going to hurt you."

# 3

Valerie Essex epiphanised in front of me—as though she'd sprung up out of the ground—and exclaimed, "Oh heavens, Matt, I'm *so* pleased about the things that are happening at the Codrington Colony, all those young artists from California, and famous people and the publicity in the papers. And you mustn't think we theatre people are hanging back either."

"Certainly not," I said. I knew that one hell of a lot of Sherbourne and Essex money had gone into the theatre project.

She said, "Matt, I've just got to tell somebody about our good news. Oh Matt, I'm so happy. I just got a telegram. We're going to have the Dominion Drama Festival in Stoverville next spring, in the new theatre. Mr. Pearson is coming for the official opening, perhaps for the final adjudications too. It's going to be the last week in April. Isn't it exciting? You see . . . we've got everything in Stoverville now . . . everything. Art and music and theatre . . ."

"Why Val," I said, "that's just bloody marvellous. Have you thought of anybody for adjudicator?"

"Oh Matt . . . we're going to have the star from Stratford. You know who I mean. Adam Sinclair." She stood watching me as I adjusted the expression on my face—I had so nearly burst out laughing. I felt the muscles in my cheeks and at the corners of my mouth contract suddenly and twitch, and I underwent that peculiar sensation, quite involuntary and therefore hard to overcome, which signifies the need for nervous release, whether of tears or laughter. A precise quality of feeling often induced by sadistic tickling during kinky sex. I felt so improperly excited by this news that I nearly insulted poor Valerie.

If she really wanted this adventure, deeply wished the presence of "the star from Stratford" at the forthcoming Festival, then by God she should have it. I thought of Adam in the Beverly theatre on matinée afternoons in the mid-thirties, wailing as people rubbed sticky candy in his hair, an action which overtly assigned to him a female rôle. I thought of the ripping noises as people pulled his pants down, the squeals which accompanied these torments. I remembered the intimate pose of his head close to mine as we took the long walk home in spring Saturday twilight, my fear of being drawn into alliance with him. And then I thought of his strange metamorphosis from "Putty-face" to leading man, his apparition in the window of Murray's as well-tailored young radio actor. There had been our late-night passage through the fireplace of Forest Hill, and much much more, Lord, Lord!

I pondered the fateful production of *The Seagull*, I visualised the viridian corpselike sheen of Adam's body on the hearthrug, the night before they interviewed him for Stratford. The complex intrigues of Mrs. Roop's boarding house. Adam's attempted rape of my shrinking person, *on the final night of my honeymoon, if you can imagine*, the cataclysmic thunder and sweeping rain that same night, when at last Skip Manley got the tent up. And then the Adamitic exile in the UK. The steady progress towards a leading place in the profession, the triumph of *The Caretaker* following hard upon the temporary setback of *Claude and Gertie*, the hilarious communications from my brother Tony, Adam's union with Sadie, the recent silence. You either had to laugh or cry, and when I say cry I mean weep buckets. But I couldn't weep buckets, I had other things on my mind. Edie was out at the cottage making provisional sketches from photographs for a book we hoped to do together. She didn't require my immediate presence, but I wanted to be with her and the children at the lake. I had it in mind to spend a few days walking from Stoverville to Athens and beyond, and was intending to leave the next morning. It would have been the height of imprudence for me to develop any line of argument or analysis with Valerie about Adam Sinclair's appropriateness as an adjudicator in the still somewhat inwards-looking, even parochial atmosphere of Stoverville in 1966. At the same time I had to say something at once or break into uncontrollable laughter, tears.

"Oh, ah, yes, I see," I said. "Well, that ought to be very interesting."

My mouth stopped twitching. Perhaps this non-committal reply would channel nervous impulse into less dangerous expression. I still wanted to laugh hysterically, and my knees felt trembly and weak with loss of voluntary neural control. I started to gabble the first words that came into my head.

"Let's see," I said, "have you met Adam? Wouldn't he have seen you as Perdita at Hart House?"

This was an inspired guess. Valerie blushed deeply and slowly. I saw the blood rise first in her pretty cheeks, then on her throat; at length it quite o'erspread her chaste bosom. I mean it. She went red all over and began to giggle. "It's all too long ago for anybody to remember," she said with delighted embarrassment, "but I ought to have known that you would."

"Would what?"

"Remember."

"Oh, that, there's nothing to that. It's a trivial gift and I wish I didn't possess it. It's simply that I don't seem able to forget anything. It has something to do with the way my life works out its highs and lows."

"I don't understand you."

"Something to do with memory clusters." I thought I'd better change the subject. "I remember you as Perdita very vividly. You were delightful, Valerie, gorgeous. But for the life of me I can't remember who played Florizel in that production. It's in there, and it'll come back to me."

She started to speak.

"No," I said, "no, don't say the name, let me work on it. Did you encounter Adam at that time?"

Still a bright pink at all visible points, probably at all invisible points too, Valerie inclined her head silently.

"And that was what, twelve years ago?"

"I was Perdita in 1954."

I hate that way of talking about one's rôles. She hadn't *been* Perdita. "Twelve years. Have you seen him since?"

"I went to every Stratford play for the first three seasons," she said. "*All's Well, Richard, Shrew, Measure, Oedipus* . . ."

"We always called it Edie-puss," I said. "Did you know that Edie painted James Mason's mask for Oedipus?"

"*Caesar, Merchant.*"

She wasn't listening to me; she continued her recital of the Stratford repertoire for the first three years. "It was after he played Bassanio that he got his TV series and his London offers."

I saw where her motives inclined. "I'd forgotten his Bassanio," I said. "It's a pretty good part if you take it the right way."

"He was incredibly good," said Valerie, rubbing her toe on the sidewalk. "He was so convincing in the casket scene. He seemed so much in love, it made me cry for him."

The text of *Merchant* began to come back to me. I had worked through it line by line with Bea Skaithe—and where was she now? Poor old Bea.

"Lorenzo has the best speech in the play," I said.

"Oh he does not," said Valerie with a toss of her head. "Bassanio has better speeches and Antonio has better speeches and so does Portia. And so does Shylock. And so does Old Gobbo."

"If you say so, Val." I didn't want to spoil her pleasure and her triumph, but I had mixed reactions to the notion of Sinclair in Stoverville; the very phrase "Sinclair in Stoverville" possessed intoxicating and dramatic overtones. I wondered where Sadie was, and what she might be up to. Last I'd heard she'd been in Hollywood looping a film in which her co-star was Charlton Heston, the first of a famous science-fiction series played in monkey-makeup. Sadie, as she has developed into ripe womanhood, looks good in anything. In glossy fur and big false ears she was smashing, but all that is another story. The thought of Adam Sinclair and Sadie MacNamara set upon the unsuspecting citizens of Stoverville made me shudder and recoil.

"Have you asked Adam about this?"

"We have friends in common," she said grandly. "I know how to get in touch with him, and I have a letter from him, a signed promise. He'll be here all right."

"It'll be interesting to see somebody like Adam Sinclair in town. Have you considered where he's to stay?"

She eyed me with the air of someone who cherishes an *arrière-pensée*.

"Oh no," I said. "No, not me. Not us, Valerie, please. Uh-uh. We couldn't take it on, I mean that. We've got the three young children, and the Codrington place is full of pictures and artists. There's no scope for entertaining. If you're going to have Adam Sinclair in Stoverville for a week . . ."

"Monday to Saturday . . ." she demurred.

". . . you're going to have to entertain him. It's true that there will be plays to see every night, that is, if the theatre is able to mount a different show every night," I said. I gestured widely. We were standing in front of Stage Stoverville, formerly the old Lyceum Theatre, and before that the Opera House, on King William Street at the west end of the business district. The doors leading into the foyer were wide open, and there were large cardboard cartons bound with metal stripping, broken pieces of ceiling tile, and all the customary ingredients of building renovation, lying outside the doors, inside on the new carpeting, and all over the foyer. It was a messy scene.

"Listen," I said, "aren't there going to be any living quarters in Stage Stoverville: perhaps a suite for the manager? He'll want some privacy, you know." I felt a renewed impulse to laugh crazily. "Frankly," I said, "I don't believe the Royal Edward would be the hotel for Adam. It seems to have gone downhill over the last decade. You can't risk having him stay there."

"I don't see any element of risk," she said.

"Take my word for it, there would be risk," I said. "Have him to stay at your place, or arrange an invitation to Robinson Court for the week. The house is still one of the two showplaces of Stoverville, and either Angela or Esther could arrange it."

"Nobody knows where Angela is," she said musingly.

"Nonsense, she's in Montréal, that's a matter of public record."

"Montréal's a big place, and she doesn't live in the English district."

"If you can contact Adam, you can certainly trace Angela Robinson."

"She's very elusive."

"What about Esther?"

"Esther's gotten mighty peculiar these last few years. She's very nearly a recluse."

"In Robinson Court?"

"That's right."

"What does her father think of that?"

"Uncle George?"

"Is he your uncle too? I know he's Dougie Crum's uncle."

"He's half Stoverville's uncle. I don't know for certain. I was brought up to call him Uncle George. He doesn't seem to be a very attentive father. He allows Esther and Henry the run of the house, and she acts as her father's hostess when the house is open. I don't think he pays very much attention to her otherwise."

"He'd have to be here all through the Festival, wouldn't he? He'll want to entertain Mr. Pearson at the opening and on the last night. Get George Robinson to house Adam. If he thinks there's any chance that Sadie might come along with Adam, he'll break his neck to make them happy. He's not at all a backward host, you know. I remember he was all over my father at our wedding, even if he did call him 'a profoundly disturbing, alarming, manifestation of History's Will to REVOLUTION.'"

"Did he say that about your father?" she breathed.

"He did indeed, and what's more he said it *after* the Prize Address. Plenty of people who had hard things to say about my father before he won the prize never had the guts to say anything afterwards. I'll do George Robinson credit. He wanted to entertain my father, but he never tried to hide what he thought of him."

Valerie made a sour face. She said, "He's gotten onto some very important committees during the last few months. He must have hated being out of the House from 1963 to 1965. I think he's had a terrible effect on Esther and Henry. I think their marriage is about at the end of its rope."

"Everybody's marriage is always at the end of its rope," I said. "That's the normal modality of the state. Except for Edie's and mine of course."

"What about George and me?"

"Well, you too, naturally. We don't want to take care of Adam Sinclair, Val. Get George Robinson to put him up; he can afford it." I had private reservations about this advice. George Robinson, veteran legislator and companies director, had not been wholly sane, in my view, for a number of years. One saw him regularly on the streets of Stoverville, more particularly when the House wasn't in session, mumbling to himself, strolling down King William Street with that characteristic half-limping gait as though one leg were perceptibly shorter than the other. For long, with a short interruption from 1963 to 1965, and apparently for the foreseeable future the member for Stoverville/Smith's Falls, George Robinson had in recent months begun to attain a much more significant and influential stature in caucus and even at sub-cabinet level, than one could reasonably have expected from a man of no discernible talents or gifts, his enormous inheritance of wealth apart.

Only a few weeks before my conversation with Valerie in front of Stage Stoverville, he had been named Parliamentary Secretary to the PM. An extraordinary development! Eastern Ontario, from time immemorial intensely Conservative in its voting patterns, was now blessed with a representative just below cabinet rank destined, some said, to rise much higher in the course of the disturbances which must inevitably agitate the federal Liberal party upon the retirement of Mr. Pearson, a development which could not, it was widely prophesied, be long deferred.

George Robinson was at this time sixty and more; there could be no serious question of his obtaining the succession to the ruling PM. At least one would never have thought so. But he might be a strong contender during the early ballots, able to influence the final choice. This bore thinking over. In the meantime he would make the best conceivable host for both Lester Pearson and Adam Sinclair, a bringing-together of opposites in some way intensely characteristic of Canadian life which makes—I know I shouldn't put it this way—strange bedfellows. There were no solid reasons why Adam and the PM should not be lodged in adjacent rooms in gilded Robinson Court. And if young Angela Mary Robinson, now twenty-one years old and much changed from when I had glimpsed her as the baby princess on the last train from Westport, should turn up in Stoverville for a visit at any time in the course of the last week of next April, she might take lessons in rôle-playing from two masters, the Prime Minister and "the star from Stratford," lessons which—if all one had heard about her were true—would immensely forward her own change of rôles. One often heard from Maura Boston that young Angela was getting up to some pretty weird antics, that she called herself by the French translation of her Christian names, *Marie-Ange*, that she had been taken up by the Québec intelligentsia, all sorts of things. She might perhaps take lessons from Mr. Pearson in the cause of *bonne entente*, and would certainly profit from close observation of Adam Sinclair's mercurial behaviour.

George Robinson was supposed to be worried about his daughters. One of them had turned French, and the other had married perhaps the most withdrawn man in the united counties of Leeds and Grenville, who now practised withdrawal with his shrinking wife Esther, behind the lowered window shades and drawn curtains of Robinson Court. Esther too had taken the last long train ride on the SWLSRR; those princesses were hovering in ghostly air all around me, invisible presences, slowly beginning to take form before me. I took another long hungry look at Valerie, thinking how she, on the streets of Stoverville, and Edie, out at the lake waiting for me or perhaps not thinking about me at all, composed the central polarity of my life. Before Edie there was Valerie and after Valerie only Edie.

"I've got to get out of town," I told Val, who was joined in the precise instant by her husband, the Reverend George Essex, pastor of Saint Saviour's, Anglican, and prominent local man of the theatre. I don't speak satirically; George had done some very fine work in association with the Stoverville Players' Guild, as their director in a series of those plays which lend themselves to staging in a church. There are a surprising number of such plays and George had an aptitude for finding them: pageant plays, miracle plays, *A Sleep of Prisoners*. He was an able amateur director and an actor of some real talent, with clear unaffected speech and much authority in his physical presence. I like George Essex and I approve of him, not necessarily the same thing, and I thought he was wonderful with Val, very good for her.

I don't mean to suggest that George Essex had in any sense "taken Valerie off my hands," or that her decision not to marry for several years after I'd first known her was in any real way connected with my marriage to Edie. Valerie had introduced me to Edie, after all. I mean, my God, I can't be expected to feel guilty about everything. George was the right man for Valerie, and they worked together marvellously. They joined hands now, and insisted that I follow them around the parking lot to the back of the theatre.

"Listen, you two, I can't hang around here this afternoon, I've got a lot of things to do. I'm going away for a couple of weeks. I've got to meet Edie out at the cottage." This last was an untruth; we had no firm appointment. Edie had simply asked me to join her and the children whenever I had something definite in mind as the text for the book we were supposed to be preparing. I'd had a text in mind right along, but had wanted to see some of her sketches first, before fixing anything too unalterably in place. Collaboration is never easy.

"Come on around here," commanded Valerie. They led me through the weeds which grew at the side of the parking lot next to Stage Stoverville and down a slope of gravel and blacktopping around the corner of the theatre building to a point just at the exact centre of the back wall.

"Now look up," said Valerie softly, "look at all that brick-work."

I craned my neck and stared up at the point where the line of the roof met the sky. "It must be a hundred feet," I said, feeling dizzy.

ABOUT# The Scenic Art

"It's a hundred and ten feet high," said George Essex with pride. "We think it must be the largest single expanse of brick between here and Toronto."

"It's quite a wall," I said without thinking, "you ought to put a mural on it."

"Yes, maybe," Valerie said, "or we might mount a signboard there. You were wondering if the theatre could house six productions at the same time. Just look at that fly gallery, Matt. Isn't it magnificent?"

She was perfectly right. I'd gotten used to thinking of Hart House Theatre, which is underground and has no place in which to fly scenery, and the Stratford Festival Theatre, which has a thrust stage and requires relatively little set construction, as the typical Canadian theatres. I knew little or nothing of the technical aspects of stage-management, especially that part of it which has to do with the storage and mounting of set-pieces. This art may be in decline; the finances of the commercial theatre make the single-set production more and more the norm. Room in which to arrange the elements of several successive sets, in such a way that they can be lowered into place in a few moments, is less and less required, and less and less often provided, in contemporary theatre-architecture. Stage Stoverville was in no way deficient in this regard. It had enough space in its flies to house the scenery for major operatic presentations on a grand scale. In the event, ten months afterwards, the technical crew of the Drama Festival were able to store the sets for six different plays in the flies and wings of the huge structure.

"It was first called the Opera House, you know," said George Essex, "and it was built for grand opera, with two balconies and two stage boxes on either side of the proscenium arch, four in all. And caryatids, holding masks in front of their faces, formed in plaster on the columns beside the boxes. And about ten tons of art plaster cornucopias and festoons and swags, the lot. You never saw so much gilt and red plush in your life."

"Sure I have. I've played the Royal Alexandra. How many does this house seat?"

"Originally around fifteen hundred. The auditorium

wasn't nearly so grand in conception as the stage facilities. If you look at the plans in section, you can see that the stage, the wings, the flies, dressing-rooms, and storage space, and the foyer and service areas, are almost three times the size of the auditorium. There was never that great a population to draw on, but there were actually fourteen hundred and seventy-eight seats, with places for standees. There was a sizeable orchestra pit, with entrances for the musicians to either side underneath the stage. We found music stands for more than thirty musicians stored backstage."

"An organ?"

"No, an organ was never put in, probably because either a pianist or an orchestra would be present. The architect was Colonel Wood of Detroit, the same man who designed the Grand Theatre in London and the Star in Toronto. They were all part of a single circuit for vaudeville and travelling musicals, managed by the famous Ambrose Small, you remember, the man who disappeared without trace. You ought to see the old playbills and posters. We're having some of them cleaned and restored and we're going to display them under glass in the foyer. You'd be surprised at the people who've performed in our building. The Hart House String Quartet, Kathleen Parlow. The San Carlo Opera Company."

"That sounds fairly recent," I said. "Those are names I remember from when I was a child. Was it still called the Opera House at that time?"

"No," said George. He took a notebook from his pocket and consulted it gravely. "They changed the name to the Lyceum when the sound system was installed for talkies. The talkies and radio killed vaudeville. And the theatre never did well as the Lyceum; there was too much competition from the Famous Players house along the street. I don't believe the Lyceum was ever more than a third-run movie house."

"There were only two movie theatres in town," I said.

"When it became a movie house, the management let all the interior decoration go downhill. They painted over a lot of it, which was bloody criminal, and they closed off the second balcony. Most of the original décor was by Briffa of Montréal. There was a ceiling painted to resemble the night sky, with

# The Scenic Art

electrically illuminated stars in it. There were artificial windows opening on paintings of the Italian lakes; there were bare-bottomed cherubs, and fish that spouted water like fountains! You can't imagine what it was like. But all through the thirties and forties the box office kept shrinking."

"They used to have shitty movies," said Valerie. "I wasn't allowed to come here, even in a crowd. My mother said that we might pick up things. I didn't realise what she meant at the time, but I suppose she was thinking of vermin. Only tough kids came here. They showed Bowery Boys movies, and Veda Ann Borg movies, and I remember seeing posters with Belita and Vera Hruba Ralston on them. Finally they closed the building about a decade ago."

"It's been used from time to time for public meetings," said George, "and when the city took it over for taxes they installed a permanent maintenance man to look after the boilers and the duct-work, a stationary engineer with third-class papers. The place hasn't been allowed to fall completely apart, but it badly needed renovation."

"Look," I said, "I've simply got to say good-bye for the moment. I've got a flock of things to clean up at the Codrington Colony before I leave town. If you don't mind, I'll excuse myself."

"Look at that beautiful expanse of brick," said Valerie dreamily. "It certainly would look marvellous if somebody were to do a mural on it."

"Oh no you don't!" I said, gasping. "Why it would be a five years' job like the Sistine Chapel ceiling. You'd have to have scaffolding and you'd be working outside in all weathers. Who could you get to do it?"

They looked at each other connivingly.

"You raised the subject," said George insinuatingly.

"Maybe I did, I'm sorry," I said. "If I ever suggested such a thing to Edie I'd be getting myself into big trouble. You can't dictate to Edie or any real artist. I'll tell you what, get hold of her through the summer and show *her* this wall. It's one hell of a wall, I'll grant you all of that. I see that it begs to be painted on. Something nice and bright in a weather-resistant exterior paint—you'd be able to see a thing that size quite clearly from out on the river as the ships go by. It would become a landmark. But I wouldn't propose such a thing to my wife if my life depended on it. Why don't you go and talk to Maura Boston at the Codrington Colony offices. She might be able to pick out an artist who would accept a commission."

"To tell the truth, Matt," said Valerie, once more colouring delicately, "we were hoping we could find somebody to make a cartoon for a mural, squared off for enlarging to scale. We could find volunteers to apply the paint."

I took another look at the roof line, a hundred and ten feet above us. "That's a hell of a height. It may not look like much from down here, but if you were up on top of that you'd be scared shitless, excuse me, Valerie."

"That's exactly what I said to George," she said, laughing.

"And him in holy orders."

"George never minds what people say in front of him," she said, smiling at him cheerfully. "He's not the sort of priest who wants to put a damper on everything."

"I know. I've watched him directing," I said. "And I've listened to his sermons. Tell you what, you know where our cottage is. Drive out and see us; we'll go for a swim or a sail and talk about it. Good-bye now!" I turned tail and beat it, climbing up a crumbling bank and crossing the parking lot at a jog-trot. When I looked back a few minutes later, I saw that they were still standing at the back of the building, looking up admiringly at the vast expanse of weathered red brick which formed the rear wall of the theatre.

It was a monumental structure, by much the largest building in the city. I waved to them but they didn't happen to see me. Then I crossed King William Street and moved quickly along past the front of the theatre, heading eastwards across town towards our house. I always have trouble speaking of it as our house; it always seems to me to be the Codrington house, not my house, although I've spent half my life there. I knew that it would be thronged with visiting day-trippers and young, nameless painters from California and suchlike places, tracing the visionary element in art from the inspiration of Mrs. Codrington's twelve wonderful works, now definitively arranged in the new gallery at the top of the house. I had no objection to that, how could I? I'd been largely responsible for putting the whole enterprise on foot. All the same, I felt squeezed out by the pressure of circumstance, and I knew that this first summer's operation of the Codrington Colony for the Encouragement of Visionary Art was going to encounter exactly the same kind of birth pangs and growing pains that had plagued the Stratford Festival during the first few seasons of its operation. So too would Stage Stoverville struggle and agonise to be born.

Like every great Canadian undertaking, Stage Stoverville would be born from its social matrix only after quakings, rumblings, threatened abortion or miscarriage. The whole undertaking eventually began to be associated in my thoughts with the exactly parallel evolution of the world's fair in Montréal, the glamorous, wildly successful Expo 67. Not very long after my conversation with George and Valerie outside the theatre, it began to be clear that the week during which the Dominion Drama Festival was to be offered in Stoverville—the most exciting and *mouvementée* week in the history of eastern Ontario—would coincide with the week in which Expo 67 was to open. The Drama Festival was to run from Monday night, April twenty-fourth, through its closing ceremonies of Saturday night, April twenty-ninth, just about the pleasantest week of the year in a town like Stoverville, the rains of early spring by then normally over, May flowers close at hand.

The Friday night performance during the Festival would conflict with the formal opening ceremonies of the most imposing Centennial project of them all, Expo 67. Obviously the Prime Minister could not attend both. If he were to be present at the triumphant rituals in Montréal, ribbon-snippings, speechgivings, banquetings, dismissals of disagreeable political opponents, such as the inaugural of a world's fair would provide, he could not possibly be in Stoverville on the Friday night. For several months following my conversation with George and Val, the Festival organisers lobbied the Prime Minister's office in order to get a written commitment that Mr. Pearson would be present on the opening Monday and the final Saturday. At first there were demurrals from Ottawa. George Robinson, roused from dogmatic slumber by the urgings of his honorary niece, now began to exert himself on the Festival's behalf. A long and highly secret process of negotiation developed, about which somebody certainly ought to write something someday, in which the principal agents were Uncle George Robinson, Liberal member for Stoverville/Smith's Falls, Mr. Pearson's *chef de cabinet*, a now forgotten political nonentity who was for a brief time something of an *éminence grise*, the rising young member from Montréal who now became for a short period one of Mr. Pearson's two Parliamentary secretaries, and finally, at one moment or another during the long run up to the Centennial Year celebrations, my father.

Three powerful MPs, the head of the PMO, the Prime Minister himself, they constituted an extraordinary quintet, a kind of ad-hoc sub-committee presiding from on high over the centennial celebrations of a small eastern-Ontario city with very far-reaching results. The whole of that time was for me a pause in history like that preceding the San Francisco earthquake or the eruption of Krakatoa. There were continual subterranean portents, shifts of rock-strata of different mass and geological character, emissions of fierce heat, disturbing sudden noises. I was better placed than anybody else to register these disquieting occurrences. I used to get long letters from Dad, keeping me and Edie abreast of what was going on in Ottawa. As time passed, it began to be evident that the minor issue of Mr. Pearson's personal schedule of appointments during the last week of April 1967 was assuming the character of a test-issue. An Ontario-Québec confrontation.

The good citizens of Stoverville had every right to expect Mr. Pearson to participate fully in their centennial project. The Centennial of Confederation was Mr. Pearson's personal baby, just as the new Canadian flag had been. Eastern Ontario must necessarily take a great place in any such observance. The first Prime Minister of Canada had been a Conservative from Kingston. The great university of the region had supplied, and continued to supply the Civil Ser-

# The Scenic Art

vice of Canada with many of its most distinguished officers, right up to the level of Deputy-Minister, sometimes beyond. Some people—misguided as they might be—considered the federal Civil Service to be a fiefdom of Queen's University. There could be no doubt whatsoever that eastern Ontario had exercised an influence in federal politics out of all proportion to the region's wealth, which was never great. Political IOUs remained in existence in great numbers; these might now be called in to insure that when Stoverville celebrated Centennial Year with the great undertaking of a week-long Festival at Stage Stoverville, the PM, and the sitting member for Stoverville/Smith's Falls, all those members of the bureaucracy—and their name was legion—who had local affiliations, and hordes of simple Ottawa and district citizens with cousins or friends living in Stoverville, Cornwall, Smith's Falls, Prescott, Gananoque and Kingston, would be present at the ceremonies, not just on opening night, but for most of the week, and especially on closing night, which would be a time of prize-giving, an awards banquet without the necessity of the ingestion of creamed chicken and *petits pois*.

From Belleville to the Québec border along 'the Front,' that is, the district bordering Lake Ontario and the Saint Lawrence, it was next to impossible at that time, and for many years afterwards, to find a single Liberal member of the federal Parliament. George Robinson was then, had been for most of two decades, the only Liberal voice in a solid bloc of eastern Ontario Conservatives. This was the more surprising, as the Robinson fortune was a very great one, and massive commercial undertakings usually associate themselves, in North America, with the forces of the political right. In Canada, there being no simple consistent ideological striations of political opinion from far right to extreme left (and thank God for that), party affiliation isn't always an accurate reflection of one's personal political views. In New York State, George Robinson must have been a Republican. He couldn't have escaped being a Republican, and not a liberal Republican like Nelson Rockefeller either, but a real genuine solid old-time cigar-chomping supporter of Bob Taft, an Ohio political luminary in whose company George Robinson had sometimes been photographed, once in fact at the 1952 Republican National Convention at which Bob Taft was General Eisenhower's only rival for the Republican nomination.

George Robinson couldn't approve of General Eisenhower, whom he considered an adventurer, a man without real political convictions. He was never really reconciled to the naming of the principal works along the Saint Lawrence Seaway after the celebrated commander of the invasion forces on the Normandy beaches. The two men met at the opening of the Eisenhower Locks, in the company of the then mayor of Stoverville—my father-in-law Earl Codrington—and they were coolly polite to one another, but that was all. Uncle George didn't much like John Diefenbaker either, on the grounds that Diefenbaker wasn't an honest Conservative but a CCFer in drag, a prairie populist radical who wasn't any more legitimately a Conservative than Major Coldwell or Andrew Goderich.

You couldn't find any specific reason in anything Uncle George said why he should profess membership in the Liberal Party of Canada. But then you would have had to look hard in all directions to find a legitimate Liberal ideologue in 1949 or 1953 under Mr. St.-Laurent, in 1965 under Mr. Pearson. Like so many members of the Liberal Party, Uncle George Robinson belonged to it because he didn't belong to anything else. He had a perdurable attachment to power and unformed centralist allegiances. He liked things pretty much the way they are, so long as the status quo could be gilded with a superficial progressivism, the electorate be persuaded by successive moderate social measures that life was getting better and better, more agreeable and more rewarding, at not too rapid a tempo. Everybody in Stoverville was perfectly aware that George Robinson was much more opposed to profound social change than any of the Conservative MPs from the constituencies roundabout. If he chose to identify himself as a Liberal, that was a harmless eccentricity in a man so rich. And anyway he had an in with the federal government, and might someday be in the Cabinet as Fisheries Minister or Minister of Northern Affairs.

However he might finish his political career—and a man in his strange physical and mental condition might well live to his century, sitting in Parliament the whole time—George Robinson was the only red face, so to speak, in a sea of blue noses. His electors ought to be encouraged by the federal Liberal party and by the government (same thing?). Belleville and Cornwall could plead with the PM's office for his attention to their Centennial projects; their pleas would have to go unheeded. There were the needs of Québec to be borne in mind as always. But the solid constituency of Stoverville/ Smith's Falls, that was a mode of being, in the language of modern Protestant theology, wholly other. The Robinsons' commercial interests extended far and wide. Robinson Pharmaceuticals was in the mid-nineteen-sixties in process of evolving into a multinational corporation, one of two Canadian organisations at that epoch truly deserving the title, the other best known under its name of listing on the New York Exchange, Distiller's Corporation.

The Robinson interests had not for many years maintained their head office in Stoverville. The financial officers were housed at first in Montréal, finally in Toronto in the Commerce Court complex. Production facilities for the organisation's various lines of popular patent medicines were scattered across Canada, though no longer in the province of Québec. Latterly the corporation had found itself obliged to diversify its holdings at the same time as a major move into US markets became mandatory. Three old and much-advertised US brand names were acquired: a chest rub, a salicylate analgesic, and a line of antihistamines. But expansion in the retail drug trade was not the solution to the corporation's Canadian and American tax and cash-management problems. Other products, other forms of enterprise, would have to become available to RobPharm if investment opportunities were to be maximised; there was such a lot of money lying around.

In the mid-nineteen-sixties, George Robinson found himself locked in close and apparently interminable debate with his son-in-law, Esther's husband Henry Golmsdorfer, whom I have described as the most withdrawn man in the united counties. He was certainly all of that, and he may have been the most acute investor in Canadian finance and company development all the time he practised withdrawal behind the drawn window shades of Robinson Court. It was Henry Golmsdorfer who directed the RobPharm invasion of US markets, and the later diversification into the great new technologies of the last third of the century.

When Uncle George was invited to throw his weight as Parliamentary Secretary (one of two) to Mr. Pearson behind the proposal to have the PM present at the Drama Festival as its presiding genius, he seized upon the idea with concentrated enthusiasm. He saw the occasion as perhaps the climactic celebration of his financial and political career. He hoped to announce major modifications of the corporate structure of RobPharm during the last week of April 1967, with the Prime Minister at his elbow. A way could certainly be found, perhaps by judicious subsidy, to associate the scenic art to the manufacture of proprietary nostrums and auto parts. He might endow some annual award. The Secretary of State ought to be present at the concluding awards ceremonies as well as the Prime Minister; the occasion would make the front pages of every Canadian daily, even though Expo 67 had opened the day before.

Publicity of this kind would make clear to Henry Golmsdorfer and the officers of the corporation that investors' acumen needed at all times to be activated and controlled by political clout. Every major Canadian business enterprise had a Cabinet Minister in its pocket, he judged, or if they didn't they certainly ought to. He intended to stand this trend upon its head. He wished to become the Canadian Cabinet Minister who had a major investment program and a major industrial and commercial organisation in *his* pocket. This wouldn't be an absolute novelty in modern Canadian political and financial history—a few others had worked the trick before him without being suddenly shunted to the siding of the Senate—but it would be unique in the emergent world of the mid 1960s. George Robinson was always thinking about the Rockefellers and their bank these days.

Sometimes George regretted his knee-jerk low opinion of that so-called liberal Republican, Nelson Rockefeller, wishing that he hadn't allowed himself to be photographed with his arm around Bob Taft's shoulders. But the thing was done; there was no point in vain regret. There was no point thinking for a single moment about close combat with the Rockefeller interests; only a very idle fellow would consider such an undertaking, and Henry Golmsdorfer, withdrawn, anti-social, and alien in behaviour as he might be, was in no sense idle. Not long after the restructuration of RobPharm, towards the middle of the sixties, Golmsdorfer installed a computer terminal in the music room at Robinson Court, an innocent-looking box. It was a decade before anybody else in Stoverville knew what a computer terminal was, and much longer before any other citizen of the city even suspected how such an object worked or what it could do.

George Robinson wanted Lester Pearson in Stoverville for the whole week following the opening of the Festival on Monday, April twenty-fourth, 1967, and he desired it so much that he was ready to spend most of the preceding winter in elaborate subterranean manoeuvrings designed to produce the effect. He would throw open Robinson Court to the Festival staff. Its gracious reception rooms, the ballroom, the extensive library, the floral conservatory, the palm court, the billiard room, the smoking room, and all the other rooms except for the private apartments, could be employed in entertainments and Festival business; never mind that Esther and Henry were gravely inconvenienced for many weeks. This was after the computer terminal went in. Once that piece of equipment was installed beside a gilded concert grand from Steinway, George Robinson would have died rather than admit strangers to the music room. He learned to operate the queer, mysterious, almost magical equipment when he was past sixty-five; it was a pretty sight to see him deploy his newly acquired computer literacy. His final years were much comforted by his possession of the most advanced, state-of-the-art, computer and information processing equipment, by his constant playful use of Henry's much prized word processors and copying machines, and by the support of his other newer son-in-law, Duncan McCallum, a man who devoted himself entirely to mastery of these devices. Their few intimates used to declare that it was charming to watch the elderly public man huddled together with his son-in-law over the desk of one of the information banks, working out instantaneous inventory control of, say, glove-compartment locks produced in one of the corporations' subsidiaries in Woodstock, Ontario, or some other masses of obscure data which might not directly affect day-to-day RobPharm Corporation actions but could provide advance notice of sudden unsuspected favourable investment opportunities for private capital, which even Henry and Esther might have overlooked. It was a remarkable fact that George Robinson, after sixty-five, grew more expert in the deployment of the new information technology than Henry Golmsdorfer ever did.

The Prime Minister a week-long resident of Robinson Court, with Adam Sinclair and Sadie MacNamara installed in an adjacent suite. When George Robinson thought this over he could hardly contain himself, and would not allow himself to be turned aside from pursuit of this goal for fully ten months, from the time when Valerie Essex first came to him with the hazy nebulous outlines of what grew to be the final specifications for the momentous occasion. This happened on the day following my conversation with Valerie and her husband—also, most inconveniently, named George—at the exact same time, as nearly as I can reckon it, as I was standing in the middle of the fields eight miles north of town, knee deep in wildflowers, envisioning the ten brilliant princesses on their last railway ride: Valerie, her sister Mary, Esther Robinson and her baby sister Angela, Maura Boston, poet and curator of the Codrington Colony, Sallee Lennox, Faunce Crum, Rhoda Maguire from Athens, and Nancy Wiltse from the Wiltsetown Road.

And Edie Codrington.

"That Codrington girl won't have anything to do with this, will she?"

"Codrington girl?" It took Valerie a moment to realize that Uncle George was talking about Edie.

"You know who I mean. Earl and May-Beth's girl, and that husband of her's, young Goderich, the antiquarian. They're the ones who've disgraced King William Street with their art circus."

"You mean the Codrington Colony?"

"I certainly do mean the Codrington Colony, as you call it. Not a block away from my grounds. I've actually found painters—painters!—trespassing on my frontage on the river. I can't think what old Senator Maclean would have said about it. It was Flora's fault; she was always too friendly with May-Beth Codrington. Now the Maclean place has gone to seed, and the Codrington house, a decent enough establishment in its way, though nothing like Robinson Court, has been ripped open to make an *art gallery*. I don't know. I have to ask myself if this is the way we want to go in Stoverville. The artists, the mad poetess . . ."

"Do you mean Maura Boston?" asked Valerie stiffly.

"Who else? Now there's a family with a demented streak a yard wide."

"But Uncle George," said Valerie a little guiltily, "none of the people you've named have any connection with the Players' Guild or the Festival staff. And the theatre is a much saner and more wholesome thing than poetry or painting. I've heard you say so yourself."

"I'm not saying I don't intend to work for the Festival," said George Robinson. "I have it in my mind to do big things for the Festival. I think much more can be made of it than that caravanserai of Earl and May-Beth's."

It was clear that the emergence of the Codrington Colony into wide public prominence without his assistance had left Uncle George feeling left out, superseded, a bit on the shelf. "I would have given them every assistance in my power," he grumbled, "but that daughter of theirs and her husband, and Sallee Lennox and their crowd, they had to get the whole thing up among themselves without so much as a nod in my direction. I'd have been delighted to help. I suppose that simply because they're linked to the famous Nobel Prize winner, who happens to be a member of Parliament for a party that has never held office and will never hold office federally, they imagine that they can do without George Robinson's influence. They've got another think coming. Nobel Prizes don't count for all that when they're fifteen or sixteen years in the past. How many people ever speak of that man now?"

"I don't know, Uncle George, I imagine a good many do."

All at once the old paladin changed his tone; he laughed at her gently. "You're perfectly right, Valerie, a good many do. I can't disguise it. Andrew Goderich is a powerful man, and I don't suppose that his son is such a bad fellow either, though I'd like him better if he had some sort of profession. He simply married the Codringtons' girl, and I suppose he lives on their money. What does he do for a living? What is he doing at this moment?"

At that moment, as nearly as I can figure from things Valerie told me afterwards, I was running along the abandoned right-of-way of the SWLSRR, rapt with my vision of old times, the last train, the ten noble ladies.

"Matthew does plenty of useful work, Uncle George," said Valerie. "The art colony was his creation, and it's brought all sorts of publicity to Stoverville. That's exactly why I've come to you. We need support for our project, just the way the Codrington money, as you call it, has supported the art colony and the visiting painters' program. If you want to create a rivalry between the two activities, so be it. But put yourself behind the Players' Guild and Stage Stoverville and next year's Drama Festival, and take my work for it, you'll never be disappointed."

"I know that, my dear, and I'm going to take you on. I'm throwing all my influence behind you and your actors. We'll let them know that we native Stovervillians can get up to things in the arts, the same as anyone else. I'll interest Esther in the affair. We'll see if we can't persuade young Angela to spend some time at home for a change. With her energy she might be a distinct asset."

Angela Mary Robinson was the child of her father's middle years, and he invariably spoke of her with every sign of exhaustion. She was now in her early twenties, very seldom seen in Stoverville, said to be connected with left-wing Québec politics in some mysterious way. Once or twice a year she would appear at Robinson Court, coiffed, made up, and dressed in exotic fashion. She had something of her father's air of latent *monomanie*, a deliberately cultivated inconsequence.

"We'll have to make certain that some of those Québec elements don't work against us," said George Robinson with immense satisfaction. He loved political intrigue, and saw in this question of Mr. Pearson's appearance at the Festival an opportunity for crypto-political mischief-making of a high order.

That afternoon, he shared an exquisitely served luncheon with Valerie at Robinson Court. Whatever might be spoken against the Robinsons, that they were superannuated, no longer a functioning element in real Canadian life, troglodytes, economic royalists, all these charges and others besides, they nonetheless perfectly well understood how to hire servants and retain their loyalties. This light collation was served off unpretentious English stoneware, on the main terrace behind the wing of the house that overlooked the river, so deftly and unpretentiously that you might imagine that you hadn't done something so physical as eat a meal at all, if it hadn't been for the airy exquisiteness of the trout, the perfection of the anonymous *Entre-deux-mers*. In fact the Robinsons were extremely rich, something it did Valerie good to remember. She enjoyed being on these intimate terms with her titular Uncle George, and intended to go on making good use of him. That he was making even better use of her, all the time enjoying her little strategems, concealing his perceptions from her as he made up his mind what to do, didn't alter Valerie's enjoyment in the least when he announced his decision over crème caramel.

"We'll put on a display that will make the Codringtons sick as mud," he said with a grin.

"But Uncle George, Mr. and Mrs. Codrington have been dead for some time."

"I'm talking about the folks over at the Codrington Colony for the Encouragement of Visionary Art."

"I believe you know all about them; you've just been teasing me."

The veteran public man made no direct reply. He said, "Those Goderiches."

"I've already thought of asking Edie to do a mural on the rear wall of the theatre." She was surprised at her uncle's reaction.

"That's all right. There's nothing wrong with that. The girl's good, isn't she? A good painter, I mean."

"Oh yes."

"Rope her in for any practical help you can get. I'll pay for the paint. Hah hah! A painting on the back wall of the building. You mean outside? Showing? So you could see it from the river?"

"Exactly."

"Hell of an idea," siad Uncle George Robinson. "You'll require scaffolding, such as they had in that movie about Michelangelo."

He was still capable of surprising you, thought Val.

"... scaffolding, yes sir, and a team of painters to put the paint on under the artist's supervision. They might be house painters or industrial painters. What do you fancy for a subject? Nothing like those things of May-Beth's. Don't want to give people thoughts of the life to come, do we?"

"Uncle George, have you ever actually seen the Codrington paintings?"

"Not actually seen them, no. I might just have seen the one of Phil Horsbaugh in the robes of Judas, hah-hah."

"They wouldn't frighten anybody; they're much more inspiring than frightening. But I do agree with you that we need a large-scale design on some simple colourful subject that can be seen from a long way off."

"And you're going to invite the Codrington girl ... Mrs. Goderich ... to take charge?"

"Only to prepare the design. She needn't work on the actual painting."

"I wouldn't want this to become another Codrington project, my dear."

# The Scenic Art

"No, no, nothing at all like that. It's going to be a Stage Stoverville undertaking, in association with the Dominion Drama Festival."

"Then I'll willingly lend Robinson Court for an headquarters, and you can billet your adjudicator with me. I'll have our projection room made ready. His wife too, if she turns up."

Valerie nodded. "I didn't know you had a projection room."

"Yes, we've got a little movie theatre just off the conservatory; we used to use it for birthday parties. I'll keep after the Prime Minister's office to make certain of his commitment. It seems to me that he should open the Festival and close it, and be in attendance for at least one other night."

"That would be simply perfect if you can arrange it."

"April twenty-fourth to April twenty-ninth. I'll invite him to be my house guest for the inside of the week. There's nothing in Ottawa to equal Robinson Court, you know."

"I don't suppose there is," said Valerie, looking around her approvingly.

Conversations like this, fraught with consequences for many who don't take part in them, persons in some cases many miles distant when they take place, seem to have a mysteriously effective method of diffusing themselves, perhaps through the thin upper atmosphere, in such a way as to make those for whom they mean big trouble shiver with apprehension, though they have seen and heard nothing of them through the corporeal senses. When I confronted my wife on the sundeck of our summer home, on the night after this exchange of views between two redoubtable plotter/planners, I almost knew in my living flesh that there were going to be unhealthy corollaries to my inadvertent observation that the back wall of Stage Stoverville was just a nice size for a mural.

The observation and its implications were seated very uneasily at the back of my mind—and in the pit of my stomach like an ill-digested dinner—as I held my wife in my arms and enjoyed with her the midnight stillness of the lake. We said little, and retired to bed soon after my arrival at the cottage. I have the sense of tossings and turnings, of disquieted slumber, following my arrival; there remains an impression of mild guilt. I could swear to myself that I hadn't in so many words volunteered Edie's assistance on the mural project. I thought over my exact words, as carefully as my memory would permit. George and Val had led me very cannily into temptation. Quite possibly they had had no notion of painting the back wall of the theatre. Certainly when the proposal popped out of my mouth I had had no formed intention of suggesting Edie as the only possible executant of such a work. No *formed* intention, certainly. But she had unquestionably been at the core of my thinking when I made the fateful remark which set the wheels turning.

How naturally we invoke metaphor to excuse ourselves. "It just popped out of my mouth." "At the back of my head." "Set things on foot." Organs of speech, thought and locomotion appeared to be in some obscure way connected to my ensuing apprehension of mild guilt. What do we mean when we say to ourselves, "It was at the back of my head"?

At the age of thirty-six I had no sense at all of the multivalent structure of human motive, no grasp of its intolerably perplexing location in the world. *Where is motive?* Where is the back of the head? Is motive perhaps the sub-structure of the real, the mode of being so much more real than anything else, that everything that is is an expression of it, while it remains inexpressible? Obviously there is one mode of being in the world which is inexpressible, because beneath everything else. What awareness of Edie's right to free agency was merged in my thoughts with my foolish sudden remark?

"It's quite a wall. You ought to have a mural painted on it."

I had no business to say that. I ought not to have said it. It was going to mean trouble. We were already committed to a piece of work to be undertaken together. I have observed elsewhere that kisses and threats are the marks of married collaboration on serious work. I always supposed that our collaboration was to be constructed on a foundation of close communication and intense mutual awareness. What demon had possessed me to open my mouth?

It was a week before I could steel myself to mention the matter to Edie, very cautiously. She repudiated it at once, with some show of anger.

"You what?"

"I only just mentioned it, and I see now that it was stupid."

"That's right, it was stupid. You didn't make any commitment of any kind?"

"How could I? I don't make commitments for you."

"The hell you don't!"

"Oh come on, Edie! When have I ever involved you in something that you didn't know about, or against your will?"

"And you say that Adam Sinclair is going to be mixed up in this Festival bullshit?"

"I had nothing to do with that, and you know it. Adam is the last person in the world I'd have picked for that assignment." The more ridiculous aspects of the situation suddenly struck me and I burst out laughing.

"I fail to see anything in the least funny about this," said Edie grimly.

"Mike Pearson, Adam Sinclair, Uncle George Robinson, George Essex, Sadie MacNamara, old Uncle Tom Cobbley and all. And you don't see anything amusing about it?"

She relaxed far enough to allow a concession. "It might involve certain necessary absurdities. I guess it deserves a mural, an allegory of art and politics."

"That's my good girl."

She called to Andrea, who was spending the morning at work on some drawings of her own in the dim recesses at the back of the cottage, "Darling, would you bring Mummy her sketchbook and pencils?"

"How can you use a five-year-old child as a messenger?" I said easily, thinking to even up the score a bit.

"I let her play with them. It teaches the child a sense of fair exchange."

Andrea pushed open the screen door and handed her mother a dog-eared sketchbook and a fistful of pencils, most of them much shortened by sharpening. Almost the first manual skill Andrea had mastered . . . the use of the pencil sharpener. She ground all pencils that came into her hands down to needle-sharp points, with great gusto. Now she turned and gave me a marmalade-scented kiss. "Hot in the back room," she said.

"We'll go for a swim in half an hour."

"I want you to keep a close eye on me," she said.

"I won't let you out of my sight for a second," I said.

"You walked all the way out here," she said, eyeing me appraisingly. She squeezed my forearm; her hand tickled. "Aren't you tired?"

"Not a bit. I'm having a good rest."

"Don't get yourself too tired," she said, peering into my face.

"I promise I won't."

She ambled away to the back of the cottage talking to herself, from time to time breaking into song. I looked across the picnic table at Edie, who was scribbling frantically in her sketchbook.

"Throw me out a title," she mumbled without looking up, "some sort of evocative phrase."

"For what?"

"For the back wall of the theatre. Tell you what, I wouldn't mind doing something for them, as long as I don't have to supervise the actual painting, and as long as they agree to maintain and restore the work from time to time with fresh paint. I don't even feel certain what sort of paint you'd need over brick. You'd have to scour the surface and apply an undercoating, some sort of primer/sealant. You'd have to make sure that the bricks were sound, not too sandy or wind-eroded." She bent her head and made some more quick passes with a pencil. "I'd better make some notes. Do you happen to know the dimensions of the wall?"

"I just happen to have them with me," I said happily, feeling my neck. "From ground level to the roof line is a hundred and eight feet, with another two feet of footing showing at the bottom."

"How wide is it?"

"I'll have to check that," I said, "but it would be about

seventy-six feet wide, I should think. I can get the exact measurement from George or Val."

"You wouldn't bleed it right out to the edge of the wall. That would involve some loss of quality along the ground-level edge; there would be dust and dirt on it, and there would be oil smears on the ground. Isn't there a parking lot out back?"

"Right."

"I'm thinking seriously of something enormous, with a vertical of ninety feet and a horizontal of sixty, nice proportions and a huge space. Ninety by sixty, why that's . . . what?"

"Enormous," I said, "monumental."

"Don't keep saying 'monumental,' for God's sake."

"Sorry," I said, "did I say it before?"

"No, but you might say it again at any moment."

"It works out to fifty-four hundred square feet."

"Monumental!" she said. She whistled between her teeth. "That's six or seven times the floor space in this cottage, do you realise that? Let's see, how would it work out? Suppose you make your cartoon to a scale of one inch to a foot? No, that won't do. I can't get any detail into one-inch squares, and they'd have to work from the squares." She grew very excited. "Maybe some of your young visionaries could be hired to apply the paint. What size cartoon would two inches to the foot give us? That's one sixth the size. If your horizontal is sixty feet, the lower edge of the cartoon has to be ten feet and the vertical will be fifteen."

"It would be a lot like scene painting."

"My God, you're right," she said. "That's exactly how you'd manage it. You'd have some flats made, ten feet by seven and a half precisely, two of them. One for the lower half of the picture, one for the upper. Or wait a second, hold it, even better. Even better by gollies. Now look Matt, here's how we do it, just make a mental note of this will you, till we get a chance to write it down somewhere. What we'll do is we'll have the men at the store make up four large canvasses mounted on stretchers, just like what I use for painting, only bigger. Is there a word like 'triptych' only for something with four panels?"

"Quadriptych," I said.

"Really?"

"If there wasn't before, there is now."

"Right, now we know what to call it, our quadriptych. I'll get the staff at our plaza branch to do this for me. They've been selling canvasses from there for ten years; they must know what one looks like by now. You want visionary art? I'll give you visionary art! Wait till they get a load of this. I'll get four large canvasses run up, five by seven-and-a-half, do you see? That will give me four surfaces to work on, each one corresponding to one quadrant of the finished picture. When they come to apply the paint to the wall, they can work on two sets of scaffolding right next to one another. I'll have them start at the upper edge and work down. They'll have to prime the wall first and then apply at least two coats of paint, maybe three. It'll take time. They'll have to prepare the wall as soon as possible. You can mention that to Valerie if you're talking to her on the phone after supper. Scrape it and clean it and fill in any cracks and pitting. Planing and pointing. We might be able to apply a couple of coats of primer this fall, to preserve the surface through the winter. I don't think we ought to put the paint on till next spring."

"Would it be finished in time?"

"In time for what?"

"For the Festival opening on the twenty-fourth of April."

"Oh certainly, if they get started early in March. Good drying weather, and that's very tough paint, and anyway it'll be covered in tarpaulin all the time until the opening, the unveiling. What a grandiose conception. I'm deeply indebted to you, my darling, so come here!"

She led me around the corner of the picnic table by the hand, and gave me a heartfelt kiss when I sat down beside her. "Look here," she said, "this is what I have in mind. We'll have these four canvasses five feet by seven-and-a-half each. I'll make my sketches; then I'll execute the four quadrants of the picture on the four canvasses in the scale of two inches to a foot. Then the painters will have four easy-to-handle working

# The Scenic Art

renderings to scale, which they can easily take up on the scaffolding. We can square off the wall this fall, and get it all ready for execution. The scaffolding can go up the first week in March, and we'll have the picture in place with two good coats on it by the day of the opening; it can be touched up later if necessary. I expect they'll want to unveil the thing that afternoon, right?"

"Oh sure, sure, why not?"

"And they'll have the Prime Minister to do the unveiling, with Adam and Sadie standing around taking bows, correct?"

"If they can. I'm sure that's the sort of occasion that George and Valerie envisage."

"And why bloody not? I tell you, Matt, and I mean no disrespect to me old Mum when I say this, I'm going to do a this-worldly painting. None of this visionary shit."

"Have you got a subject in mind?"

"You're damn' right I have. 'The Genius of Politics Introducing Dramatic Art to its Ideal Counterpart.' How do you like them apples?"

I said, "It'll kill them in Stoverville."

We don't have a telephone in our cottage. I had to drive into Athens that night to give Valerie the good news of Edie's proposals. Valerie in turn was bursting with Uncle George's reaction. From the moment of that first meeting of minds the mural was an accomplished mental fact.

"What would Edie charge for the design?"

"She empowers me to say that she will present it to Stage Stoverville without charge, the expenses of its realisation, the paint, the preparation of the surface, and the later preservation of the work, to be defrayed by you. She wants a written agreement which lays this out. Neither of us wants to see the picture executed, then allowed to weather and peel. How does that sound?"

"That's beautiful, very generous. We can sit down with Mr. Fitzsimmons . . . it is Mr. Fitzsimmons, isn't it?"

"Yes," I said, "he does all the legal work for Codrington Hardware and Builders' Supplies. Since 1867. And he handled the founding of the Codrington Colony. He'll know what we want. It's a question of making sure that the work survives in good condition."

"Oh I know, I know," said Valerie.

"It isn't like a play production," I said, slightly maliciously. "It's supposed to be permanent."

"I do see that," said Val. "Can you let me know what the subject of the picture will be?"

"Sure. She's calling it, 'The Genius of Politics Introducing Dramatic Art to its Ideal Counterpart.'"

"My goodness!"

"She'll have sketches ready for you when we're back in town after Labour Day. It will be a representational design with Shakesperian associations."

"Marvellous. We can't wait. I'll hang up now, so I can tell George about it. He's sitting right beside me."

"George is going to love it. But remember, Val, the expenses won't be small. The paint has to be absolutely first-quality. You'll have to hire scaffolding, and people to put the paint on, maybe from the Codrington Colony."

"The very place," she said. "Look Matt, I've got to go. I want to tell my hubby."

"It has to be a first-class production," I said, "we insist on that."

Valerie exclaimed, "So do we!" Then she hung up abruptly. I chuckled to myself all the way back to the cottage.

The book Edie and I had been working on got sidetracked indefinitely after she took the decision to proceed with the mural. I still don't understand exactly what it was about the conception that attracted her so much. There couldn't possibly have been any element of competition with her mother's famous works. The two women painted in totally different, even opposed, styles. One of the things that pleased me about the undertaking was that visitors to the Codrington Colony, once they had digested Mrs. Codrington's twelve fabulous works, could make a short trip across town to study Edie's mural, comparing for themselves two wholly distinct notions of pictorial organisation.

I remember the summer of 1966 at the lake as a time in which I was continually retrieving sheets of paper from the

# The Scenic Art

sundeck floor, smoothing them out, then collecting them for my private amusement. Edie considered this a cheeseparing habit, probably psychologically undesirable.

"Those roughs have no value whatsoever. I can't think why you bother to hang on to them."

"I'm not keeping them with the idea of selling them," I said indignantly. "I'd never try to make money out of you, not that way. But I don't believe they're worthless at all, not at all. And I should think you'd be flattered by my wanting to retain them."

"Oh God!" she said.

But I was proved right when we moved back to town for the fall. I'd picked up and preserved in a file forty to forty-five pencil sketches and coloured studies in watercolour or gouache, and a few pastels, which she'd done in a great hurry through July and August. When the time came to describe the mural to the financial officers of Stage Stoverville, we had this material ready to show them.

This was just as well. The renovation of the theatre had cost tens of thousands of dollars. The final cost may have run into six figures, just how far into that bracket remained matter for conjecture, perhaps for subsequent investigation. The officers of the organisation were starting to feel their necks a bit, as the accounts came in for final settlement. They had to invoke a couple of penalty clauses in the sub-contracts too. The electricians had been behindhand, as the electricians always are in the completion of new circuitry, some of it heavy-duty wiring needed for the stage lighting. Plumbing had been well in arrears. Revenue from the first season of plays would be nowhere near what had been estimated. The Players' Guild had originally projected a full fall/winter season of eight plays, September through April, with professional directors from Montréal and Toronto hired for two of these productions. One of these directors had to be paid off without having done any work, because the theatre wasn't ready for September. Other losses were sustained for the same reason. By early October it was clear that existing financial conditions would not permit an eight-play season, nor would production facilities be available for any such elaborate undertaking. After several postponements, after workmen had to be booted out of the lobby with some show of physical force, after legal action had to be threatened to make certain sub-contractors returned to the site to do their contracted cleanup, it was at length clear that the earliest date at which a first play could be mounted in the renovated building was very late in November. When this was established for certain, the joint executive committee of the Players' Guild and Stage Stoverville (afterwards a united operation) held an emergency meeting in mid-October and scrapped the eight-play season.

A drastically truncated four-play season would be launched at the end of November with a production of *A Streetcar Named Desire*, a Stoverville première, with Valerie Essex in the leading rôle, the staging in her husband's capable hands, a company of local actors to undertake the remaining parts. Such a production could be presented at relatively low cost; no professional outside assistance need be engaged. Everybody in Stoverville knew how a southern accent sounded. The set could be minimalist in execution, possibly a vivid illustration of the virtues of economy of means. Anyway, *Streetcar* is actor-proof. Anybody knows that.

It was while this initial show was in rehearsal at the end of October that Edie's designs for her mural were shown to the now closely united officers of Stage Stoverville and The Players' Guild, united in recognition of admiration for the proposed mural, fused by bitter recognition of practical administrative necessity.

I have to explain now that the Players' Guild and Stage Stoverville had never previously been the same entity, either legally or in spirit and direction, at any time after the original decision was taken to re-model the Lyceum Theatre. The decision to re-model was unquestionably the brain child of Players' Guild people, Valerie and George Essex and the "theatre crowd" of Stoverville. Every population centre has a "theatre crowd." London, New York, Toronto, Stratford, Stoverville. And they are invariably the same blend of the talented and the less talented and the untalented, the able, the willing, and the emotionally crippled. Theatre crowds never

# The Scenic Art

vary in their elements, although the range of talent from the abysmal through the exalted is usually narrower in the smaller centres. Not always, though.

Valerie Essex might have functioned as a leading actress in any but the most rarefied theatrical atmospheres. She was no Vivien Leigh, but she could certainly play Blanche Dubois. George Essex was no Lee Strasberg—and a good thing too—for Strasberg could never have made a place for himself in Stoverville. I say this without the smallest ironic intention; irony would be grievously out of place in this summation. There are certainly national, and even local trends in stage direction, and Lee Strasberg was definitely not of the school of Stoverville. Nor would he have functioned acceptably at the Abbey Theatre, nor at the Old Vic, nor at the *Comédie Francaise*.

The theatre crowd of Stoverville had its roots in the English provincial theatre on the one hand, and the American little theatre movement on the other, both traditions perfectly appropriate to a small Ontario city in possession of an excellent theatre, a limited audience and limited funds, no new playwrights, and no fully professional actors. The members of the Players' Guild had almost all at one time or another done some work in or related to the professional theatre, or to the semi-professional university theatre. One or two of them had made radio commercials, another had played in summer theatre in the eastern townships of Québec. A couple of others had played small parts, years before, on CBC-TV Drama. Valerie Essex had been a promising leading lady at Hart House. Out of these disparate elements a small company of quite decent actors and actresses had drawn together. They had a place to present their work, a small amount of money for production expenses, one local stage designer of considerable competence and even originality, and the friendly backing of the local daily paper.

Among the elements of a really professional theatre, they lacked any sort of serious criticism, a committed and vocal audience who knew dramatic literature more or less well, any formed awareness of the value and use of art to society, and an original playwright or two, or three. There was no Synge, no

O'Casey, no Shaw or Chekov or Yeats or Strindberg, living in or near Stoverville.

I don't mean to offer a damaging criticism of the true worth of life in the city at that time or since. A society can't be tested only by the degree to which the theatre and the other arts flourish in its soil. But if this is a reasonable partial measurement, a bench-mark of the worth of Stoverville life, its geniality, its mental vitality, then the small eastern-Ontario city passes the test with an honourable rating, but does not stand high. It's probably impossible for a community of this kind to harbour any kind of original artistic and social independence, in the last third of the twentieth century. Eighty to a hundred years earlier, a few small cities in North America had achieved a qualified artistic independence. Hollywood is the most pressing example. A whole new form of entertainment which altered the life of humankind, with none but the most tenuous relationship to the French cinema, for example, sprang in the course of a decade from a town of a few thousand on the slopes near Los Angeles, itself a city with no claim at that date to metropolitan status. There are a few other cases, but on the whole the great art of modern times has been produced in the metropolis. Stoverville, no metropolis, has given us no new work in the theatre, but by the fall and winter of 1966/67 was capable of mounting a season of four plays with admirable competence, varying from production to production in excellence, but at a consistently better than adequate standard.

This development of a virtually professional standard of performance was what finally killed the Drama Festival movement. When the first organisations associated with the Canadian Drama Festival movement appeared in the early nineteen-thirties, there had been no permanent professional theatre companies in Canada whatsoever, except for touring troupes from England or from New York. There were scarcely any Canadian playwrights writing in either French or English. The Drama Festival movement began with muddled ambitions. Was it meant to create a class of professional actors and actresses, stage designers, lighting specialists, directors? Was it meant to promote the performance of new Canadian plays?

# The Scenic Art

Was it meant merely to perpetuate the ensemble styles of the English touring companies and provincial repertory theatres, or the completely distinct style of the commercial Broadway theatre? At that time there were no men and women in Canada with any clear understanding of these questions, much less their answers. Forty years after, there existed a large community of professionally trained players, a large number of theatre schools and faculties of drama, at least one professional theatre company in every large Canadian city, and the beginnings of a Canadian playwriting movement—without any writer of unquestioned gifts having been drawn into this development.

The evolution of this new professional theatre made the Drama Festival movement superfluous, and the institution withered and died, not too long after the notorious Dominion Drama Festival of Stoverville in April of Centennial Year. Perhaps the intense feelings and fiery competitive rivalries displayed on that occasion were the signal of a new birth in the country. One would like to think so, but the mists haven't yet sufficiently cleared away from the embattled scene for such a judgment to be made. What led up to that week of high drama, on and off the stage of Stoverville's new facility, was: incessant strife, grave misunderstanding, intrigue, diplomatic *va-et-vient*, psychological horror, civilised refusal to give battle, the works.

The testing stresses of that winter and spring began in October with the matter of the relative powers of the management of the completed theatre building (the Civic Committee for Stage Stoverville) and the company of actors who were going to use it, the Stoverville Players' Guild, who would probably be the only consistent paying tenants of the building. The proposed renovation of the structure had been set on foot by the Players' Guild. They had mounted three or four shows at different periods in the dusty, cobwebbed, shadowed house. In 1963 or 1964, they started a campaign to have the theatre redesigned for their use, as Stoverville's principal observance of Canada's Centennial. The idea found favour with the city's residents. It had the support of the *Intelligencer* and its publisher and editor-in-chief. There seemed to be a general disposition to let the actors take legal authority for the undertaking, but as soon as the question of ownership of the property surfaced, it was discovered that the corporation of the city of Stoverville held title, because of a long-outstanding lien against unpaid taxes. The previous lessee of the theatre, a small film-distributing company based on Ottawa, had been very glad to see the title to the building, in which they had no financial interest, clearly in the hands of the city and its legal agents. Nobody seems to remember who actually owned the property before it was taken over by the municipality, and that is a question—a fascinating question—into which I cannot allow myself to enter. All we need to know is that in 1964 the city owned the building and all its adjuncts, fittings, demesnes, stock and lot.

The city couldn't simply give the building or the use of the building to the acting company. The interests of the city's bond and debenture holders, and its ratepayers, were obviously at risk in any such proceeding.

Do I need to point out that it is because of this kind of reasoning that the arts don't really effloresce in Stoverville? I don't? Terrific!

A long, tedious, sometimes almost violent, wrangle was unwinding itself all through the summer and fall of 1966, from that day in July when Valerie accosted me in front of the theatre and gave me the news about the Festival until the dark and ominous Friday night in late October when the combined executive committees of the Civic Committee for Stage Stoverville and the Players' Guild met to look at Edie's cartoon and working drawings for the mural on the back wall of the theatre. It was their shared enthusiasm for the drawings that drew the rival bodies together—something I'd never have predicted. Edie and I were sitting in the foyer of the theatre while this final meeting was taking place in the administrative offices, just to the left side of the foyer and up the stairs as you enter. There must have been fifteen people at that meeting. The Civic Committee for the building included the mayor, two other members of city council, the city clerk, two representatives of the ratepaying electorate, both women and both friends of Valerie Essex, the head of the Stoverville

# The Scenic Art

Board of Education, and the chief librarian of the Stoverville Public Library. A very responsible and judicial body, though not perhaps a judicious one.

The executive of the Players' Guild comprised six persons, I think. Everybody was there that night. How well I recall it. They had been arguing for four months about how the enterprise was to be managed, as the renovations dragged on past one deadline after another, and the bills kept coming in, the estimates being exceeded. Cost overrun. A term which was to become part of the familiar vocabulary of private and public finance over the next fifteen years, now began to surface in the collective consciousness of these two bodies for perhaps the first time. All of the members of those two committees laboured for a year and more under the delusion that the extra and wholly unlooked-for costs were simply the result of the renovations having been carried out against a pressing deadline.

The overtime charges and the rising costs of materials, paint, electrical circuitry, lumber, the sudden unforeseeable leaps in price, the scarcities, the arrogance of skilled tradesmen. All these things were as marvels and wonders, signs, portents, to the citizens of Stoverville and their representatives. They believed that after the Centennial Year events would resume their customary character and pace. Prices would stabilise. Skilled tradesmen would learn, by gollies, where they got off.

The twinned executive committees never realised at the time, though a few of them grasped it later, that the birth throes of Stage Stoverville were an emblem of the changes in the metabolism of Canadian economic life which would produce the characteristic high inflation rate of the nineteen-seventies. Too many wishes chasing too few pleasures.

Without in the least understanding what was happening to them, and around them, in the summer and fall of 1966, these good innocent folk battled one another, each one quite sincerely wishing only the good for their city and their new theatre. Weeks, months, went by. No revenues were vouchsafed to help pay for the renovations. By late October it was clear that the two committees would have to merge in a single entity which should be responsible for both finance and artistic management. Edie's cartoon was the catalyst which effected this wonderful and, as it seemed, almost unthinkable union.

They all loved the sketches and the cartoon. It is true to say that some—many—of the details of the treatment of the faces in the layout weren't perfectly decipherable. The final realisation of the picture was to be on such an enormous scale, sixty feet by ninety, that the most accurate scale drawing could not give an unimpeachable account of the immense final effect when the panel should be unveiled.

We got summoned to the manager's office around eleven-fifteen. It was thick with cigar smoke; there had evidently been some drinking going on. Nothing scandalous, at the same time not typical of a council meeting. The ordinary respectable comportment of the town's executive officers had visibly been modified by contact with show biz. Everybody sat around in shirtsleeves. The ladies present had removed the jackets of their neat suits. I was surprised at the size and agreeable proportions of the room, which resembled a corporate boardroom. That the theatre didn't have a full-time professional manager was an extra surprise, when you considered the scope of these offices.

It turned out that there wasn't going to be a resident manager of that type. Executive authority for the emergent Stage Stoverville was to be vested in a board of directors, self-perpetuating, to take office as from this night, with three members drawn from the Players' Guild, three from the Civic Committee, and a seventh, the chairman, with a tie-breaking vote, to be named by the mayor and council after a brief period of public consultation. This whole arrangement sounds ominous, but in fact it worked extremely efficiently for the next several years. As Valerie remarked, the representatives from the Players' Guild were the only ones who knew the actual day-to-day problems of running a theatrical season. Their close technical know-how allowed them to bamboozle—her word—the city's people by presenting them with firm estimates, hard facts. And the first chairman of the board proved to be an excellent choice, no mere gavel-wielder, acceptable to both factions and a sometime amateur actor himself, an occasional yachtsman and sculler, never lucky in boats, Edie's old boon companion Dougie Crum.

Dougie and Edie had spent one particular happy hour together in the long ago, out in the middle of the river off the coal docks, clinging to the hull of the capsized *River Lady* while the upper laker *Lemoyne* stood by, hove to, ready to come to their assistance, an indelible part of Stoverville social comedy. Those two idiots had cost the steamship company thousands of dollars in lost time and fuel, to say nothing of the difficulty, even danger, in keeping a great vessel dead in the water in that current, in that narrow fairway. The *Lemoyne*'s boat fished Dougie and Edie out of the water and towed the waterlogged hull of *River Lady* into a salvageable location near the shore. In an hour the incident was over and the vessel on her way through the islands once again. In 1966, a score of years after this bit of adolescent tomfoolery, Dougie Crum was the big cheese at Stoverville Trust, and a director of the steamship line whose vessel had plucked him and Edie from the deep. Such, such, are the joyous ways of the coiling intercircles of Ontarian business and financial life. Dougie was the ideal man for the chairmanship of Stage Stoverville. He was related closely by marriage to *both* the Macleans *and* the Robinsons, an almost unique double-first which connected him by cousinage with just about everybody in the united counties who was ever likely to amount to anything fiscally or monetarily— his own choice of terms.

The only other candidate for the board chairmanship ever considered by the mayor of the epoch was poor old Bert Invergordon, a man long since exhausted by the fervours of the chase, now living out his span of years under the assiduous, watchful care of his fourth, *much* younger wife, in the huge limestone Invergordon fortress at the east end of town. Genial as he was, Bert could never have coped with the exactions of the frequent committee meetings. Dougie appeared to be a shoo-in, the right man in the right spot. He was there on the night that the merger of the committees, and the approval of the design for the mural, took place, in the capacity of either city councillor, or chairman of the Board of

Education. I forget which. If you stick around town long enough and keep your nose clean, you're apt—if you don't watch out—to serve in both positions more than once.

About midnight that night a unanimous vote of approval gave the go-ahead to the design for the mural, and funds were allocated for its completion. Edie presented her design to the united committee as her gift to the Centennial celebrations. In return we got a written statement guaranteeing the quality of the materials to be used, and the means of preserving the work in existence. I'm not sure that the members of the joint committee who voted the work into existence had any idea what the wall was going to look like with the mural on it full-sized. Sixty by ninety is an enormous space, and the little details given in the sketches would be blown up to overwhelming proportions.

Reviewing what happened afterwards with the advantages—always questionable—of hindsight, I can see that they understood the Shakesperian references in the picture, the explicit invocation of *The Tempest* as the source for the work, and the modified Shakesperianism of the costumes in which the three principal figures in the mural were clad. I still don't think that there was anything in the least disrespectful or satirical in those costumes. They were simply executed in a kind of neo-classical style, not in the norms of present-day dress. Given the subject, 'The Genius of Politics Introducing Dramatic Art to its Ideal Counterpart,' it seemed perfectly appropriate that Prospero, Ferdinand, and Miranda might stand for these three personifications. Prospero as the genius of politics. Ferdinand as Dramatic Art. Miranda (the wonderful one) as the Ideal Counterpart.

The problem for the designer was to select modes of costume which would not too much suggest Malabars of Toronto, or the provincial Shakesperianism of the Earle Grey Players. What robes should these ideal beings wear? I still maintain that Edie's solution was perfectly acceptable and well within the canons of good taste. What was wanted was something Grecian, something Keatsian perhaps, timeless and classical.

She had to grapple with that conundrum while the affairs of the Players' Guild surged rapidly onwards, now that the constitution of the joint committee was agreed upon. *Streetcar* was already in rehearsal, the theatre ready for occupancy, the "Joint Board" solidly in place. It was the Joint Board which now gradually gathered to itself all authority for the many functions which were to be presented in Stage Stoverville, public meetings, conferences, small conventions, art exhibitions, presentations of travelling musical events of various kinds, all that. As soon as the organisational disputes were resolved, the usefulness of the renovated theatre building became clear. It was seldom dark for as much as a week after that, some sort of event or other proving available for exhibition almost continually, often on terms highly favourable to the Joint Board.

One of the successes of later years was a newly fledged concert series which presented young artists from the conservatories of Montréal and Toronto, touring on a concert circuit which included Stoverville, Kingston, Belleville/Trenton, Port Hope/Cobourg, Cornwall and Sherbrooke. Pianists, violin and piano duos, a piano trio, string quartet, vocal ensembles, the whole range of a professional concert series: they all came to Stage Stoverville, and after a couple of seasons were a consistent draw, one of the unlooked-for surprising successes of the Joint Board. Friday night, to everybody's astonishment, became accepted in Stoverville as the night for chamber music. The concert series became one of the indispensable features of a Stoverville winter season.

The Players' Guild productions, however, were from the first the most important revenue-earners for the Joint Board. It was not much more than three weeks after the fateful October night on which all difficulties seemed to be settled that they obtained the use of the stage for final rehearsals. The opening night of the very first semiprofessional production of the Stage Stoverville Players' Guild (now the official name of the company) took place on Friday night, November twenty-fifth, to a tumultuous reception, one of the landmark events of modern Stoverville history. For once we got everything right.

The whole evening worked out like clockwork. To begin with, the renovated theatre looked marvellous, splendid, ornate. The caryatids, the scrollwork, the volutes, the swags, all the rich traditional plaster trim, had been picked out in gold or silver. The walls were shining clean. All the seats had been repaired or replaced, and were covered in heavy dark blue plush which conferred an agreeable warmth. The stage curtain had been repainted according to its original Arcadian design; all the lights sparkled. The house was sold out. A full house in the new seating arrangements was eleven hundred and twenty-eight, less comps and house seats. There were no standees, as the sale of standing-room had been vetoed by the Fire Department. There were no empty seats anywhere that I could see.

In the packed foyer, one saw *le tout Stoverville*, my dear! Simply everyone was there. The mayor of course, and every member of city council, all looking singularly uncomfortable in their formal attire. I don't seek to give the impression that these were rented dinner clothes, for they weren't. Most of the richer businessmen of the city possessed a tuxedo at that time, for wear at the Country Club or at various holiday functions or superior funerals. Opportunities for dressing up were limited however, and Stovervillians were as a rule ill at ease in boiled shirt and starched collar. Wives fared better in dinner dresses of real elegance, the most striking of them obtained through the good offices of Sallee Lennox, herself attired for the opening night in a *tailleur* of great distinction.

Edie had allowed the Joint Board to mount some of her sketches for the mural in the foyer, as the first of the many art exhibitions which were to be housed there over the following years. There were about a dozen black-and-white and watercolour renderings on show. I noticed no small number of the opening-night crowd going from one work to the next, spelling out their titles, and examining the details of the sketches with close attention. This seemed genuine interest, which I took for a hopeful augury. And the play itself was a great triumph.

I'm not that crazy about the writings of the late Tennessee Williams, I'm bound to admit. I don't think that he ever really detached the narration of his own emotional confusions and his fantasies from the actions represented in his plays. Much of the success of any production of *Un Tramway Nommé Désir*—to give the delightful French title of the work—will depend upon the spectator's gradually increasing suspicion that Blanche is an expression of male homosexual passivity. Her dependence on the kindness of strangers has far too distinct overtones of the sort of kindness to be found in the lavatories of bus stations during ambiguous sexual encounter. She isn't like any woman ever to be encountered on land or sea, but she very much resembles the sort of diffident uncertain, not very young, male homosexual much written about in the period following the second World War. Blanche insistently recalls characters like those in the fiction of Gore Vidal or James Baldwin who seek out rough trade in the delicious expectation of being buggered, beaten up, or both. And what is to be said of Stanley Kowalski, if not that he is such a not-very-young person's fantasy of extremely rough trade? Kowalski is the archetypal dockworker or sailor or marine or leather-clad motorcycle cop, sadist and rapist, whose sexual orientation is the more ferocious as it doubts itself. This is the right way to read *Streetcar*. It seems difficult to believe, but this is the way the Players' Guild performed the work. Valerie Essex had very little in her appearance suggestive of homosexual youth, but for whatever reason, whatever nuance of lighting or vagary of costume or coiffure or gait, she recalled to everybody in the audience (at some or other level of perception) just such a personality. Valerie is a beautiful woman, but the costumes, and one particular costume—a slip, stockings and pumps—and her slender blondeness, and something in the set of head, arms and shoulders, insistently recalled a little male in his twenties.

This impression wasn't specific or named; nothing in the text underlined it; there were no sneering or hinting intimacies. But the performance had an inexplicable nervous heat, an edginess to it, that made the audience discomforted and responsive, that uncomplaining and encouraging cluster of tired businessmen and nice women. They may not have understood what was being done to them, but they certainly loved it. The romance of the defenceless 'invert' appealed to them at a perceptual level very rarely discovered in Stoverville life, and they responded by voting the production a triumph and sending their friends to see it in great numbers. During the two-week run, people came from all over the region, from Kingston and Cornwall, Smith's Falls and Gananoque, from as far away as Belleville/Trenton, to see the play.

At some point towards the end of the first week a reviewer from Ottawa saw the play and wrote it up in the *Journal*. Since none of the actors or crew received any payment, the play made money and paid quite a handsome return to the Joint Board. No rental had been charged for the use of the theatre; the maintenance staff were paid by the Joint Board, and the production costs, royalties, costume rental, purchase of makeup and other incidentals, were borne by the Players' Guild. Box-office receipts were paid directly to the Joint Board, who then returned a pro-rata percentage of the total to the Players' Guild to subsidise further productions. This arrangement had the great advantage of taking the Players' Guild out of a purely amateur situation and giving some continuity to its season. If the standard of quality of the first show could be maintained through several plays into further seasons, the venture might prove self-sustaining. Eventually a native playwright might emerge to provide the group with script material which reflected local life. This development would probably occur a long time in the future; there could be no question of risking an Eastern Ontario play during the first few seasons. In fact such an event has never yet come to pass.

There was one small technical problem in the production—otherwise triumphant and universally approved—of *Streetcar*. Accents. It seemed as if every amateur actor in the Stoverville region had his own idea of a southern accent, which he or she claimed was the right idea, no other need apply.

I have often noticed that every Canadian thinks he can do a southern accent, and no Canadian ever does one in the smallest degree convincing. The producers of *Streetcar* never thought of bringing in somebody from Louisiana to vet the

# The Scenic Art

rich variety of accents which the production yielded. The fact is that people from eastern Ontario are uniformly unconscious of the rich, thick texture of their own accent, so distinctive a mixture of Protestant Scottish and Irish English, so immediately audible if you don't happen to come from there. A Stovervillian, or some lad from Arnprior or Pembroke or Perth, will tell you that he speaks a neutral English, neither American nor British, but the fact is that he speaks something strongly reminiscent of the dialect of an Orange conventicle in Glasgow or Belfast. I suppose nobody ever hears his own accent.

The Players' Guild continued to have problems with accents, in their second and third productions of the first season. Nobody seems to have mentioned to them that the southern speech of *Streetcar* as they gave it, had been ludicrously unlike any actual southern American dialect, whether black or white. There must be dozens of dialectal variations of southern English. Perhaps there are hundreds of them. And anyway it was a mistake to give Stanley Kowalski a southern accent. I always wondered why they did that.

I was never closely in touch with Players' Guild internal affairs. I took it for granted that George and Val were running the show, but there were sixty or seventy other people actively involved in Guild affairs, and it may have been some other element in the organisation which plumped for the next choice of play. This was in fact a double-bill, an evening of Irish theatre with *The Shadow in the Glen* as the curtain-raiser, and a very very enchanted production of *The Countess Cathleen* as the main event. The second production under the new dispensation was probably doomed to relative unsuccess, after the triumph of *Streetcar*. Valerie took no part in the Irish double-bill, and George didn't direct either play.

The Irish material came on late in January, when a third show was already in rehearsal, as if an insurance policy against a failure was desirable. I've always suspected the Guild wanted to have something ready to rush into the breach, should the two Irish plays fail to make a favourable impression. At the same time, it suggested a will-to-fail to announce, even before the Synge/Yeats evening came on, that a "surefire New York comedy hit" was to be the third production of the season, in the event the old Holm and Abbott laff-riot *Three Men on a Horse.*

The two Irish plays were just too goddam literary. As somebody said in another context, "I don't think real poetry is ever as poetic as this." The actors had poetry coming out of their ears. I would not try to make good a claim to have heard any actual begorras, or references to the wee folk, but notorious Irishisms hovered in the air awaiting utterance during performance. Audiences were kind, fairly numerous, but never really taken out of themselves, and there was the recurrent problem with accents. Everybody imagines he can do an Irish accent (Sure and tiz the foine toime yez'll be havin', ochone, ochone, ye've kilt me darlint bhoy intoirely) just as everybody thinks he can do a southern accent (Sho'ly to goodness, honeychile, ah' jes' love y'awl.) He can't, and he shouldn't be encouraged in the delusion, particularly if he happens to be a semi-professional actor working in a little theatre in a smallish community. I would not have tried Yeats and Synge on a Stoverville audience, then or now.

What would I have tried? To have great art you have to have great audiences. What sort of play was the right sort of play for Stoverville round about 1967? Maybe there wasn't one. To perform plays, you've got to have audiences that really like plays, really care about the strangely distorted language and speech of the theatre, as provincial Italians really like the tenor voice raised in florid aria, as businessmen profoundly approve of Monday night NFL football.

I do not know how or why social forms or art forms generate that kind of understanding and commitment, but I do know that there was no such natural understanding and commitment to the real arts of the theatre in Stoverville in 1967. People there went to the theatre out of a more or less vague sense that they were doing their duty to the community, for which they expected a return in this world or the next. Or they went half-expecting to see their next-door neighbour, or that girl who sang in Saint Saviour's choir, make a fool of herself. They might have gone because they had a relative in the cast, or simply out of curiosity. But they did not go for the same reasons that impelled them to watch Hockey Night in Canada on TV—surely the true native cultural form of group commitment and enjoyment of that period in central Canada. Churchgoing too provided opportunity for common worship and enjoyment, but the histrionic arts? Uh-uh. Not then, and probably not now, in Stoverville or Toronto or Montréal. Certainly not for most people. The theatre in North America is invariably "in the hands" of an interest-group. The group varies, but the social captivity is a constant. In New York the theatre is "in the hands" of the ticket brokers, and managers of group theatre outings for out-of-towners. In London in the nineteen-fifties it was securely in the grasp of the H.M. Tennent organisation, though there was a residual commitment to agreeable social comedy mounted by independent producers for the dwindling band of admirers of Ben Travers or Dodie Smith.

Folks in Stoverville, as in most other places in Canada, go to the movies or watch TV or go to church (if they're into middle-age) with unreflexive simple enjoyment. There are still a surprising number of people around who actually enjoy churchgoing. They meet their friends, hear the news of the past week, make themselves feel virtuous—a feeling never to be scorned. There is, in short, a felicitous, perfectly genuine sociability about churchgoing, or moviegoing, or TV watching, in Canada, that isn't characteristic of the theatre or ballet or opera or other musical events, or at poetry readings. These latter goings-on are cultural, not sociable; you aren't expected to enjoy yourself, and you don't enjoy yourself. I have met few Canadians who actually derived pleasure from observing ballet performances, and fewer still who enjoy the cavortings of the mime. The arts of the drama are minimally more popular, but partake really of the nature of lip-service to moral self-improvement.

I have no idea where the reading of books stands in this order.

But I do know Synge and Yeats were not the stuff to give the troops at Stage Stoverville in Centennial Year. Nowadays in our community theatres we give the troops regionalist plays about old-time murderers, work-plays exhibiting the emergence of our native peoples into critical self-consciousness, exhibitions of female insurgence, semi-mime plays in which actors become tractors, always with intensely boring effect. Canadians hate being entertained; they fear it. Official Canadian cultural policy seeks to replace entertainment by cultural uplift, wherever gaiety and good spirits show their charming selves. We are never, by any mischance, to feel good about ourselves. Succeed as an entertainer, and you will be driven out of Canada with oaths and curses echoing behind you. Think, only think, of those disgusting repellent sermonettes which the CBC televises as dramas. Docu-dramas. Works about people who have "prolms". Urban prostitutes of all sexes, drug addicts, the Dene nation, oppressed women in clumps, and of every size and shape.

So if I were to propose a season of plays for Stoverville in Centennial Year, or at the present time, I would not know where to begin. The third play of that inaugural season was a decent gesture in the direction of simple entertainment, *Three Men on a Horse*, a charming and exceedingly agreeable farce-fantasy about a pudgy young accountant in Brooklyn who discovers one morning that he can predict the winners on the day's racing cards, while travelling to the office on the bus. He's called "Irwin," and the name is always pronounced "Oiwin" in any production of the work; this is traditional in the rôle. I've never seen the play on the stage. I missed the Stoverville performances. But I've seen the movie, one of the best screen comedies of the middle-thirties, starring Frank McHugh and Joan Blondell, and boy, is it endearing! You can't dislike the story or the actors, especially when you remember that the States was only beginning to come out of the worst after-effects of the great Depression. Escapist fantasy? A poor clerk who can guess today's winners? I don't think so. The social comment is never overt. The play and the film functioned perfectly when they made you feel good, feel pleased, feel that things aren't as bad as right-thinking people claim. The exact same function was discharged by the Rogers/Astaire movies, which had no redeeming social teaching whatsoever. There was nothing to be done with them but look at them. Why *should* anybody dance? Yet those movies pos-

# The Scenic Art

sessed and communicated an extraordinary airy grace, which was the product of weeks and months of disciplined, arduous rehearsal. As a boy, I supposed that Astaire's routines were improvisations, that he just walked into them, and invented them spontaneously as he went along. I still find it hard to believe that this wasn't so. In much the same way, I imagined that Groucho Marx ad-libbed his lines. I had no notion of what civilised controlled art went into Groucho's effortless spontaneity.

I was once invited to dinner at the home of a poet-professor in Toronto, a small affair, only six of us sat down, the poet and his wife, a well-known historian and his wife, Edie and me. There had been a gala week of ballet performances in the city, and all the talk was of this *entrechât* or that *pas de deux*, conversation to me stupefyingly boring and pretentious. At one moment just before we went in to dine I seized the opportunity to remark how much I hated and despised the classical ballet, that it was the flower of that most repellent of societies, late Czarist Russia, that nobody should encourage young girls down the path of tortured metatarsals and anorexia, that the whole tradition was alien and offensive to our lives. I then stated that the greatest dancer of the century was unquestionably Fred Astaire, and that any honest person who had ever seen him perform would at once acknowledge this.

Gasps and horrified silences. Warning grimaces from Edie. I might as well have mooned the horrified dinner party. And yet, much later in the evening, replete with the poet's good food and softened by friendly chat, the history professor drew me aside in the hall, looked round warily for his consort, then mumbled, "You know . . . what you said about Fred Astaire . . . you know, you're right."

Shortly after this he began to weep nostalgically and had to be taken home.

Very hard to get a Canadian to admit how much he has loved Fred Astaire. To a Canadian that perfection of form, that joyous grace, that insouciance and savoir faire, that evident and obvious sense in which Astaire is primarily a matchless comic dancer, these elements of life are deeply suspect, and we are fobbed off with ballet dancers whom nobody really enjoys. Who are the great performers of our century in North America? Astaire. Crosby. Cagney. My God, Jimmy Cagney, what speed, what purity of definition. Jimmy Cagney is the only movie star I know, Astaire set apart as a special case, whose style of speaking and movement dictated the actual cutting of his films. The rhythm of the edited shots is visibly determined by the way Cagney moves, by the brilliant poetic rhythm of his reading of his lines. Speed. Verve. Comedy. Even when Cagney is acting the part of a killer, his rhythm is always light, up on the balls of his feet like a boxer or a dancer. He was an excellent dancer, and like Astaire's, his is a comic presence, as his persuasive performance as Bottom, in Reinhardt's *Midsummer Night's Dream* demonstrates.

There have been Canadian entertainers with gifts resembling those of Astaire and Cagney, though none of that importance—and don't talk to me about Mack Sennett and Mary Pickford. Sennett, a master of body movement and comedy rhythm, did none of his work in Canada, and neither did Mary Pickford, and anyway Lillian Gish was the greatest actress of the silent screen. But there have undeniably been great Canadian entertainers—never *in* Canada. Who has there been, on the Canadian stage, with the exuberance and presence of Astaire or Cagney or Olivier or Jean-Louis Barrault? This range of experience is denied to Canadians; we refuse it, we won't allow ourselves to have it.

Try to select the appropriate season of four plays for Stoverville in Centennial year, or any year, and see what you can come up with. I can't do it. I wouldn't do Shakespeare, I'll tell you that, and I wouldn't do any Canadian play that I can think of except one or two of James Reaney's. I certainly wouldn't undertake an entire season of Reaney. I think the difficulties are clear enough. We have no performance tradition of our own. We have no committed and eager audiences. We have no dramatists of more than very minor gifts. (A Rick Salutin Festival? A Michel Tremblay Festival?) There seems to be an instinctive, rooted fear of the dramatic impulse and the scenic art, set into the hearts of Canadians, throbbing between systole and diastole. This is not necessarily a Bad Thing. Israel is not a people of the drama. Islam repudiates the drama. The Covenanters found no good in it. I can get by without it.

A season of four plays for Stoverville without any accents, not southern, not Irish, not Brooklynese? Let's see, what can we pick? I think I'd open with *The Kildeer*, follow it with *Claude and Gertie* and *Luther*, and finish with *Three Sisters*. The Players' Guild really would have some hope of getting through the first three of these with few scars, and those honourable. I don't feel certain about the Chekov, but at least you can do it in the ordinary speech of eastern Ontario, a region much like that evoked by Chekov's masterpiece.

I have always thought that the Russian drama of provincial life suits Canadian companies and audiences right down to the ground.

So there's a choice for you. A fantasy-play by a really good Canadian poet; a comedy by a Canadian writer permanently resident in England—and my brother, God love him—a play about the origins of the Protestant mentality, and finally a play in apparently naturalistic, simple speech, which happens to describe eastern Ontario with great exactitude, while remaining one of the two or three greatest masterpieces of the drama since Shakespeare and Molière.

I would not choose any Shaw play for my imaginary Players' Guild of this or any year. Shaw bores my ass off; his moralism and his detestation of sexuality, his cockiness and inhumanity, the interminable debates, the dated issues . . . away with him, let me not see his ugly red beard, or his any other parts. And if by mischance we are to grapple with GBS, let our choice of play not fall upon *Man and Superman*. And if—which God forbid—we should undertake a production of *Man and Superman*, let us at no time set ourselves up to rival Charles Laughton and his drama quartet by including the monstrous third act of the play in our production. I should have thought that reflections like these would at once cross the mind of any director undertaking to do this piece in modern times. But not the Players' Guild. Oh no! They decided to crown their first season with a production of a major modern classic, as they thought. So they produced *Man and Superman* (idiots, knaves, proud boasters) with Valerie Essex as Ann Whitefield—tragically miscast in my opinion—and George Essex directing and playing Mendoza, the bandit, who is transformed into the Devil in the celebrated third-act debate.

I don't know how many people remember the First Drama Quartet, founded and taken on tour by Charles Laughton in the early nineteen-fifties. I'm not absolutely sure that I remember who the other members of the group were, but memory proffers the names of Cedric Hardwicke, Charles Boyer, and Miss Agnes Moorehead, and memory seldom errs.

If these were in fact the four players involved, the rôles would obviously have been distributed like this: Boyer: *Don Juan*. Laughton: *the Devil*. Hardwicke: *the Statue*. Miss Moorehead: *Dona Ana*. What Laughton did with that ghastly third act was to produce it as a very carefully directed dramatic reading, with the four players in evening dress, each one standing at a lectern with a script in hand. After a few moments they would set aside the script and start to act out the roles, at the same time preserving the illusion of a static reading; there was no attempt to dramatise the lines with movement or broad gesture. An occasional use of handkerchief, or flourishing of wrist and hand was permitted, not more. In this form, the *Don Juan in Hell* scene was an extraordinary success, and it spawned a series of successors which toured the continent in rehearsed dramatic readings: *The Caine Mutiny Court Martial*; *John Brown's Body*.

Laughton was a great actor and director. More than that, he had a highly ingenious moral intelligence. He originated and perfected in one leap a form of dramatic entertainment which nobody else has practised with similar success. Certainly the Players' Guild were not up to the challenge. They made two serious mistakes at the start. They treated the third act as an interpolation having nothing to do with the rest of the play, and they rehearsed it apart from the rest of the cast, treating it almost as a separate production. In effect what they had was a three-act production of *Man and Superman* in period

# The Scenic Art

costumes, plus a long dramatic reading of *Don Juan in Hell*, done in modern evening dress as a wholly independent piece.

What they ought to have done was to cut the play ruthlessly, and incorporated the third act into the main action, if they meant to do it at all. They didn't have any actors as good as Laughton, Boyer, Hardwicke and Moorehead. They simply weren't up to the exigencies of the highly artificial form of the dramatic reading. If they had pared their show down to about two hours, twenty minutes, NOT four hours, then disaster might have been averted. But nobody ever consulted me about this, and there was no reason whatsoever why they should have consulted me. Edie and I had our hands full by this time with the preparations for putting the mural on the back wall of the theatre, which had been pointed and scoured and primed in the previous November. At the end of February two more coats of priming were applied, and fortunately the spring of 1967 was dry. The scaffoldings were put up at the same time as rehearsals started on *Man and Superman* and *Don Juan in Hell*. I recall that the actors used to come out of one of the emergency exits at the back of the stage area to watch the painters at work and try to guess what the final image would look like. This they were unable to do because the paint was applied in a highly unusual way.

Photographs of the provisional sketches of the picture were now commonplace in Stoverville; some of them were still on the foyer walls in the theatre; others were displayed in the Public Library and at the offices of the Board of Education, but the full scope and application of the pictorial image was still highly secret. Edie chose to use a very heavy, rubber-based, exterior glossy enamel, in the primary colours and black and white, with occasional hints of green. The effect of the finished work was meant to be that of a giant piece of pop art, an image bigger than that of Graham Sutherland's gigantic wall-hanging behind the altar of Coventry Cathedral, which is about seventy feet from bottom to top, and is the second largest picture I can call to mind. Edie wanted to suggest a mammoth imitation of a frame from a comic strip, somewhat in the manner of Lichtenstein, though without balloons of dialogue.

The workmen started from the top of the building, working on twin scaffolds side by side, enlarging each successive two-inch square to the proper proportions, in the colours which her code-sheet dictated. They painted downwards for a day, left the new paint uncovered overnight to dry, then returned to the freshly painted squares on the following day and applied a thick second coat. Working in this way, covering up the image with tarpaulin as they proceeded down the wall, they were able to keep the total image in its final appearance a secret until the formal unveiling took place.

The painting and the work on *Man and Superman* went on simultaneously, but the actors met the public first. They took the three-act version of the play to Ottawa for the Eastern Ontario Regional Festival, where they won the competition without working up a sweat; there were only four entrants, and the other productions, even the entry from the Ottawa Little Theatre, *Hay Fever* treated as a gay romp, were not really up to competition standard. Triumph at the regional level dictated an appearance, as the host organisation, at the Dominion Festival—the resemblance to the playoff system in Stanley Cup competition was clear, and was probably encouraged by Festival officials. Late April is hockey playoff time in Canada. The Stoverville win at Ottawa was discussed in the Kingston and Stoverville dailies exactly in the language of post-season competition in the NHL.

STOVERVILLE ADVANCES TO FINAL
*SUPERMAN* PICK OF CHAMPIONSHIP SERIES
SMART MONEY ON SHAW ENTRY IN
BESSBOROUGH TROPHY SHOWDOWN

These headlines sound as though I'd invented them with some satiric intention, but that is not the case. Each of them appeared in an eastern Ontario newspaper, and not on the entertainment page or the sports page, but on the front page where, for once in a way, a cultural event was the hot story of the month. The Dominion Drama Festival wasn't front-page news when it was held in Toronto or Vancouver or even Winnipeg. But to editors in Kingston or Cornwall, Ottawa or Stoverville, the final playoff round for the Bessborough Trophy (presented like national prizes for football and hockey by a Governor-General) was a two-week-long circus, bringing onto a local stage many persons of national and even international prominence. It must be noted that there were five daily newspapers in the region at that time, including three with nationwide reputations for excellence. There were three television stations, each of them mainstays of their respective networks, two CBC affiliates and a CTV station, CJOH, the voice of Seaway Valley, broadcasting on channels eight and thirteen.

Eastern Ontario, after all, lies almost at the centre of the most highly developed and complex communications network in human history, that of the American and Canadian northeast. Just as you can reach the New York State Thruway or the Pennsylvania Turnpike or the American Interstate system in a couple of hours' drive from Stoverville, so Stoverville is bang in the middle of an enormous population and its radio, TV, newspaper and wire-service network. Because Stoverville—a very small city—is a couple of hundred miles from Toronto or Montréal, doesn't mean that it is an isolated outlying burg, not these days. Tastes, manners, opinions, moral judgments, in Stoverville in 1967 were probably just slightly behind the standards of Columbia University or the campus at Berkeley. Stoverville didn't join the revolution but it certainly knew about the Beatles and Richard Nixon.

Immediately after the Players' Guild won at Ottawa, the final schedule for the week of the Dominion Festival was released to the press. It went like this: the Festival would be preceded, on the afternoon of Monday, April twenty-fourth, by the formal unveiling of Edie's mural. There was a great to-do in the national press about a completely fictitious rivalry between Edie and her mother, what used to be called "media hype." I don't know who started the story that Edie was burning to show the world that her mother's notion of visionary art was outmoded, superseded, and unsuited to the spirit of the 1960s. I suspect that George Robinson's office may have had something to do with the circulation of this base canard. Whatever the source, the media gave the unveiling tremendous coverage, largely because the Prime Minister was to perform the unveiling with Adam Sinclair at his side, and perhaps Sadie MacNamara too. Sadie's monkey movie was in release just at that moment, playing to capacity houses. Some kinky people may have expected her to show up at the Festival opening wearing her furry makeup. In this they were to be disappointed.

After the unveiling there was to be a formal dinner for the Prime Minister and his suite, the adjudicator and his consort, if she showed up, the directors and certain executives of the competing theatrical troupes (but not their actors), and for the newly named Minister of Justice, who had been Mr. Pearson's other Parliamentary Secretary—together with Uncle George—until a few weeks before the festivities, but who had just been named to the Cabinet, much to George Robinson's chagrin. That this great dinner was to be tendered by Uncle George himself at Robinson Court, now the headquarters of Festival Week, was no adequate solace for his wounded feelings. He had not hoped to be named Minister of Justice; he'd wanted Trade and Commerce or at the very least Revenue. But nothing was forthcoming at that time; this gave the opening banquet an undertone of tension which may have had much to do with what ensued.

After the banquet, and sundry irregular cocktail parties for actresses and actors, there was to be the first-night gala performance, a presentation by Pile of Bones Workshop, of Regina, of their all-new production of their adaptation of the famous Canadian novel *Who Has Seen the Wind*. It was felt by everybody that the opening of the Festival in Centennial Year must feature a Canadian play; there probably couldn't have been a better choice.

Tuesday night was to include a performance in French of *Le malade imaginaire* by Molière, in the impeccable style of the Montréal company *Les petits frères de l'enfant Jésus*.

Wednesday night: the University of Manitoba Dramatic Club from Winnipeg with Pinter's *The Caretaker*.

Thursday night: the London, Ontario, Little Theatre, with *Who's Afraid of Virginia Woolf*, in a production which, as events showed, overstressed unduly the play's homosexual subtext, much as the Stoverville production of *Streetcar* had done.

Friday night: a company from Calgary whose name kindly time has erased from memory, in a wretched performance of *The Taming of the Shrew* in Western costume. Aha, I've remembered the name of this troupe: Stampede Theatre.

And then on the last night of all, beginning half an hour early at 8:00 PM sharp, the host organisation's gala production of *Man and Superman* with the third act included for this performance only. We were to be exposed to the integral version of Shaw's text, and never mind how long it took to get through it.

I don't think I've ever seen a small city of some twenty to twenty-five thousand souls so flooded with publicity coverage. It was as if the Second Coming of Jesus had been announced, either for the official opening of Expo 67 or the unveiling of Edie's mural, and nobody knew for sure which it was to be except perhaps the Holy Ghost. We had priority as to date in Stoverville on that cool bright April twenty-fourth. The opening of Expo was to come on the following Friday. Media interest in the Montréal event would peak later in the week, but on Monday Stoverville had the attention of the wire services and the TV networks and the regional newspapers pretty solidly concentrated upon the local scene. I've never before or since seen so many microphones on a Stoverville lectern.

The crowds started to gather on the parking lot at the back of the theatre by ten in the morning, though the unveiling wasn't slated to take place until two-thirty. There wasn't a cloud anywhere in the sky. The temperature was around sixty-five, with a light breeze blowing. No predictions of rain.

There was one small technical hitch. The rear doors of the theatre, through which the materials for each of the six Festival productions had to be delivered, were blocked by the temporary platform erected for the unveiling ceremonies, and there were occasional clashes between security guards and stage managers from Regina and Montréal about mode of entry to the rear. Fortunately it proved possible to prise open a seldom-used fire door on the east side of the building, through which entry could be effected, the offstage storage areas gained. We didn't want too many deliveries going through the rear doors anyway, since truck wheels raised dust in the parking lot which might adhere to the fresh paint of the unveiled mural. There was already a tarry crust, mixed with dust from the gravel, beginning to build up at the bottom of the wall, which had been brushed and scrubbed clean some months before. The whole vast expanse of paint was hidden by tarpaulins suspended from sturdy piping fitted just below the roof line. There was a pull-away release cord attached, which led down to the speakers' platform. A tug on the cord by the Prime Minister would trigger the clips which retained the tarpaulins, which would then fall away to either side of the wall, revealing the whole expanse of the picture in a few seconds. Attendants were stationed at either corner of the building to gather in the fallen coverings and remove them instantly, as the crowd caught its first sight of the mural.

The cloudless sky and the position of the afternoon sun ensured that the picture would be brightly illuminated, without direct rays falling on the surface to cause glare. We couldn't have wished for better weather for such an event. You could see from the way the sun fell on the tarpaulin that the picture would receive an agreeable even light without distorting shadows. There are no tall trees at the back of the theatre to cause unwelcome shade, and the ground slopes down from the parking lot towards the river in such a way as to make the building highly visible from the decks of passing vessels. An ideal location.

A bit before two PM the dignitaries began to assemble on the platform . . . not too many dignitaries because it was a small platform. I had refused to mount it, preferring to stand at the back of the crowd a goodly distance from the formal proceedings. I'm no dignitary. I thought, and I still think, that the mural is so big that you have to be quite a long way away from it if you're going to take it all in. You can't make too much of it if you're standing right below it. I don't believe that Adam, for example, ever got a really accurate impression of the effect.

By two-twenty-five there were two remote trucks for the TV networks all set up and ready to shoot, stationed to either side of the back lot, with sound equipment, stationary cameras mounted nearby on pylons, shoulder-held cameras moving around the edges of the crowd, which I estimated at just below four thousand. Nobody came by with loaves and fishes. But you could peek in the doors of the remote trucks and look at the monitors and listen to the chatter of the switchers. It was rumoured that the CTV crew were providing a feed through the facilities of WWNY, channel seven, Carthage-Watertown, to NBC in New York. If this was true, it was most likely because of the promised appearances of Sadie and Adam.

Very promptly at two-thirty a group of the elect appeared around the corner of the building in a straggling row, herded along by the Mayor and by Dougie Crum in his capacity as chairman of the Joint Board. Dougie was wearing his morning clothes; the stiff collar made him look exceedingly uncomfortable. Others in the party wore less formal attire. Edie looked unostentatious, inconspicuous, sardonic. Mr. Pearson looked exactly like himself. The Minister of Justice, for whatever reason, appeared impatient and ill-at-ease. He stood next to Adam Sinclair who had, like the Prime Minister, the public personality's faculty of being immediately recognisable in any attitude.

There were a few speeches. The Mayor led off, keeping his address tactfully and mercifully short. George Robinson came next; he had his customary comic difficulties with the sound-amplification system, but managed to communicate some effective observations about the key position of Stoverville in the tri-cities triangle. His views were received with applause and real enthusiasm by the crowd.

Adam didn't speak.

I kept looking around for Sadie but there was no sign of her.

Edie was asked to say a few words. It was getting on for three-fifteen by now, and the usual late-afternoon breeze was getting up. It was hard to catch more than occasional phrases.

". . . originally my husband's idea . . . owe him every credit for the conception . . . the theatrical associations . . .

Shakesperian elements the best in English drama . . . our national heritage . . . prominent figures of stage and screen . . . political wisdom of our leaders." She stopped, looked around nervously, and retired to the rear of the platform.

The Mayor gave an encouraging nod to Mr. Pearson, who stepped to the front of the platform, seized the release-cord with both hands in the manner of a man much habituated to opening bridges, pronounced a formal invocation in words which I didn't catch, and tugged briskly at the cord. It worked like a charm; the two halves of the veil were rent apart and fell at once to the ground, where they were bundled up and unobtrusively removed. We all craned our necks and gazed up at "The Genius of Politics Introducing Dramatic Art to its Ideal Counterpart." Slowly at first, and then with increasing vigour and volume, the crowd, now in numbers about five thousand, began to chuckle, giggle, chortle, snicker, laugh outright, hoot, howl. Edie carried off all the honours of the afternoon, the rest nowhere. She had given us an inordinately funny, really comic, play on Canadian politics and art.

Everybody had been aware that the Prime Minister and Adam Sinclair appeared in the picture, and that Sadie Mac-Namara was likely represented as well. What nobody had grasped from the sketches was the laughable accuracy of the three caricatures which identified the three personages present in the picture. They were plainly identifiable as Prospero, Ferdinand, and Miranda. Mr. Pearson appeared as Prospero, the Genius of Politics, right in the middle of the picture in the strongest stage position, holding Ferdinand (Adam, Dramatic Art) paternally by one wrist with his left hand while introducing him to Miranda, who stood in an upstage left position, embodying the Ideal Counterpart of the histrionic impulse; this was the Sadie MacNamara image. What nobody was quite prepared for was the almost Bugs-Bunnyish brilliance of line in the portrayal of these three figures. Their execution strongly evoked the great days of the Warner Brothers animation team of the late nineteen-thirties and early forties, the days of Bob Clampett, Michael Maltese and Friz Freleng. One looked for Daffy Duck to make a

# The Scenic Art

sudden appearance, perhaps in the costume of Ariel, which would have been perfectly appropriate to the scene as represented. The designer of the work, known widely as an admirer of the art of animation, and as a proponent of the Warners group in particular, had resisted the temptation to introduce Bugs or Daffy, Porky or Elmer, perhaps for reasons having to do with copyright; there was no Ariel figure anywhere in the picture.

There was however a teeny-tiny Caliban away down at the left corner of the frame. This mythical, purely Shakesperian earth-monster was presented like a midget in a gorilla-suit, a figure strongly suggestive of the demonic underworld.

The thing that surprised me most about the mural was the prominence of certain details when enlarged to this size, hints and half-statements which had been almost invisible in the scale of the sketches. The most striking and persuasive of these elements was the strongly pop-art feeling of the whole panel. Everything in it looked as if it had been designed for a feature-length animated cartoon of *The Tempest*—not at all an untenable artistic conception—which had been brought to the late stages of the art-direction, then abandoned, perhaps because of cost. The picture might have made a billboard for such a production, with a promotional legend splashed across it:

ADAM SINCLAIR AND SADIE MAC NAMARA IN WILLIAM SHAKESPEARE'S *THE TEMPEST* WITH LESTER PEARSON AND FEATURING BONZO AS CALIBAN . . . COMING SOON TO YOUR NEIGHBOURHOOD THEATRE . . . A WARNER BROTHERS CARTOON FEATURE

The enormous size of the mural brought other details into sharp realisation. The costumes worn by the three figures were a bit too sharply stylised for audience-comfort. There was more than a hint of the science-fiction Saturday-matinée serial of the nineteen-thirties, with Mr. Pearson in a costume perhaps best suited to Doctor Huer in *Buck Rogers* or Doctor Zharkov in *Flash Gordon*.

Adam Sinclair, representing Ferdinand, and Dramatic Art, looked strikingly like some caped crusader of the comic books.

The ideal Counterpart of Dramatic Art, the wonderful girl, Miranda, unquestionably a penetrating caricature of Sadie MacNamara, had more than a suggestion about her eyes and her dependent spit-curls of the early-thirties cartoon personality, Betty Boop.

The effect of the mural was slow to realise itself fully, but after some moments of inspection by the audience in the parking lot, a very large number now began to cheer and stamp their feet rhythmically. They laughed and shouted and in every way signified their approval of the work. I noticed the TV crews busy at their tasks, attempting to move the heavy pylons with cameras mounted on them back down the side street as far as cables would allow, so as to get better wide-angle shots of the building, taking in as much of the scope of the mural as possible. The effect on colour television must have been dramatic indeed.

The dignitaries on the platform seemed to have formed widely divergent reactions to the work. Standing right there next to the surface, it must have been hard for them to look up at it so as to get a unified impression of the whole. Whether or not they liked it, they would have at most a partial impression. They would have to return to the site later in the day or week, taking up a position at some remove from the building, in order to absorb a total and unified impression. Their first reactions were obviously not definitive, but they were certainly varied. You could tell this from the way they stood. Mr. Trudeau, the new Minister of Justice, was poised with his back to the audience, which now began joyfully to disperse. Mr. Trudeau had his head bent between his shaking shoulders. It was hard at first to judge what emotion had moved him; then it became clear that he was choking with laughter. Mr. Pearson's behaviour gave nothing away. He moved easily among the crowd of notabilities, shaking the extended hands, and exchanging polite conversation with those around him. George Robinson had turned an agreeable shade of purplish-red, whether from the rising breeze or from suppressed emotion could not be determined. Adam Sinclair stood rooted to the spot, his head angled sharply backwards as he studied the expanse of painted brick above him, seemingly estimating whether or not Sadie had upstaged him. On that score he could have no complaint. His neatly caricatured features were almost too plainly visible. Edie had rendered him in a perfect caricatured likeness; any filmgoer in the English-speaking world would have said at once, aha, Adam Sinclair. The likeness was a handsome one, even flattering in certain respects. At the same time it had aspects that a critical viewer might receive with disfavour. The rendering of the features could not conscientiously be described as virile or masculine. There was a stealthy roguishness about the glance and the attitude of the figure of Dramatic Art.

Perhaps any figure representing Dramatic Art must contain hints of the enacted, the cleverly simulated, a touch of rôle-playing, of the *roman a clé*, even a smack of what might be described as closet-drama. These nuances were all present in the rendering of Adam's features. They hadn't been visible in the sketches, and I resolved to demand of Edie how this had come about. I looked for her but couldn't spot her; she had evidently slipped away among the now rapidly dispersing crowd. As a figure familiar on King William Street from long residence, she could readily sink into the background, attract no unwelcome attention. A celebrity attracts no autograph-seekers on the streets of his native place, as Jesus knew.

I was obliged to content myself with a consideration of Adam's posture from afar off. It was clear that he was none too pleased with his own appearance as given by Edie, perhaps because his wife had received such sympathetic attention. Where Mr. Pearson had been treated as a sage of science-fiction, and Adam's emotional orientation was left widely open to question, Sadie had been treated with magnanimity, even with pardonable exaggeration of her unquestioned beauty. There were suggestions of all the fairy princesses of popular culture: loose flowing tresses, a bosom delicately full, a slender waist, clearly an ideal evanescent loveliness. There was little of the caricatural in the portrayal. This was possibly an early, not-quite-conscious manifestation of the articulate feminism of the following decade. I met Edie at a cocktail party hosted by Dougie Crum towards five that afternoon. We were to dine with Dougie and his wife, then proceed to the theatre for the formal opening of the Festival proceedings, including addresses by Mr. Pearson, the president of the Dominion Drama Festival organisation, and Dougie himself, as representing the host company. It had fallen to Dougie to present the adjudicator to the audience, a task which I did not envy him. We expected to see Adam at Dougie's party, and Sadie too. But Sadie had not yet arrived in the city and Adam was nowhere to be found. Edie and I spoke about him briefly at Dougie's place.

"You were a little hard on Adam, weren't you?"

She eyed me guardedly. "I've never been really keen on finding the boys in bed with my husband."

Thirteen years ago, I thought. "He wasn't in bed with me in any but the most technical sense," I said stiffly. "He met with stern rebuff at all points."

"I should hope so."

There was sharp feeling in Edie's rejoinders, and I chose not to pursue the matter. Not long after we decided to forgo dinner with Dougie on some pretext, and left the party at the stage of the second drink, in some instances the third, when hilarity was beginning to supplant nervous and mental fatigue in the assembly.

We walked across town at riverside, intending to approach the theatre from the angle at which the mural would be seen from the water. It was the first week of Daylight Saving time; the light was still almost that of mid-afternoon. We strolled up the slope from the river around six-fifteen. We could see every part of the mural. The image gained greatly in precision and definition at this distance, much the same way as coloured slides of paintings give them a hard-edged sharp focus, greater clarity of composition than the ordinary gallery prospect. I was delighted to see how fresh and shiny the paint looked, and how bang-on the colours were, the reds really red, the blue and yellow devoid of obvious subtleties but full of attack. The picture really did look like an enormous rendering of a full-page layout in a comic book, and the flavour of *Flash Gordon* was intensified by distance.

As we drew closer we noticed a single figure moving irresolutely around in the parking lot as if seeking a favourable viewpoint for inspection of the picture, yet finding none. It was Adam Sinclair, and his step was unsteady. This seemed an unpromising augury. We gave him an exaggeratedly wide berth as we came up the street on the east side of the theatre. Towards seven PM we were seated in a neighbouring Chinese restaurant poking at egg rolls, waiting for the dinner for four for two. Chicken with almonds, fried shrimp, sweet and sour, an unsettling repast. The bits of paper embedded in our fortune cookies in no way partook of the gnomic or sibylline. Mine said, "Help, I am a prisoner in a Chinese bakery!" Edie's was darker in tone. "A dark man loves you from a distance." We laughed a lot at this. I'm not as dark as all that.

By now men clad in dinner jackets and ladies in long dresses were filing past the front window of the New Nanking Grill; some of them gazed in at us attentively, nodding in uneasy recognition. We paid our bill and attempted to merge inconspicuously into the throng; in this we were partly successful. We got past the television cameras and lighting standards, and the microphones of CKSI without incident. Unfortunately the series tickets which we had been given were almost exactly in the middle of the front row, the piano in the orchestra pit and the conductor's podium directly in front of us. There was no loss of visibility, as we were looking slightly upwards at the playing area, but we could be seen from all over the house, and our seat-mates in the front row were persons of real celebrity of local, national and international repute. Edie and I found our own exposed location discomforting.

The Prime Minister and the Minister of Justice were seated exactly in the middle of the row. George Robinson and the Mayor of Stoverville, and their ladies, were on the other side of them. Dougie Crum and his wife were next to Mr. Trudeau on his right; then there was an empty seat. I think it must have been reserved for Sadie, who was expected to turn up from one moment to the next, flying in from Toronto in a two-engined, propellor-driven Beechcraft. The Stoverville airstrip will not accommodate jets. Next to Sadie's empty place sat Adam, and next to him were our two seats. All these folks were already in place when we came in.

As this was the front row, it was simple for each person in turn to slide along the front of the row in order to mount the stage and say a few words. An unspoken agreement at once established itself between me and Edie that I must be the one to sit next to Adam. I could not have exposed her to a weeklong emission of radiation such as issued from his physical presence. Adam was sitting scrunched in a ball, his head immobile, as if the vertebrae of his neck had somehow locked in place, making rotation of cranium on shoulders impracticable. He said nothing to us as we seated ourselves, indeed seemed scarcely aware of our presence as the introductory speeches went on. There were only four of them.

Dougie Crum spoke first, as chairman of the Joint Board, welcoming this distinguished audience. He would say no more than that he was proud above all things to have been asked to take the affairs of Stage Stoverville in hand. This was going to be a never-to-be-forgotten week. We had with us tonight . . . he called upon the mayor to invite our Prime Minister to open the Festival officially, but first—he had forgotten to do this—he would simply mention that our adjudicator, the distinguished star of stage, screen and television, Mr. Adam Sinclair, would provide a short preliminary assessment of the merits of the individual productions after the final curtain of each performance. Audiences were urged to remain in their seats until Mr. Sinclair had concluded his remarks each evening; they promised to be of the highest interest to lovers of the theatre. A full and final adjudication would take place at the conclusion of the Saturday night performance of *Man and Superman* by the host company. And now, without further ado . . .

The mayor, and Mr. Pearson, and George Robinson (quite unbidden) mounted to the stage, where the mayor, a tactful and diplomatic gentleman, requested our local MP to introduce the Prime Minister, just in case he needed to be

# The Scenic Art 235

introduced in Centennial Year, largely his invention (cheers), though introduction of Mike Pearson must now be superfluous in any gathering. The mayor concluded his remarks and returned to his seat. George Robinson, to everybody's surprise, said little. He wished only to present to the throng a man who ... and he developed the "a man who" form of words for three or four minutes before concluding with the phrase, "the Right Honourable Lester Bowles Pearson, PC."

The Prime Minister spoke very sensibly for less than three minutes. He was especially pleased to see how strong was the representation in the Festival of entries from western Canada, something which, he managed to suggest, demonstrated the close ties of his party to the interests of that part of Canada. There was also present a French-language troupe, possibly some of its members were in the theatre tonight—he hoped that they were—who would perform Molière *dans la langue de Molière*. An adjudicator could not have been named of greater accomplishment and judiciousness than that famous star, whose performances at Stratford, Ontario, as elsewhere, were rightly famous, Mr. Adam Sinclair (applause). It was to be hoped that Mr. Sinclair's lovely wife would favour us with her presence at some point in the course of the week. While he could not be with us, most regrettably, for every performance in the Festival, he promised to attend on the closing night, this coming Saturday. Everyone would understand that Stoverville's great sister city, the metropolis of Québec, *la ville de Montréal*, would naturally expect him to be present at the inception of their great Centennial Year undertaking, the world-renowned Expo 67. But he would surely be with us again on the day after Expo 67 opened, and he wished all the competitors in this year's Dominion Drama Festival the very best of Canadian luck.

The actual performances began with this note of competition strongly present in the audiences' thoughts. At the end of the week prizes and trophies would be awarded in numerous categories: Best Actress, Best Actor, Best Supporting Actress, Best Supporting Actor, Best Director, Best Production, Best Scenic Design, Best Performance of a Canadian Play, plus a number of others whose specific nature escapes me. There was a genuine, hard-fought competition going on all week, very much like the competition of professional sport, perhaps a tennis tournament in which the "seeding" arrangements are laid down by the organisers of the tournament so as to favour, quite openly, the competitors whom the paying customers will want to see in the finals. You never want to see your big box-office draws knocked out in the early rounds, and you therefore arrange matters so that they don't run into formidable competition too early.

In a somewhat similar way, the productions which come early in any Festival week are not expected to go anywhere in tournament competition, so to speak; they're in there to fill out the program, give pro forma representation to some chronically dissatisfied region of the nation, perhaps to be fobbed off with some minor award, Best Canadian Play (often Only Canadian Play) or Best Stage Lighting. The token French-language show often gets worked in towards the beginning of the week. And any production which has to follow four or five opening-night addresses faces an almost insuperable obstacle—the problem of obtaining the attention of an audience already overstuffed and drowsy with food and drink and bored out of their skulls by crypto-political observations from dignitaries. This word "dignitary" doesn't really mean what it purports to mean. It really means "person who bores your ass off at the openings of things."

Pile of Bones Workshop of Regina were not able to overcome this handicap with their version of *Who Has Seen the Wind?* The text of the play, clearly related to an excellent and widely known novel, lacked the spaciousness and mysterious openness of the book. Perhaps Mr. Mitchell's book goes better on the screen than the stage. In the nineteen-seventies it received an adequate film treatment which, however, broke no box-office records. The movie had a lot of visual breadth; you could see a long way across its photographed prairies, and it conveyed vividly the vertiginous feeling, often a characteristic of the smallest prairie settlements, of an immense space beginning at the end of the next block, just at the edge of town, a treeless unhedged immensity where the sky seems to press upon the ground. In Saskatchewan townsites of these proportions, Aylesbury or Pense, I have sometimes experienced the eerie conviction that eternity begins just overhead or just around the corner of the next street but one.

No stage version of the novel can convey this radical space-vertigo; it is simply too shut-in, too obviously taking place in a built-up enclosure, for that actual reeling motion of the head, neck and shoulders to be induced in performance. The notorious difficulty in production of the cliffside scene in *King Lear* will bear me out. The scene is described to Gloucester by Edgar as though they two were standing at the edge of an immense drop—which of course cannot be presented onstage, though it might be in a film. Edgar has to *trick* Gloucester into believing that he has cast himself from this great height and somehow miraculously survived his fall. The scene can only with great tact be brought before an audience. "Hangs one that gathers samphire, dreadful trade."

Adam's remarks that night, perfectly forbearing and well considered, dwelt on the problem of realising a sense of spatial immensity, of infinity, on a small stage area in a walled theatre. He considered briefly the supposed advantages in this respect of outdoors theatres, and rejected them because of difficulties in projecting subtleties of speech. He spoke about the notorious problems of the Shakesperian chronicle plays, particularly *Henry V*. "Can this wooden O contain the very casques that did affright the air at Agincourt?" He demanded rhetorically, supplying a negative answer. He said that he would like to see this cast in a movie made from the novel (none of them appeared in the later film version). He raised a laugh in the audience by admitting that Pile of Bones Workshop appeared to be a shoo-in for at least one major award.

He was less tactful and accommodating towards the company which appeared on the Tuesday night, *Les petits frères de l'enfant Jésus*, from Montréal. It appeared that Adam knew next to no French, that he considered it a ridiculous affectation in the Festival organisers to throw a sop to official bilingualism by including a French-language play in what was really an English-Canadian enterprise, founded by a British Governor-General, the Earl of Bessborough, with whom the people of Québec could in the natural order of things feel no true sympathy. Was anybody in tonight's gathering really entertained by watching a play in a language of which they were totally and cheerfully ignorant, trying to laugh at the right time at jokes which they didn't really find at all funny? The production values of this performance were solidly in the tradition of the French theatre, quite foreign to what audiences in Canada and the United States were accustomed to. There had been a good deal of silliness, frippery and frou-frou, which he personally was prepared to allow a certain validity in a Parisian production of the work, but not perhaps in one from Montréal. It seemed to be perpetuating a performance tradition which meant nothing in North America. Much more to the same effect.

The adjudicator's voice wavered and lost volume from time to time that night, and his hearers were unsettled by the rambling, and unnecessarily political and sociological implications of many of his remarks. It was the opinion of most of the audience that dramatic criticism was one thing, and political comment another, especially during Centennial Year. Thank God Mister Pearson hadn't heard those remarks about official bilingualism.

Sadie still hadn't turned up. Her empty front-row seat loomed like some grave philosophical vacancy of Heideggerian or Sartrean stripe in the ontological structure of the event. Forgive the language. Well . . .

People opined that Adam Sinclair and Uncle George Robinson were sitting up late together every night at Robinson Court. Why didn't they get out more?

The Wednesday night show was the first one which some wiseacres tipped as the winner of the award for Best Production, Best Direction. *The Caretaker*, presented by the University of Manitoba Dramatic Club, obviously included in its cast no contender for the Best Actress award, but it did exhibit an amazingly solid grasp of the necessities of ensemble playing, of timing, by the three college students who took the three parts. The players who personated Aston and Mick were particularly good, their rôles better suited to their years than that of the old vagabond Davies. The actor who played Mick, the smallest part in the play, was especially good. Of course Adam had played the rôle himself in the West End, in the original production of the play, replacing Alan Bates. He spoke at the conclusion of the Festival performance with nostalgia, and with a recurrence of the wandering, rambling, quality to his discourse, which had alarmed and in part alienated some of his listeners the night before.

"Love this play . . . *love* love *love* it. Gorgeous dialogue. Simply gorgeous. Non-professional can't see what's involved. I tell you, lies in the mouth like maple syrup. Take that speech where Mick describes the renovations in the kitchen. He's never going to renovate that bloody kitchen. He knows it. Davies knows it. You and I know it. Aston of course is a stunned bloody cunt, right out of it in some fairyland of his own. You talk about your lobotomies. That second-act curtain speech of Aston's is the greatest dramatic speech in modern drama in English. Very tough to put across, I can tell you. The pauses . . . my God . . . those . . . pauses. You can hear the audience trying to fart quietly. You know, everybody, I played Mick in *The Caretaker* in London in 1960. I can't say I created the part, but I was close. Just before that disaster, *Claude and Gertie*. But that's all ancient history; you don't want to hear about that cartload of old rubbish. I'm not going to go on about that. I'm going to put it behind me. Rise above it. Ancient history. The fellow who played Mick tonight, whatsisname? Got my notes here somewhere (business of fumbling in dinner jacket pockets) aha, here they are, the little rascals. He should have described that kitchen interior just a little more lovingly. You want to push the idea that he's just as obsessed as the others. The voice of pure reason, he ain't. They're all bonkers. As a matter of fact, I don't believe there's any such place as Sidcup. Sidcot. Whatever. That's a P.G. Wodehouse name. You can't really trust anybody."

Thus, and much more, Adam on Pinter.

The University of Manitoba looked like a pretty good bet for one of the major awards, maybe Best Performance, Best Production, something like that. Opinion swerved even more strongly in their direction after the events of the ensuing two nights, which were widely open to interpretation; neither of the presentations of Thursday or Friday night rising to more than very modest standards of excellence, both giving great offence to the adjudicator.

On Thursday night the London (Ontario) Little Theatre favoured Stoverville audiences with their production of *Who's Afraid of Virginia Woolf*, then almost a new play, just in its first season of availability for amateur and little-theatre performance. Somehow the director of this presentation had gotten lodged in his head the notion that the two main characters, ostensibly husband and wife, are *really* (what do stage directors mean by this word?) a male homosexual couple. Their shared fantasy about a dead child comes from the depths of their sexual infecundity. I believe that some such rumour about another Albee play, *Tiny Alice*, was then in circulation to the effect that the author intended this title as a reference to the term for the male buttocks, in homosexual cant.

I've never met a male homosexual—or a female one, for the matter of that—who referred to people's rear-ends as "Tiny Alice," but let that pass. The fact of the matter is that the director from London (Ontario) had decided that *Who's Afraid of Virginia Woolf* had this congeries of hidden meanings, this gay *subtext*, as they say in the theatre. It has never been clear to me how anybody can fix the exact limits to the ambiguities embedded in the dialogue of a play in such a way as to be able to state specifically what the subtext is. Certainly any work of narration of the smallest degree of artistic sophistication will have what used to be called undertones (or sometimes overtones) of implication which allow for variety of interpretation. This is a commonplace. To go from there to the position that the undertones or overtones of the text supply a parallel subtext which is as precise as an inner voice in a written-out fugue, and as audible, is probably not defensible; it is invariably wise—and I put this forward as a general rule—to stick pretty close to what the words say. If the play is set on the seacoast of Illyria—there being no such place—you choose some actual seacoast as an analogy. You don't conclude that because there is no Illyrian seacoast, you can produce *Twelfth Night* as though it were taking place in present-day Toronto, or up in a balloon, or in the *art-déco* interiors of the *Queen Mary* in 1935. You can't arbitrarily lay it down that Feste is gay, that Olivia is fat and fifty. There are limits to these so-called undertones or overtones, which bungling stage-directors regularly transgress, giving rise to what one great critic has called "the theatre of the Bright Idea" in a famous essay entitled "Doing Shakespeare Wrong." That was the American critic Eric Bentley, also celebrated for his work on Shaw, *The Playwright as Thinker.*

Now just as there is a theatre of the Bright Idea which ruins much Shakesperean production (Tony Guthrie himself not exempt from its glittering attractions) so there is of the plays of Albee, which seem to lend themselves to bizarre and indefensible readings. *Tiny Alice,* for God's sakes! The Thursday night production of *Virginia Woolf* was particularly rich in idiocies which somebody had mistaken for Bright Ideas. George was portrayed as the passive partner in this putatively homosexual union, Martha as a slob drag-queen. Gee, but it was awful!

Nobody can understand the inner structures of homosexual experience but those who have undergone it, but everybody can guess that two conditions press harshly on the homosexual man as he grows older, in contemporary North America: the sense of the impermanence of affection, the difficulty of sustaining it into the last part of life, and the necessity of childlessness. It seems likely that grave and tormenting loneliness must still be the lot of the aging homosexual male. I've never been able to see this as particularly "gay."

If Albee's plays, and *Virginia Woolf* in particular, are parables of homosexual marriages and their inevitably sterile and deeply alienated consequences, we might expect to find this suggested somewhere in the texts. I've read over *Who's Afraid of Virginia Woolf* from time to time, and all that I can figure out about Martha is that she is female, female, female, if anybody is. On any other interpretation Elizabeth Taylor's success in the part becomes a bitter and crude joke at the expense of the actress.

I've got Adam Sinclair on my side. The production of *Virginia Woolf* offended him deeply at some visceral level of apprehension. He was shaking visibly when he got up to go onstage with his notes at the end of the performance. Once or twice during the evening I saw him sneak a snifter from a pocket flask when the house lights were down. I don't want to go into what Adam said. I felt so sorry for him. There were moments when he seemed in the position of a fox at bay, with the pack snarling at him. He wasn't perfectly steady on his pins, but I think most of us wrote that down to fatigue. By this point in the week we were all feeling the strain; it was the most hysterically intense week in the history of Stoverville, if you ask me. There were murmurs, more than murmurs, of displeasure at Adam's failure to deliver formal and lucid assessments of each production as they succeeded one another. I've often wondered since if certain local wiseacres weren't perhaps making book, or taking small private bets, or running a pool on the results of the competition. All decisions were in the adjudicator's hands, and in the case of most of his provisional remarks after the individual shows, you could form no clear idea of the awards he might make. It was, however, clear that the London (Ontario) performance had affronted him deeply. Punters in the back rows must have laid off their Albee wagers overnight.

Friday, April twenty-eighth, dawned bright and clear, football weather. You half-expected men in striped shirts to be standing on King William Street blowing the whistle for the kickoff. There was about the whole Stoverville Festival an irremediably sporting atmosphere, a touch of the Stanley Cup playoffs or the World Series, some great contest of the turf. Thousands cheered. That Friday was a day unlike any other, charged as it was with the expectation of the citizens of Stoverville that those bastards in Montréal would persuade the Prime Minister to stay there over the weekend, wining and dining him amongst throngs of international notabilities who had assembled for the opening of Expo 67. He wouldn't show for the closing of the Drama Festival, said the wiseacres. He was the captive of the notorious Mayor Drapeau and the celebrities, and that new Minister of Justice who seemed always at his elbow. Lots of Stoverville people stayed glued to their TV sets to watch the opening of Expo 67, which went off wonderfully well. The weather, the huge crowds, the brilliant and bizarre collection of pavilions, the airy minirail, the Bucky Fuller Dome at the U.S. pavilion, the mythology of Man and His World, gleamed and glittered on millions of screens, including those of all the citizens of Stoverville who held series tickets for the Drama Festival. So the Calgary Playhouse performance of *The Taming of the Shrew* went on that night under doubly adverse conditions. The audience was over-excited and inflamed with Centennial Year/Expo 67 passions, and—as they say in the show business—the curtain was up.

It said in the program that the old farce was to be given in costumes appropriate to the Calgary Stampede; this notation alone sent a chill through the members of experienced playgoers. I saw quite plainly the shudder which passed along Adam's limbs as he contemplated his program as the house lights dimmed. Months ago in Calgary it must have seemed a Bright Idea to capitalise on the popularity of Shakespeare's worst play—unless it be *The Comedy of Errors*—by performing it *en travesti*, in clothes wholly unsuited to the text. When Petruchio made his entrance preceded by a rocking chuckwagon, connoisseurs of Shakesperean performance tradition at once gave up the game as lost. *Shrew* attracts the stage director who is full of Bright Ideas, but really, there's a limit. There has to be a limit! Stampede costumes? I couldn't believe my eyes. I thought Adam was going to choke to death over his emotions.

When I assert that *Shrew* is a rotten play, a really shitty play, I mean that it is a bad play *by Shakespeare*, and that a bad play by Shakespeare will be better than the best play by anybody else, Chekov and Molière alone excepted. I'm no Bardolator, but I'm perfectly able to see that Shakespeare is by much the greatest of dramatists. I would not have the temerity to assert that *The Taming of the Shrew* is a worthless play. It holds the stage. I suspect that it is Shakespeare's most often performed work. It forms the sub-structure of an enormously popular musical comedy which *is*, I think I may say, a worthless piece of shit. I've seen *Shrew* done by children, by film stars, by clowns, by college girls, by highly gifted actors, by the inmates of a lunatic asylum, by nuns, by apprentices at a famous theatre-school.

I've seen it done on a bare stage, and with several elaborate sets, as a musical révue, and as a treat for SM freaks who really dug the spanking scenes. Like all of Shakespeare's work the play has some mysterious quality of universal appeal. I confess to certain mixed feelings whenever I catch sight of women staring, fascinated, at poor Katharine kicking as she is held firmly in place across Petruchio's knee. Sexual spanking has its place in the hearts of most of us, though not in the heart of A. Sinclair. The scene I have in mind seemed deeply repellent to him. And I noticed once more his sudden recourse to a flask concealed in the recesses of his dinner jacket. He would bob his head down like some feeding bird, and ingest fluid with a half-sucking, half-swallowing movement of the head. At least he wasn't on something more immediately deranging like coke.

When the curtain fell on this most lamentable comedy, Adam was visibly almost beside himself. He spoke little from the stage that night, contenting himself with a brief review of other ways to approach *Shrew*, seeming to hold that there is now no viable way to bring the work onstage and that it had therefore better be left alone. Do some easy Shakesperean play, like *Hamlet*, he seemed to imply. Or perhaps *Lear*.

Later that night Edie and I looked in very briefly at a party for the players from Calgary given by Sallee Lennox in the hinder parts of her shop on King William Street. Sallee had some sort of family or perhaps financial connection with one of the producers at the Calgary Playhouse. I caught some snatches of dialogue between the director of the night's performance and Sallee herself. She is a knowledgeable theatregoer, by no means untutored in her tastes, certainly not a doctrinaire feminist, and it was clear that she had been distressed by the disagreeable nuances of certain attitudes to women implied by the Calgary production.

"But it's in the text, it's in the text," the director went on exclaiming. "Shakespeare probably detested women. I mean, I'm sure he was gay."

"You're a fool, Simon," said Sallee succinctly, and I'm sure she'd put her finger on the sore place.

We mustn't judge of the inner persuasions of our dramatists; we must take only what they offer, their words. Sometimes we shouldn't even take all their words. We oughtn't, for example, to accept every last word of *Man and Superman* as integral and necessary to performance of the play. It shouldn't be given in its entirety; it is cruelty to animals to allow it. In a brisk performance, keeping ingenious production effects and Mozartian musical interludes to an absolute minimum, *Man and Superman* requires more than four hours to get through, even if you risk doing it with a single intermission, in which case you place an intolerable strain on your audience's collective bladder. Nobody can sit through *Man and Superman* comfortably without peeing twice.

Saturday night, last night of all, and Sadie still hadn't appeared. The empty seat between Adam and me remained what it had been during the whole week, repository for Adam's coat, notebook, texts of various plays, a clipboard at which he sometimes scribbled frantically between the acts. I deposited nothing on the empty seat, would have quailed at the notion of placing some blocking article where the divine Sadie might be expected to sit. By Saturday night it was clear that though the Prime Minister had returned to Stoverville as promised, in the company of George Robinson and Pierre Trudeau, who were sitting beside him along the front row to our left, Sadie had not risen in the night. Waiting for Sadie, I thought to myself as I scanned the program, an almost metaphysical state. Immediately after I had this thought, I noticed the statement in the program that the play would be performed in its four-act text, and I rose at once, scrambled over Edie and the people to her right, and made for the gentlemen's lounge. I wasn't going to risk sitting through the first half of the play with nothing on my mind but the frantic need to urinate. I remained in the Gent's until the last possible moment, rejoined Edie over the muted protests of our neighbours, and seated myself in time to hear the powerful opening lines of the play:

RAMSDEN: Shew him in.

THE MAID: Mr. Robinson.

From unpromising beginnings, unrewarding goings-on. A word of counsel to amateur actors: if you want to do classical English comedy, do Wilde and fail. Don't do Shaw and fail. It is more honourable and more pleasurable to fail with the genuine article than with the false glee of the intellectual. What were we supposed to make of *Man and Superman* in 1967? Its dated intellectual fireworks (Nietzsche, Samuel Butler) and its laboured parody of Mozart. The *longueurs* of that intolerable third act! We had had no warning and had neither recourse nor remedy. Few were those who took their courage in their hands and bolted during the single intermission, probably because the audience had no notion what further treats were in store.

It seems in retrospect an inexplicable act of artistic impudence, egregiously over-confident, for the Stoverville Players' Guild to have undertaken rivalry with Laughton, Boyer, Moorehead, Hardwicke. They weren't up to it. I don't think I've ever seen a man of the theatre so nearly beside himself with amazed and affronted artistic revulsion, so utterly discomforted, as Adam Sinclair on that night. The occasion was an instance of the horror and the terror produced by failed art. From about 10:00 PM onwards I harboured misgivings about how the night must end. The performance occupied four and a half hours, beginning at the stipulated early curtain time of 8:00 PM. It was long past midnight when the curtain fell on the conversation of the newly betrothed pair.

ANN: Never mind, dear. Go on talking.

TANNER: Talking!

Shaw's stage direction calls for universal laughter. But the only laughter that night was the false and contrived mirth of the persons onstage. No sound rose from the auditorium barring, here and there, soft snores. The curtains parted; the

# The Scenic Art

rehearsed curtain call was enacted once, twice, no more. The performers left the stage to await judgment. Then Adam Sinclair mounted to the stage and spoke.

He stared down at us for long moments, and finally said, "Sadie, eh? Everybody's dying to see Sadie. I'm dying to see Sadie myself, come to that. I want the key to the beach house, and never mind community property settlements. Tony was right, you know, he said straight out from the start, 'Stay away from the little Schatzenberg, Sinclair, she'll drink your blood.' He had the goods on her, Tony knew. He didn't know about some things but he knew about her all right, Tony Guthrie, that is. Always talked like a sergeant-major on the drill square. 'You horrible little man, you,' he used to say, and then I'd always get it right. Tony . . . or am I thinking of Tony Goderich, maybe that's it, maybe it was Tony Goderich who warned me to stay away from the girls, that awful Strathdrummond, that Millen woman, and you, Edie. Yes, you!! I see you down there. Think you're just such a smarty-pants, don't you, with your caricatures fifty feet high, think I don't know what you're on about, protecting your precious little hubby from the lads. I wish Binkie could get a look at you, my pet, poor Binkie, he was always so kind to everybody. He wanted to put on *Claude and Gertie* and that's as much as you could say about any man; he was the noblest old queen of them all, he'd have put money into *Claude and Gertie*. My only limited success, well, call it my only failure, twenty years in the profession, but one was enough. It's done for me, I tell you, I'm done for, sob, boohoo, crocodile tears. How did I ever let myself get mixed up with those Goderiches anyway? Tony warned me, 'Stay away from the little Schatzenberg, Sinclair.' That must have been Tony Goderich in 1960 when we did *Claude and Gertie* at the Criterion. God that was a stuffy theatre, full of stuffy stuffy people and that stuffy stuffy Canadian play. Binkie must have been mad for me or mad for Tony, it's the only rational explanation, and Tony wouldn't give Binkie a tumble because Tony's just mad for someone else. 'The one I love belongs to somebody else.' I'm not telling, you won't get a syllable out of me, but this little dickie bird knows something he won't tell, no no no not a teeny smidgen of a tale from me. Nobody messes with Kid Sinclair of the White Horse Tavern and gets away with it, you varmints. Stick 'em up! And the first one who says, 'Stick what up?' gets plugged right in the family jewels. Oh Sadie, Sadie, you've put paid to my account, and here we all are, me and this gaggle of Robin Goodfellows, Puck U. The hockey players' university. Waiting for Sadie. It sounds like something by Sam Beckett, and the ending's just the same, Sadie won't appear tonight, not on this stage nor on any other stage, because the divine Sadie has left me and taken the family jewels with her, not that they were ever up to much, you get my drift, baby? Tony told me not to take Sadie, but no, I had to have a cover, I thought people would notice if I stayed single, I had to have a girl around with those awful things sticking out in front of her like cold mutton. Well, the thing of it seemed to be that she'd agree to it. She knew it was a press party; we needn't have anything to do with one another just so long as we framed the marriage lines and hung them over the four-poster. Mrs. Adam Sinclair, isn't that a hoot, my darlings? There's only one person anywhere in the world who might pass as Mrs. Adam Sinclair, and it is not Sadie MacNamara. Man delights not me, no, nor woman neither. Women to Grimes are an enigma, so you can take it from me, you lovely creatures, that Sadie will not ring tonight, Sadie is not going to appear, the little monkeyface, the little lucky piece. Waiting for Sadie but Sadie ain't going to show, that's the hell of it, Godot ain't gonna rain no mo'. Oh thou infernal desperate damned villain. No exit. And speaking of hell, what did you think of tonight's show? Yes, what *did* you think of tonight's performance? Have you got any wild rice? No, but we can irritate some for you. What *did* I think of *Man and Superman*? Sadie could have played it. She has the ruthlessness and the big tits, but this nice woman, what'shername? Not a chance in hell, miscast, too sweet. For Ann Whitefield you need a cross between Eleanor Roosevelt and Gina Lollobrigida. I speak with pardonable exaggeration. It's simply an impossible part, who's to play it? That mamma's boy, what he knew. How he knew! Every time he went to the well with the pitcher out came mamma. Candida.

Ann Whitefield. Lady Cicely Waynflete. Major Barbara. Eliza. Saint Joan. Mummy mummy mummy the curse of the mummy's tomb, don't I know it well? And nothing will do but they have to take on this impossible play, and worst of all they do the third act. Nobody does the third act, my angels, a solecism, simply not done. Laughton could get away with it in dramatic readings because he didn't do the whole play, and he had competent professional actors to work with, and you don't. Nobody seems to understand the difference between an amateur and a professional, why is that? You wouldn't take out all your own teeth. The fate of the man who draws up his own will is notorious. You don't really want the policeman in the ambulance to deliver your baby (uggghhhh!) if you can possibly avoid it. But you want to do your own acting. Any poor sod who can hold a pencil is a writer. Some doctor goes to a Harold Town exhibition, walks along the paintings and says out loud, 'Ah yes, he's a bit further along than I am.' Can you beat it? Everybody's an actor. You just memorise your lines, that's easy enough, and then you stand up and say them. People ask me what the director *does*? They can't see anything for him to do. Why is that man waving his arms in front of the orchestra? Why do they bother to have a writer on a Groucho Marx movie, when Groucho can just make it up as he goes along? Can't you *see*? I mean, can't any of you see at all? You, Matthew Goderich, it's you I'm speaking to, down there beside that bitch of a consort of yours. Don't imagine you can hide from me by shrinking down in your seat like that. House lights up, please, come on, let's have them up so everybody can see him wriggling down there like a worm on a hook beside his friend the Prime Minister, and his friend the Minister of Justice and the local Member of Parliament and the local notabilities. They all look pretty much the same with the lights turned out, I expect, just like you and me, skinny and frightened or fat and frightened. What a gang of right-thinking Canadians! And not a Frenchman in a carload, thank God. I hate the French as much as any good Canadian, arrogant sons of bitches, all of them, a good enemy and a bad ally, and the French police are the worst in Europe. Molière, what a lot of poo. Nobody laughs at the jokes in seventeenth-century comedies, certainly not Shakesperean jokes. 'I meddle with no man's business but with all. Your trade, you saucy knave, your trade? Marry good sir, I am a shoemaker.' Whoever laughed at dialogue like that, that wasn't a hypocritical snobbish dupe? The jokes in Shakespeare aren't funny; they're dated incomprehensible stupid puns, and then you come and you laugh politely and hope you've laughed in the right place. The kind of idiots who don't know whether to applaud between the movements of a string quartet, and then applaud during a four-bar rest, oh God, it's all so dreary and I'm going to have to spend the rest of my life working amongst you. Molière. Molière. I ask you as a friend and a brother, which of you gives a shit about Molière? I don't, and I'm in the business. I mean, how dare you laugh at Molière? You don't know what he's on about and neither do I and the hell with him anyway; comedy isn't funny. You take Shaw, now. Who laughs at Shaw? I'll tell you who I laugh at, I laugh at Wilde. I laugh at the cucumber sandwiches and those two terrible little girls, such a pair of girls as were never met with on land or sea. And what I'd like to know is, who was Oscar thinking of when he invented Gwendolen and Cecily? Some disgraceful pair of charmers, I make no doubt, about seventeen. Oh the times in my life when I'd have given everything I possessed to get myself up in drag as Cecily to charm the birdies out of the trees. Not Gwendolen. Gwendolen's too butch. She's simply going to grow into a second Lady Bracknell, but that's all right, it's a great part. I fully expect to be cast as Lady Bracknell one day: we all come to it. But my dears, there was a time not too long ago when I could have played Cecily with hardly any problems, with a cinch and an uplift. About thirty pounds and twenty years ago, just about the time when that creature Matthew Goderich re-entered my life, and then, oh the torment. Why couldn't he have left me alone? Why did he have to share a dressing-room with me and sit all week letting me make him up, looking up into my eyes with his big round baby-blues, or were they browns? I forget. Sat there all week and let me pat his cheeks with just a light dusting of talcum to tone down the highlights, and then I'd always do his eyes last of all with some lake liner all dripping and gooey. Heaven, simply heaven, but do you think he ever gave poor me a tumble? Not a wink, not a sign, he might just as well have been the straightest of the straights, but we know better, don't we, ducks? Matthew and the dignitaries, oh, it is to laugh. Right next to Sadie's vacant seat and then the Prime Minister and you can't get any more of a dignitary than the Prime Minister. More of a dignitary than that and you're playing to an audience of kings and queens. I've done that. We've all done that, but we never handed out any prizes for it, and now I'm supposed to give out the prizes like a queen at a Boy Scout Jamboree. Best actor, best actress, best this and that. I know but I won't tell. It's funny how power emasculates some of them and makes others even sexier, Somebody told me once that Eisenhower—or was it Montgomery—couldn't get it up once, during the whole of World War Two. Isn't that cute, isn't that true? It's no sin to be Prime Minister but it doesn't help. Pardon. Pardon me. I've said more than I ought. I should know better. Best actress, is it? Edie Goderich, that's my choice. Come on up here, Edie, and take a bow. For her performance in *I Was a Male War Bride*, ladies and gentlemen, and what the hell, for her art work. The Genius of Politics Presenting Dramatic Art to Its Ideal Counterpart. Funny. Hah hah. I'm laughing. These are heartfelt chuckles you hear coming from my lips. Tee-hee. Why you silly woman, you silly silly woman, don't you know that if I wanted to be bothered I could walk off this stage and along the front row and give a whistle and carry your darling hubby off to the ends of the earth, or anyway Toronto, and there wouldn't be one little thing you could do about it, but who can be bothered? You're all so sexless, such a collection of withered-up prunes with all the juice squeezed out to make morning drinks for dowagers. You, Matthew Goderich, and you, Mr. Prime Minister, you're so, so, shrunk. You're so wrinkled, my dears. You know you don't really care one bit for this acting nonsense and this writing nonsense and this ballet buggery. You just want to cuddle up behind a desk to read the minutes on the auto parts agreement. Now where did I get that? Oh yes, some old idiot was mumbling about it at a party this week, this interminable awful week, could it have been terrible old George Robinson? I rather fancy it was him. He. It was he. Auto parts. Get me out of their clutches, as you might say. Little auto parts joke there. Can you just imagine an auto parts number? A funny thing happened to me on my way over to the crankshaft. No, it wouldn't play. Just watch out for the future industrial strategy of our nation, friends and brothers. Who said that to me? Some cat named Golmsdorfer, now where could I have picked up a Golmsdorfer, and what would I do with one? I see the men in the white coats beckoning to me from the wings, but I will pay them no heed, I will not yield me into their automatic clutches, Lester B. Pearson. I love you, you tubby old Nobel Prize Winner, you. How do you and Matthew's daddy get along in lovely Ottawa? I've played Ottawa, but that was when I was younger and quite a lot nicer. Not that I'm not nice now, why not try me and see? There must be some of us in Stoverville, Matthew Goderich apart. Why don't we all go back to my place and have a gay old time, you know where I'm staying, don't you? In that wonderfully bogus little shack down by the riverside with the casement windows, the turrets and the slate roof. We'll all go back to my place and get acquainted. Come up and see me some time, girls. I used to be pure as snow but I drifted. God, I'm thirsty. What am I doing up here making a fool of myself just because Sadie has gone to Reno or wherever it is they go these days? It isn't that. It's just that I want my friends around me at the last because I'm no switch-hitter, you old sillies, I'm fruit. How do you like me? I'm gay. I'm so darn gay! Who wants to dance? And how do you like that, Mister George Bernard Shaw?"

He turned to one side and sidled into the wings, stage right. The thump as he fell was audible in the first three rows, the sound of a sack of cement hitting the ground. They didn't give out any prizes that night.

*   *   *

# The Scenic Art

"Why didn't you warn us?" asked Valerie Essex, sitting glumly over Sunday brunch at her coffee table. "Why didn't you give us at least an inkling?"

"I didn't know," I said. "How would I know? I'm no handholder to the stars. He'd never been that way before. Of course I know he was a homosexual. I thought everybody knew that. He always has been, and I didn't suppose he'd changed just because he got married."

"Married to that beautiful movie star," said George Essex reflectively, "and unhappy?"

"Well you heard what he said. He only married her when he began to get famous, to cover up his other interests. It's a familiar strategy in the profession. Protective colouration."

"Camouflage, I call that."

"Do you suppose he makes love to her?"

"What do you think?"

A sigh from George. "I guess not. What was it set him off, do you think? His wife not turning up, and filing for a divorce?"

Edie said, "It was all this damn' politicking, if you ask me."

"I think it was your mural, dear," said Valerie. "I saw that it took him right aback, from the very start."

"Where is he now?" said George. "Perhaps I should go to him."

"I wouldn't do that," I said. "Uncle George refused to have him back to the house. Told me straight out not to bring him around Robinson Court at any time in the future. He was wild about something, I don't know exactly what. On hot bricks. I got Dougie Crum to help me—and poor old Dougie came through pretty well under pressure—and we carried him out to Dougie's car and took him up to the Crestline Hotel, where they were very happy to have him as a guest, I'm glad about that. He's there now. I doubt that he remembers anything about last night, and I'm not going to be the one to tell him. It will all come flooding back in the course of the next few days. I understand that the studio is sending a limo from Toronto to collect the remains." I felt proud of the word "limo" which I had never spoken until that moment. "What will they do about all those glittering prizes?"

"They're holding a meeting this afternoon to choose a substitute adjudicator from among people known to have seen all the performances. I don't suppose that you . . ."

My blood ran intensely cold. "Judge not," I said, "lest ye be judged." The phone rang in the front hall and George took the call.

"He's right here," I heard him exclaim. He put his head around the door and spoke to me. "A call for you from Ottawa, re-directed from your house."

Besides fatigue and terror I now felt mystification. "I'll take it," I said unwillingly, but I cheered up at once when I heard my father's voice.

"I'm glad I got hold of you," he said, "I wanted to tell you about this, so that you don't see it in tomorrow's papers first."

I thought, what's he up to this time?

"They're sending me to Peking," he said laconically. Only a veteran Goderich-watcher would have sensed how pleased and excited he was.

"You can't go to China," I said. "We have no diplomatic representation there, none to speak of anyway."

"I'm it," he said gleefully.

"An embassy?"

"Not precisely. Chairmanship of an exploratory committee with an accreditation to seek out ways and means of establishing trade relations, perhaps diplomatic relations in three or four years."

I said doubtfully, "Is your health up to it?"

"You know that I've always wanted to go there."

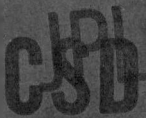

3 1221 02386 8545